NEW EDITION, *ALTERNATIVES TO VIOLENCE* WORKBOOK

© Copyright 1986, 1990, 1992, 1993, 1994, 1995 PEACE GROWS, Inc.
All Rights Reserved.

John Looney, Author

Danene M. Bender, Editor

Waring Smith, Design

Susan Shah, Composition

Rose Dailey, Consultant

Laura Weldon, Bibliography

If any of this material is reproduced for use in non-profit nonviolent training, please contact PEACE GROWS, Inc. for permission. If granted, there will be no compulsory charge but the source must be acknowledged and, when possible, voluntary contributions made to help fund the expansion of this program. For inclusions in classes or workshops for profit, or in publications or audio-visuals, a nominal charge must be negotiated. In all cases, notification of the type of usage and evaluation or other suggestions or input are requested to aid the continual upgrading of this material.

ISBN 0-9619819-4-6

PEACE GROWS, Inc., an Ohio non-profit corporation at 513 W. Exchange St., Akron, OH 44302.

PEACE GROWS, INC. develops and distributes educational resources on peace and justice. A non-profit, Ohio corporation.

at Humanity House, 513 West Exchange St.
Akron, Ohio 44302
(216) 864-5442

Dear Reader:

We wish to welcome you as the owner of the latest edition of our *Alternatives to Violence Workbook* with *Case Histories*. It represents about twenty-five years of development work including broad application and field testing.

But that development will not stop. With our continuing efforts and your suggestions, our resources constantly will be enriched.

We hope you will want to keep up with those changes. There is an easy, free way to do it. Just fill out the following form, clip it off and mail it in today. Thank you for your interest and support.

Sincerely,

Peace GROWS

Please fill out the form below, clip it off and mail it in today. Thanks.
To: Peace GROWS, 513 W. Exchange St., Akron, OH 44302.

- -

❑ Yes, I do want to keep in touch with latest developments.

❑ I would like to take the *Alternatives to Violence* Advanced Training sometime for
    ❑ deeper understanding   ❑ teaching the course myself.

Name_____ Phone_____
Address _____
City and state_____ Zip _____
Occupation and/or affiliation _____
Where *Workbook* purchased or course taken _____
Who taught the course taken _____

COURSE DESCRIPTION

Why the course?

Alternatives to Violence has been developed because of the epidemic of violence in our lives, in our families, neighborhoods, schools, communities, nation and between nations. Though the principles for the creative, nonviolent resolution of conflict have long been established, few know of them and little has been done to teach and popularize their use in our culture.

Goals of the course

Through *Alternatives to Violence,* you will learn that many creative, constructive alternatives do exist to solve human problems and overcome evil without violence or fighting. The goal is to learn those alternatives and the principles, techniques and skills for using them.

Necessarily, this only can be an overview. The course seeks to stimulate your interest for further study and practice in your own life. Its purpose is not to make you nonviolent or a pacifist. No course can do that nor is anyone completely nonviolent. But its goal is to provide you with additional choices for any situation you may need to resolve.

Guidelines for the course

Everyone is expected to participate in several ways:

1. Attend all sessions. Each one is built on the previous one. Being late is being absent too.
2. Do the assignments. They should help personalize and internalize the material for each participant.
3. Join all group discussions and activities. However, everyone has a right to "pass" providing that person still watches and listens carefully. That also is participation.
4. Honor and respect the opinions of all others. No one is to be "put down."
5. Fairly share all discussion time. Things that cannot be covered in class should be postponed until breaks or other free time to help maintain our schedule for covering the complete material offered.

What to expect in the course

Because we all have knowledge and experience to share, we will be learning from each other. We will brainstorm together. We will role play cases. We will perform simulation and cooperative games. We will have both large and small group discussions. For assignments, we will read some selected excerpts and keep a personal journal in which to record the learnings that most impress us and our feelings as we progress through the course. We may record our changes in perceptions and attitudes and our observations and experiences outside the class in witnessing or testing the principles and skills. Always we will consider not only what happened but also how and why.

Generally, we will sit in a circle facing each other so we are an integral part of what is going on. There are no "performers" or "spectators." All of us are participants together in what is hoped will be an exciting and valuable new learning experience.

©1986, 1990, 1992, 1993, 1994, 1995 PEACE GROWS, Inc., 513 W. Exchange St., Akron, OH 44302 (216)864-5442.

ALTERNATIVES TO VIOLENCE

HOW TO USE THIS WORKBOOK

This workbook aims to provide everything a person might need for participating in the *Alternatives to Violence* course under a trained facilitator (teacher). These items, in order of their sequence in the book, are:

Introduction explains why the course was developed, the goal of the course, guidelines for the course and what to expect in it, including how it will be conducted.

Syllabus presents the title and objectives for each of the twenty sessions.

Worksheet begins each session presenting the session objectives and session concepts, assignments and space for the notes and/or journal reflections.

Journal is to personalize and internalize the course material for you. This will help you learn more and remember it better. You are to record whatever you wish. What impressed you? What affected your feelings or changed your perceptions or attitudes? Particularly important is to keep in your journal a record of what you observe, experience, think about or experiment with in *Alternatives to Violence* actual applications outside of class. What happened? Why? What were the results of any experimentation?

This journal will be your own private record to encourage your most free expression and will not be examined or read by others. However, you may be asked to share things from it which you feel comfortable sharing. Your journal can be a resource for writing some assigned reflection papers.

Readings give background for considering alternatives other than violent responses.

Cases are descriptions of actual situations, recent and historic. They will be presented in various ways throughout the course. You will find cases for most sessions in the back of the workbook. The case numbers correspond to the session numbers. For instance, Case 5-A means this is an application of the principles, strategies and or techniques presented in Session 5.

Exercises and charts to be filled in will be included in the session materials as well as any other useful instructions or discussion questions.

Other assignments are in preparation for the next session and should be completed before the next session is convened. When more than one session is covered at a time, it will be necessary to do all assignments for all sessions to be covered at the next meeting and not just the first one.

Bibliography is included at the end of this workbook to suggest future reading you might like to do for further enrichment and understanding.

Future Workbook Additions - This workbook is loose-leaf so the facilitator may easily update the material and/or include appropriate material from the sponsoring institution. Likewise, participants may add notes and items they feel will be helpful to them and which they may wish to share with the class.

Finally, our plan is to update and improve this material whenever it seems advisable. Therefore, we will welcome suggestions from present and past participants at any time. Please send in your suggestions or additions for any changes or improvements. They will be most welcome.

Glossary is included in the last pages of the workbook for explaining terms used in the course.

©1986, 1990, 1992, 1993, 1994, 1995 PEACE GROWS, Inc., 513 W. Exchange St., Akron, OH 44302 (216)864-5

ALTERNATIVES TO VIOLENCE

CURRICULUM SYLLABUS

Course goals:
1. To introduce ways to solve human problems and overcome evil without fighting or violence.
2. To learn principles and skills for experimenting with and using alternatives to violence.
3. To provide, for any situation, additional choices which, otherwise, would not have been known.

Page No. 1

Course objectives:

Session 1. Kinds of violence
a. To get better acquainted with each other, the course and how it is conducted.
b. To learn the different kinds and classes of violence.
c. To define violence, differentiate it from conflict and anger and observe one successful application of an alternative to violence.

.... 7

Session 2. The nature of violence
a. To learn something of the nature of unresolved conflict and violence.
b. To understand particularly the main characteristic of violence and how that relates to starting, preventing, stopping and reducing violence.

.... 13

Session 3. Causes of violence
a. To learn causes of conflict and violence.
b. To recognize and define institutional violence and understand its effect on people.

.... 23

Session 4. Responses to conflict and violence
a. To understand better how we each respond to conflict.
b. To learn the many ways to respond and point out which this course covers.
c. To determine which responses tend to be lose/lose, win/lose and win/win and which this course covers.

.... 31

Session 5. Alternatives to violence skills: active listening, stating position clearly and obtaining all facts
a. To learn and practice nonviolent listening skills.
b. To understand the importance of stating things clearly and getting all the facts, also as alternatives to violence skills.

.... 39

Session 6. Alternatives to violence skills: handling my anger
a. To learn how to handle anger nonviolently and constructively.
b. To understand better the differences between violent and nonviolent goals, attitudes and tactics.

.... 47

Session 7. Alternatives to violence skills: handling anger of others
a. To learn principles and skills for handling the anger of another at me.
b. To learn the principles and skills for handling anger between others through third-party intervention.
c. To explore some reasons why nonviolence works.

.... 55

Session 8. Alternatives to violence skills: developing options, negotiation, mediation and arbitration
a. To define negotiation, mediation, arbitration.
b. To learn the process of negotiation.
c. To develop negotiation skills.

.... 65

©1986, 1990, 1992, 1993, 1994, 1995 PEACE GROWS, Inc., 513 W. Exchange St., Akron, OH 44302 (216)864-5442.

CURRICULUM SYLLABUS

Session 9. Alternatives to violence skills: nonviolent personal self-defense

Page No.

a. To examine cases where nonviolent personal self-defense has worked successfully and determine how and why. 75
b. To develop some basic skills and attitudes for defending oneself nonviolently.
c. To define nonresistance and distinguish it from noncooperation.
d. To probe the meaning and significance of nonviolence in our lives.

Session 10. Nonviolence as a philosophy and a lifestyle

a. To learn about the nonviolent philosophies and lifestyles of other people. 89
b. To consider how nonviolence relates to and/or is a part of our own philosophies and conduct.

Session 11. Alternatives to violence skills: group participation for problem solving

a. To learn some communication problems, in group decision making, and steps to overcome them. 113
b. To develop skills in directing group discussion toward consensus decision making.
c. To understand nonviolent leadership and ourselves as leaders and followers in it.
d. To explore the nature of power in normal authority roles and in nonviolent roles.

Session 12. Alternatives to violence skills: zeroing in on a problem

a. To learn a process for focusing a group's attention and energies on solving a problem. 125
b. To understand how to facilitate a group solution through consensus decision making.
c. To find how to plan the implementation of that solution and put it into operation.

Session 13. Alternatives to violence skills applied in the community

a. To review alternatives to violence skills for use in personal conflict situations. 133
b. To learn how the skills apply in community conflicts and examine some actual uses.
c. To understand causes of violence in our communities and the prerequisites for creating nonviolent communities.

Session 14. Alternatives to violence skills applied to global problems

a. To review alternatives to violence skills for nonviolent conflict resolution at both the personal and community levels. 143
b. To learn how these skills apply in global conflict situations and consider actual applications.
c. To understand causes of violence in the world and some of the prerequisites for a nonviolent globe.

Session 15. Alternatives to violence skills: nonviolent national defense

a. To understand better what is happening in the world's trouble spots and envision nonviolent solutions. 157
b. To examine our own attitudes toward national security.
c. To learn some creative methods for nonviolent national defense.
d. To define nonviolent national defense.

CURRICULUM SYLLABUS

Session 16. Understanding global violence—what can we do?
| | Page No. |
a. To review causes of war, violence and terrorism in the world.
b. To learn how world violence relates to the quality of our daily lives.
c. To understand how our lifestyle effects domestic and global violence. 173
d. To define simple living and see how some are applying it.

Session 17. Alternatives to violence applied to current events
a. To apply our alternatives to violence skills learning to interpret and/or resolve both violent and nonviolent situations and events as reported in our daily newspapers or on radio and TV news broadcasts. 193
b. To gain more insight into the vast need for these problem-solving skills in society and in the world.
c. To better understand how well the media reports the news and how that effects the prevalence of violence and serves our needs as citizens of a democracy.

Session 18. Alternatives to violence skills: working the system
a. To examine if, when, why and how we should get involved actively in seeking nonviolent social and/or political change. 205
b. To learn other ways of working in the United States for nonviolent improvements when the alternatives to violence talking skills fail to get results.
c. To understand those methods better and how their use is encouraged under the provision of the U.S. Constitution.
d. To practice at least one of those methods.

Session 19. Alternatives to violence skills: imaging a better world
a. To envision and feel what it would be like if there were no violence, no weapons, only nonviolent conduct in whatever framework we wish to examine: classroom, home, workplace, school, athletic field, neighborhood, community, nation, world. 221
b. To determine the needed steps and time schedule to get there. (i.e., to a world without weapons, a school without corporal punishment, etc.)
c. To realize how clearly envisioning a goal helps us get there.

Session 20. Reflection and celebration
a. To reflect on our learning experience together.
b. To show our appreciation to and thanks for each other. 231
c. To evaluate the course by pointing out both what seemed good about it and what seems to need improvement.
d. To celebrate our friendship and growth.
e. To determine, by sharing our future plans, how we can grow further in understanding and involvement.
f. To have some fun together!

Some forms for course 241

Glossary of terms 245

Organizational index 249

Case analysis sheets 257

Case histories 277

©1986, 1990, 1992, 1993, 1994, 1995 PEACE GROWS, Inc., 513 W. Exchange St., Akron, OH 44302 (216)864-5442.

ALTERNATIVES TO VIOLENCE   Session 1 Chart   6

EVERYTHING IS CONNECTED IN THE PATTERN OF LIFE

This course examines all kinds of conflict and violence at all levels from inter-personal to community to global and everything in between. This chart portrays how everything is connected. Did you ever realize that you, just by being born, are a part of each of these communities?

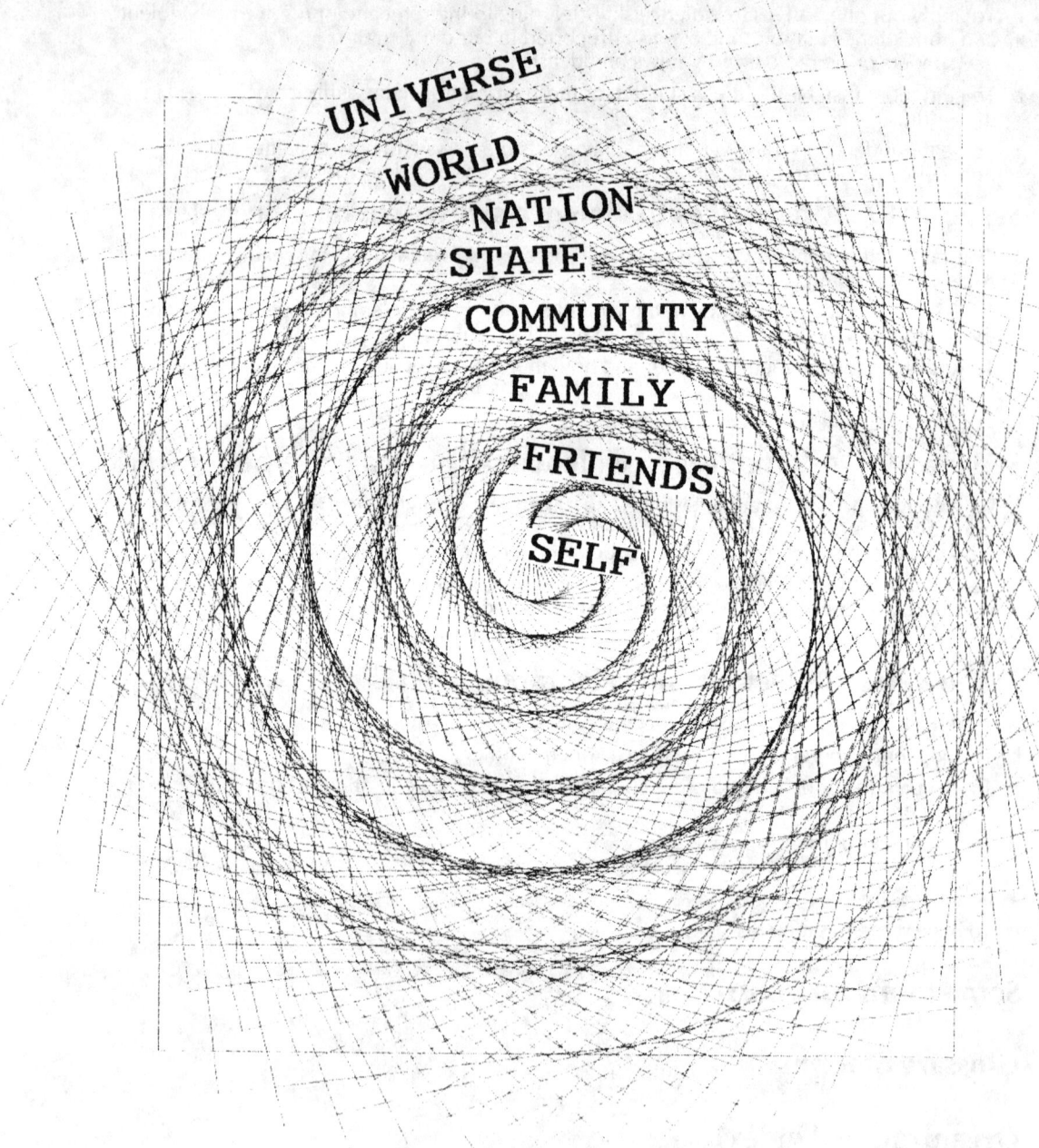

Everything in life is, in some way, connected. This means that all kinds of conflicts are possible and that all kinds of responses, violent and non-violent, are possible. In the following pages, we will be learning how to apply peaceful conflict resolution skills at every level of our lives.

This chart was developed by Sr. Rose Dailey. The spiral was created by Waring Smith and Mark Smith.
©1986, 1990, 1992, 1993, 1994, 1995 PEACE GROWS, Inc., 513 W. Exchange St., Akron, OH 44302 (216)864-5442.

Session 1
KINDS OF VIOLENCE

Objectives

a. To get better acquainted with each other, the course and how it is conducted.

b. To learn the different kinds and classes of violence.

c. To define violence, differentiate it from conflict and anger and observe one successful application of an alternative to violence.

WORKSHEET #1

(The following points will be covered in this session. Most points do not have "pat" answers, but the main thing is for you to arrive at an expression of the concepts. These questions are to help you take notes and process the material.)

1. I think an example of violence is _____

2. Some other examples I want to record from class discussion are:

3. Three types of violence are:

4. Our working definition of violence will be:

   Violence is _____

5. How is conflict different from violence? _____

6. What part does anger play?

Notes or Journal Entry

Assignments:

_____
_____
_____
_____

VIOLENCE AND TELEVISION

We are indebted to U.S. Sen. Paul Simon of Makanda, Ill.—a Democrat who in 1948 purchased the *Troy* (Ill.) *Tribune* at age 19 and became probably the youngest editor-publisher in the nation—for the following statistical extract on video and violence:

"Violence on television has risen more than 100% since 1980. From January to April [1985], prime-time television averaged 13.8 acts of violence per hour. The average child between the ages of 2 and 11 views between 27.3 hours each week. By the time a person is 16, he or she has watched more than 20,000 hours of television, including 200,000 acts of violence, 50,000 of which are murders."

The son of a Lutheran minister, Simon, 57, has authored nine books, including one with his wife, Jeanne, titled *Protestant-Catholic Marriages Can Succeed.* He also has been awarded 23 honorary doctorate degrees and since 1954 has annually disclosed his income, assets and liabilities—a record few first-term Senators can equal.

Parade Magazine, TV Roundup
12-28-85

THE VARIOUS USES OF NONVIOLENCE

For resolving conflict

A primary use of nonviolence is for problem-solving. It can be used in several ways in third-party intervention to resolve conflict between two or more opponents. Examples include mediation and crowd control or riot prevention.

The need for nonviolence in many other areas of police work is becoming apparent. It is useful in resolving neighborhood disputes, in stopping fights or arguments, and in handling criminals. Through the use of nonviolent methods, a community can work and learn together, becoming more of a community. Caring about each other and helping each other deters crime and acts of violence.

For personal self defense

Nonviolence can be used for situations in which negotiation is not an option. As pointed out in Dorothy Samuel's *Safe Passage on City Streets,* the techniques of nonviolence have been used successfully by individuals many times to repel attackers, even armed ones. Nonviolent self defense is based upon a person's refusal to act in a victim-like manner, and involves assault prevention as well as resistance.

For social protest and reform

The movement of Gandhi to free India from English control and that of Martin Luther King, Jr. to free blacks from oppressive cultural patterns in the United States are classic examples of the use of nonviolent methods for social protest and reform. They were both successful against vastly stronger forces.

Even one person can begin a nonviolent struggle against something she or he feels is wrong. Growing support may become wide enough for success. Nonviolent resistance can be for change of government as in India or for reform of government as in the U.S. It confronts established authority in either case but seeks a just and stable society rather than disruption. Nonviolent change will relieve the tensions, frustrations, and injustices that are the causes of war and violence.

For national defense

More and more people are realizing the impracticality of military defense as we are urged to spend more and more of our tax dollars for military-related expenses. Risking one million Americans' deaths in a nuclear war is not a practical defense. Nuclear deterrence doe not promote national security. It threatens it. Every arms race has ended in war, not peace. The arms race continues. Its tremendous cost impoverishes the country and the world. Yet we spend more and more because we do not realize that nonviolence has defended countries successfully. Norway's and Denmark's defenses against Hitler's army and Czechoslovakia's defense against the 1968 Soviet invasion are examples. To use nonviolence in this manner requires a new national policy decision because so many people must become involved in a trained, disciplined effort. An invading army cannot subjugate a country whose people resist nonviolently together.

Our education and culture have emphasized the military or violent history of change. If we are to have peace and security, we must teach and develop the history and the practice of nonviolence.

SUMMARY OF CONCEPTS
As related to the subjects listed on worksheet #1

1. *I think an example of violence is:*
   Any answer acceptable here.

2. *Some other examples I want to record from class discussion are:*
   Any answer acceptable here.

3. *The types or classes of violence are:*
   physical, emotional/psychological, social/institutional, condoned/encouraged, illegal/criminal, global.

4. *Our working definition of violence will be:*
   Violence is anything that hurts life.

5. *How is conflict different from violence?*
   Conflict is an opposition of ideas or actions, problem or disagreement. Conflict does not need to lead to violence. How conflict is handled determines if it is good or bad.

6. *What part does anger play?*
   Anger is an emotion common to all people; it can be good if it contributes to bringing problems out and leading to solutions. Anger and conflict, both givens, probably cannot be avoided.

Major point to remember:
- Violence is whatever hurts life.

Session 1
KINDS OF VIOLENCE
Additional reading

Carlsson-Paige, Nancy and Diane Levin. *The War Play Dilemma: Balancing Needs And Values In The Early Childhood Classroom.* NY: Teachers College Press, 1987.

Cousins, Norman. *The Pathology Of Power.* NY: Norton, 1987.

Durning, Alan. *How Much Is Enough? The Consumer Society And The Future Of The Earth.* Washington, DC: Worldwatch Institute, 1992.

Duryea, Michelle LeBaron. *Conflict And Culture.* University of Victoria Institute for Dispute Resolution Project, 1992.

Eisler, Riane. *The Chalice And The Blade: Our History, Our Future.* San Francisco: Harper & Row, 1987.

Hewlett, Sylvia Ann. *When The Bough Breaks: The Cost Of Neglecting Our Children.* NY: Harper Perennial, 1992.

Kohn, Alfie. *No Contest: The Case Against Competition.* Boston: Houghton Mifflin, 1986.

Mander, Jerry. *Four Arguments For The Elimination Of Television.* NY: Morrow, 1978.

Mansfield, Sue and Mary Bowen Hall. *Some Reasons For War: How Families, Myths And Warfare Are Connected.* NY: Thomas Y. Crowell, 1988.

Miller, Marc. *State Of The Peoples: A Global Human Rights Report On Societies In Danger.* Boston: Beacon Press, 1993.

Rich, Bruce. *Mortgaging The Earth: The World Bank, Environmental Improvement, And The Crisis Of Development.* Boston: Beacon Press, 1993.

Wachtel, Paul L. *The Poverty Of Affluence: A Psychological Portrait Of The American Way Of Life.* NY: Macmillan Free Press, Inc., 1983.

Zerzan, John and Alice Carnes. *Questioning Technology: Tool, Toy or Tyrant.* Philadelphia, PA: New Society Pub., 1991.

ALTERNATIVES TO VIOLENCE

Session 2
THE NATURE OF VIOLENCE

Objectives

a. To learn something of the nature of unresolved conflict and violence.

b. To understand particularly the main characteristic of violence and how that relates to starting, preventing, stopping and reducing violence.

WORKSHEET #2

(The following points will be covered in this session. Most points do not have "pat" answers, but the main thing is for you to arrive at an expression of the concepts. These questions are to help you take notes and process the material.)

1. What are four uses of nonviolence?

2. What principles/techniques of nonviolence listed on page 15 do you already use?

3. VIOLENCE ESCALATES. What does this mean in our lives?

4. What does this escalation of violence mean in our handling of violence?

©1986, 1990, 1992, 1993, 1994, 1995 PEACE GROWS, Inc., 513 W. Exchange St., Akron, OH 44302 (216)864-5442.

Notes or Journal Entry

Assignments:

_____
_____
_____
_____

ALTERNATIVES TO VIOLENCE

DIFFERENCES BETWEEN VIOLENCE AND NONVIOLENCE

Violence . . . . Nonviolence

Goals:

1. Defeat opponent to a finish . . . . Make friends with the opponent.

Humiliate, injure, corner and/or destroy opponent . . . . Work with the opponent to solve the problem together.

Win while the opponent loses . . . . Aim for win-win (mutually satisfactory settlement).

Attitudes:

1. Requires a strong hatred and fear of opponent to stimulate the necessary rage to attack and harm . . . . Be friendly and caring toward opponent.
. . . . Avoid any harm toward opponent.
. . . . Try to overcome opponent's hatred and fear.
. . . . Act courageously.
. . . . Think and act clearly and with self-control.
. . . . Hold firmly and calmly to your goals and values even while suffering rage or attack.

Principles and techniques

1. Attack so strongly that the opponent seems to have no alternatives or choices . . . . Keep many options open.
. . . . Allow self and opponent to change positions (s).
. . . . Avoid allowing self or opponent to 'lose face.'
. . . . Create a dilemma in which any choice results in solution.

2. Inflict all possible suffering on other . . . . Reject any and all use of violence.

3. Avoid one's own suffering . . . . Be willing to suffer oneself but unwilling to cause suffering to opponent.

This article was written by John Looney.
©1986, 1990, 1992, 1993, 1994, 1995 PEACE GROWS, Inc., 513 W. Exchange St., Akron, OH 44302 (216)864-5442.

ALTERNATIVES TO VIOLENCE — Session 2 Reading — 16

Differences between violence and nonviolence (continued)

Violence . . . . Nonviolence

Principles and techniques: (continued)

4. Use all resources to achieve victory as soon as possible ....
   - Be persistent and patient.
   - Aim for equitable solution acceptable to all parties.
   - Realize that equitable, lasting change comes slowly.

5. Use any means to attain victory ....
   - Be dedicated to justice throughout entire process.

6. Use public relations to distort truth where it serves own purposes or to cover own wrongful conduct ....
   - Be faithful to the truth at all times/at all costs.
   - Maintain exemplary conduct.
   - Maintain good public relations.
   - Create sympathy, understanding on part of public and opponent.

7. Train and discipline yourself rigidly in use of arms and techniques to destroy opponent ....
   - Use your nonviolent training

8. Act arrogantly to instill hatred and fear ......
   - Act with integrity and humility. to instill respect and sympathy.

9. Be harmful ....
   - Be helpful.

10. Rely mostly on physical resources ....
    - Rely on superior mental, creative, moral resources.

11. Stimulate hatred toward opponent ....
    - Show your opponent respect and caring. Love your enemy!

12. Ignore or suppress a problem which does violence to others when possible .....
    - Be sure all concerned know all the facts.

13. Use all possible concerted negative words and actions against opponent ....
    - Show how the change (solution) will be positive.
    - Aim for reconciliation for all parties involved.

14. Use violent actions to destroy opponent .. anticipating that he will react predictably using the established norms for fighting
    - Use unexpected, surprise, nonviolent techniques.

15. Exclude opponent in every way possible..
    - Include opponent in every way possible.

This article was written by John Looney.
©1986, 1990, 1992, 1993, 1994, 1995 PEACE GROWS, Inc., 513 W. Exchange St., Akron, OH 44302 (216)864-5442.

NONVIOLENCE: CORNERSTONE FOR A WORLD HOUSE

Martin Luther King's Nobel Peace Prize Lecture delivered in Oslo, Norway, December 11, 1964

This evening I would like to use this lofty and historic platform to discuss what appears to me to be the most pressing problem confronting mankind today. Modern man has brought this whole world to an awe-inspiring threshold of the future. He has reached new and astonishing peaks of scientific success. He has produced machines that think and instruments that peer into the unfathomable ranges of interstellar space. He has built gigantic ridges to span the seas and Gargantuan buildings to kiss the skies. His airplanes and space ships have dwarfed distance, placed time in chains and carved highways through the atmosphere. This is a dazzling picture of modern man's scientific and technological progress . . .

Yet, in spite of these spectacular strides in science and technology, and still unlimited ones to come, something basic is missing. There is a sort of poverty of the spirit which stands in glaring contrast to our scientific and technological abundance. The richer we have become materially, the poorer we have become morally and spiritually. We have learned to fly the air like birds and swim the sea like fish, but we have not learned the simple art of living together as brothers.

So much of modern life can be summarized in that arresting dictum of the poet Thoreau, "Improved means to an unimproved end." This is the serious predicament, the deep and haunting problem confronting modern man. If we are to survive today, our moral and spiritual "lag" must be eliminated. Enlarged material powers spell enlarged peril if there is not proportionate growth of the soul.

The problem of spiritual and moral lag, which constitutes modern man's chief dilemma, expresses itself in three larger problems which flow out of man's ethical infantilism. Each of these problems, while appearing to be separate and isolated, is inextricably bound to the other. I refer to *racial injustice, poverty, and war.*

The **first** problem that I would like to mention is racial injustice. The struggle to eliminate the evil of racial injustice constitutes one of the major struggles of our time. ". . . We live in a day," says the philosopher Alfred North Whitehead, "when civilization is shifting in its basic outlook: a major turning point in history where the presuppositions on which society is structured are being analyzed, sharply challenged, and profoundly changed." What we are seeing now is a freedom explosion, the realization of "an idea whose time has come," to use Victor Hugo's phrase . . . All over the world, like a fever, the freedom movement is spreading in the widest liberation in history. The great masses of people are determined to end the exploitation of their races and land . . . These developments should not surprise any student of history. Oppressed peoples cannot remain oppressed forever. The yearning for freedom eventually manifests itself . . .

> *"Each of these problems, while appearing to be separate and isolated, is inextricably bound to the other. I refer to racial injustice, poverty, and war."*

Fortunately, some significant strides have been made in the struggle to end the long night of racial injustice. We have seen the magnificent drama of independence unfold in Asia and Africa. Just thirty years ago there were only three independent nations in the whole of Africa. But today thirty-five African nations have risen from colonial bondage. In the United States we have witnessed the gradual demise of the system of racial segregation . . .

Let me not leave you with a false impression. The problem is far from solved. We still have a long, long way to go before the dream of

Nonviolence: Cornerstone for a world house (continued)

freedom is a reality for the Negro in the United States . . . What the main sections of the Civil Rights Movement in the United States are saying is that the demand for dignity, equality, jobs and citizenship will not be abandoned or diluted or postponed. If that means resistance and conflict, we shall not flinch. We shall not be moved. We are no longer afraid.

The word that symbolized the spirit and the outward form of our encounter is *nonviolence*, and it is doubtless that factor which made it seem appropriate to award a peace prize to one identified with struggle. Broadly speaking, nonviolence in the civil rights struggle has meant not relying on arms and weapons of struggle. It has meant noncooperation with systems and laws which are institutional aspects of a regime of discrimination and enslavement. It has meant direct participation of masses in protest, rather than reliance on indirect methods which frequently do not involve masses in action at all.

Nonviolence has also meant that my people in the agonizing struggles of recent years have taken suffering upon themselves instead of inflicting it on others. It has meant, as I said, that we are no longer afraid and cowed. But in some substantial degree it has meant that we do not want to instill fear in others or into the society of which we are a part. The Movement does not seek to liberate Negroes at the expense of the humiliation and enslavement of whites. It seeks no victory over anyone. It seeks to liberate American society and to share in the self-liberation of all people.

Violence as a way of achieving racial justice is both impractical and immoral. I am not unmindful of the fact that violence often brings about momentary results. Nations have frequently won their independence in battle. But in spite of temporary victories, violence never brings permanent peace. It solves no social problem. It merely creates new and more complicated ones. Violence is immoral because it thrives on hatred rather than love. Violence is impractical because it is a descending spiral ending in destruction for all. It is immoral because it seems to humiliate the opponent rather than win his understanding; it seeks to annihilate rather than convert. It destroys community and makes brotherhood impossible. It leaves society in monologue rather than dialogue. Violence ends up defeating itself. It creates bitterness in the survivors and brutality in the destroyers.

In a real sense, nonviolence seeks to redeem the spiritual and moral lag that I spoke of earlier as the chief dilemma of modern man. It seeks to secure moral ends through moral means. Nonviolence is a powerful and just weapon. Indeed, it is a weapon unique in history, which cuts without wounding and ennobles the one who wields it.

I believe in this method because I think it is the only way to re-establish a broken community. It is the method which seeks to implement the just law by appealing to the conscience of the great decent majority who through blindness, fear, pride, and irrationality have allowed their consciences to sleep.

The nonviolent resisters can summarize their message in the following simple terms: we will take direct action against injustice despite the failure of governmental and other official agencies to act first. We will not obey unjust laws nor submit to unjust practices. We will do this peacefully, openly, cheerfully because our aim is to persuade. We adopt the means of nonviolence because our end is a community of peace with itself. We will try to persuade with our words, but if our words fail, we will try to persuade with our acts. We will always be willing to talk and seek fair compromise; but we are ready to suffer when necessary and even risk our lives to become witnesses to truth as we see it.

This approach to the problem of racial injustice is not all without successful precedent. It was used in a magnificent way by Mohandas K. Gandhi to challenge the might of the British Empire and free his people from the political domination and economic exploitation inflicted upon them for centuries. He struggled only with the weapons of truth, soul force, noninjury and courage.

In the past ten years unarmed gallant men and women of the United States have given living testimony to the moral power and efficacy of nonviolence. By the thousands, faceless, anonymous, relentless young people, black and white, have temporarily left the ivory towers of learning for the barricades of bias. Their courageous and disciplined activities have come as a refreshing oasis in a desert sweltering with the heat of injustice. They have taken our whole nation back to those great wells of democracy which were

> "It is the method which seeks to implement the just law by appealing to the conscience of the great decent majority who through blindness, fear, pride, and irrationality have allowed their consciences to sleep."

Nonviolence: Cornerstone for a world house (continued)

dug deep by the founding fathers in the formulation of the Constitution and the Declaration of Independence. One day all of America will be proud of their achievements . . .

A **second** evil which plagues the modern world is that of poverty. Like a monstrous octopus, it projects its nagging prehensile tentacles in lands and villages all over the world. Almost two-thirds of the people of the world go to bed hungry at night. They are undernourished, ill-housed and shabbily clad. Many of them have no houses or beds to sleep in. Their only beds are the sidewalks of the cities and the dusty roads of the villages . . .

In a sense the poverty of the poor in America is more frustrating than the poverty of Africa and Asia. The misery of the poor in Africa and Asia is shared misery, a fact of life for the vast majority; they are all poor together as result of years of exploitation and underdevelopment. In sad contrast, the poor in America know that they live in the richest nation in the world, and that even though they are perishing on a lonely island of poverty, they are surrounded by a vast ocean of material prosperity.

So it is obvious that if man is to redeem his spiritual and moral "lag" he must go all out to bridge the social and economic gulf between the "haves" and the "have nots" of the world. Poverty is one of the most urgent items on the agenda of modern life.

Not many years ago, Dr. Kirtley Mayher, a Harvard geologist, wrote a book entitled *Enough and to Spare*. He set forth the basic theme that famine is wholly unnecessary in the modern world. Today, therefore, the question on the agenda must read, why should there be hunger and privation in any land, in any city, at any table, when man has the resources and the scientific know-how to provide all mankind with the basic necessities of life . . .

The time has come for an all-out world war against poverty. The rich nations must use their vast resources of wealth to develop the underdeveloped, school the unschooled, and feed the unfed. Ultimately, a great nation is a compassionate nation. . . In the final analysis, the rich must not ignore the poor because both rich and poor are tied in a single garment of destiny. All life is interrelated, and all men are interdependent. The agony of the poor diminishes the rich, and the salvation of the poor enlarges the rich. We are inevitably our brother's keeper because of the interrelated structure of reality.

A **third** great evil confronting our world is that of war. Recent events have vividly reminded us that nations are not reducing but rather increasing their arsenals of weapons of mass destruction. The best brains in the highly developed nations of the world are devoted to miliary technology. . .

The fact that most of the time human beings put the truth about the nature and risks of the nuclear war out of their minds because it is too painful and therefore not "acceptable" does not alter the nature and risks of such war. The device of "rejection" may temporarily cover up anxiety, but it does not bestow peace of mind and emotional security.

Wisdom born of experience should tell us that war is obsolete. There may have been a time when war served as a negative good by preventing the spread and growth of an evil force, but the destructive power of modern weapons eliminated even the possibility that war may serve as a negative good. If we assume that life is worth living and that man has a right to survive, then we must find an alternative to war. President John F. Kennedy said on one occasion, "Mankind must put an end to war or war will put an end to mankind . . ."

There I venture to suggest to all of you, and all who hear and may eventually read these words, that the philosophy and strategy of nonviolence become immediately a subject for study and for serious experimentation in every field of human conflict, by no means excluding the relations between nations . . . Somehow we must transform the dynamics of the world power struggle from the negative nuclear arms race, which

"When machines and computers, profit motives and property rights are considered more important than people, the giant triplets of racism, materialism and militarism are incapable of being conquered."

Nonviolence: Cornerstone for a world house (continued)

no one can win, to a positive contest to harness man's creative genius for the purpose of making peace and prosperity a reality for all the nations of the world . . .

All that I have said boils down to the point of affirming that mankind's survival is dependent upon man's ability to solve the problems of racial injustice, poverty and war, the solution of these problems is in turn dependent upon man squaring his moral progress with his scientific progress and learning the practical art of living in harmony. Some years ago a famous novelist died. Among his papers was found a list of suggested story plots for future stories, the most prominently underscored being this one: "A widely separated family inherits a house in which they have to live together . . ." black and white, Easterners and Westerners, Gentiles and Jews, Catholics and

Protestants, Moslems and Hindus, a family unduly separated in ideas, culture and interests who, because we can never again live without each other, must learn, somehow, in this one big world, to live with each other . . .

The stability of the large world house which is ours will involve a revolution of values to accompany the scientific and freedom revolutions engulfing the world. We must rapidly begin the shift from a "thing"-oriented society to a "person"-oriented society. When machines and computers, profit motives and property rights are considered more important than people, the giant triplets of racism, materialism and militarism are incapable of being conquered. A civilization can flounder as readily in the face of moral and spiritual bankruptcy as it can through financial bankruptcy . . .

[A] positive revolution of values is our best defense against Communism. War is not the answer. Communism will never be defeated by the use of atomic bombs or nuclear weapons . . . We must not engage in a negative anti-Communism, but rather in a positive thrust for democracy, realizing that our greatest defense against Communism is to take offensive action in behalf of justice. We must with affirmative action seek to remove those conditions of poverty, insecurity and injustice which are the fertile soil in which the seed of Communism grows and develops.

Our only hope today lies in our ability to recapture the revolutionary spirit (which brought the first settlers to America) and go out into a sometimes hostile world declaring eternal opposition to poverty, racism and militarism.

ALTERNATIVES TO VIOLENCE

SUMMARY OF CONCEPTS
As related to the subjects listed on worksheet #2

1. *What are four uses of nonviolence?*
   a. For resolving conflict
   b. For personal self defense
   c. For social protest and reform
   d. For national defense

2. *What principles/techniques of nonviolence listed on page 15 do you already use?*
   Participants will write as many of the phrases as apply.

3. *VIOLENCE ESCALATES. What does this mean in our lives?*
   Answers will vary. From the film "Neighbors" we learn violence can destroy all parties and their objectives.

4. *What does this escalation of violence mean in our handling of violence?*
   The more violence escalates, the harder it becomes to stop and reverse. Even small signs of tension or discontent should be addressed.

Major point to remember:
- Violence escalates.

Session 2
THE NATURE OF VIOLENCE
Additional reading

Dass, Ram and Paul Gorman. *How Can I Help? Stories And Reflections On Service.* NY: Knopf, 1985.

Kirchof-Glazier, Deborah. *Peace Studies Through Biology.* Amherst, MA: National Association for Mediation in Education, 1992.

Kropotkin, Peter. *Mutual Aid: A Factor Of Evolution.* Boston: Porter Sargent Pub., 1976.

Kreidler, William J. *Elementary Perspectives: Teaching Concepts Of Peace And Conflict.* Cambridge, MA: Educators For Social Responsibility, 1990.

Kreisberg, Seth. *Transforming Power: Domination, Empowerment, And Education.* Suny Press, 1992.

Lappé, Frances Moore. *Rediscovering America's Values.* NY: Ballantine Books, 1989.

Nagler, Michael N. *America Without Violence: Why Violence Persists And How You Can Stop It.* Covelo, CA: Island Press, 1982.

Prothrow-Stith, Deborah. *Violence Prevention Curriculum For Adolescents.* Newton, MA: Education Development Center, 1987.

Session 3
CAUSES OF VIOLENCE

Objectives

a. To learn causes of conflict and violence.

b. To recognize and define institutional/social/cultural violence and understand its effect on people.

WORKSHEET #3

(The following points will be covered in this session. Most points do not have "pat" answers, but the main thing is for you to arrive at an expression of the concepts. These questions are to help you take notes and process the material.)

1. What are my needs? _____

   _____

   _____

2. What are my rights? _____

   _____

   _____

3. When have I been deprived of needs and/or rights? How did I feel? How did I respond?

   _____

   _____

   _____

4. Thinking about when I have been excluded from something I felt I rightfully should be a part of, how did I feel?

   _____

   _____

   _____

5. What makes an individual fully-functioning?

   _____

   _____

   _____

Notes or Journal Entry

Assignments:

_____
_____
_____
_____

NEEDS AND RIGHTS IN THE STAGES OF HUMAN DEVELOPMENT

Many people react violently when they feel that they are being denied or deprived of their basic human needs or rights. The following list of human needs and rights may give us some insight into people's violent responses upon perceiving that they are being deprived or denied in these areas.

Human needs

1) Food
2) Shelter
3) Water
4) Clothing
5) Warmth/Fire
6) Medical care
7) Education/to know
8) To be loved
9) To belong
10) Acceptance, respect
11) Employment/use skills, talents
12) Self-actualization
13) Autonomy
14) Authenticity

Human rights

1) Right to life, liberty and the pursuit of happiness
2) Right to protect and keep self and family safe and secure—out of harm's way
3) Right to worship/freedom of religion
4) Freedom of speech/press

William Glasser's list of human needs

In his book *The Quality School*, William Glasser reduces the number of needs to five:

1) Survival
2) Love
3) Power
4) Freedom
5) Fun

These five seem to incorporate all of the needs named above and add a very important one, otherwise often overlooked, namely—fun!

According to Glasser, we will never have quality schools until we are addressing these five needs of students. Conditions are not going to improve, Glasser contends, as long as teachers, administrators, parents and the public ignore students' needs and focus on their own needs—to present a better image to pass tax levies or to reduce drop out rates or to increase test scores. Yet as these five students' needs are met, the other factors will automatically improve.

The work of W. Edward Deming inspired Glasser's thinking. The quality control and management consultant's ideas of leadership and team work instead of bossism and coercion were at first turned down by U.S. corporations. Introduced in Japan, they led to Japanese industry and business outperforming most all others.

Nonviolent, noncoercive leadership is not idealistic "pie-in-the sky." Meeting these five needs of people is essential to group performance in any field. Ignoring them has been done at great risk and loss.

This article was written by John Looney.
©1986, 1990, 1992, 1993, 1994, 1995 PEACE GROWS, Inc., 513 W. Exchange St., Akron, OH 44302 (216)864-5442.

WHAT MAKES AN INDIVIDUAL FULLY-FUNCTIONING?

The following chart shows the balance of factors needed for an individual to discover his/her talents, nourish and use them (WORTHY MISSION). An individual requires basic needs met (adequate RESOURCES), to use rights fairly (appropriate POWER) in a supportive environment (flexible STRUCTURE). How does your life measure with these concepts?

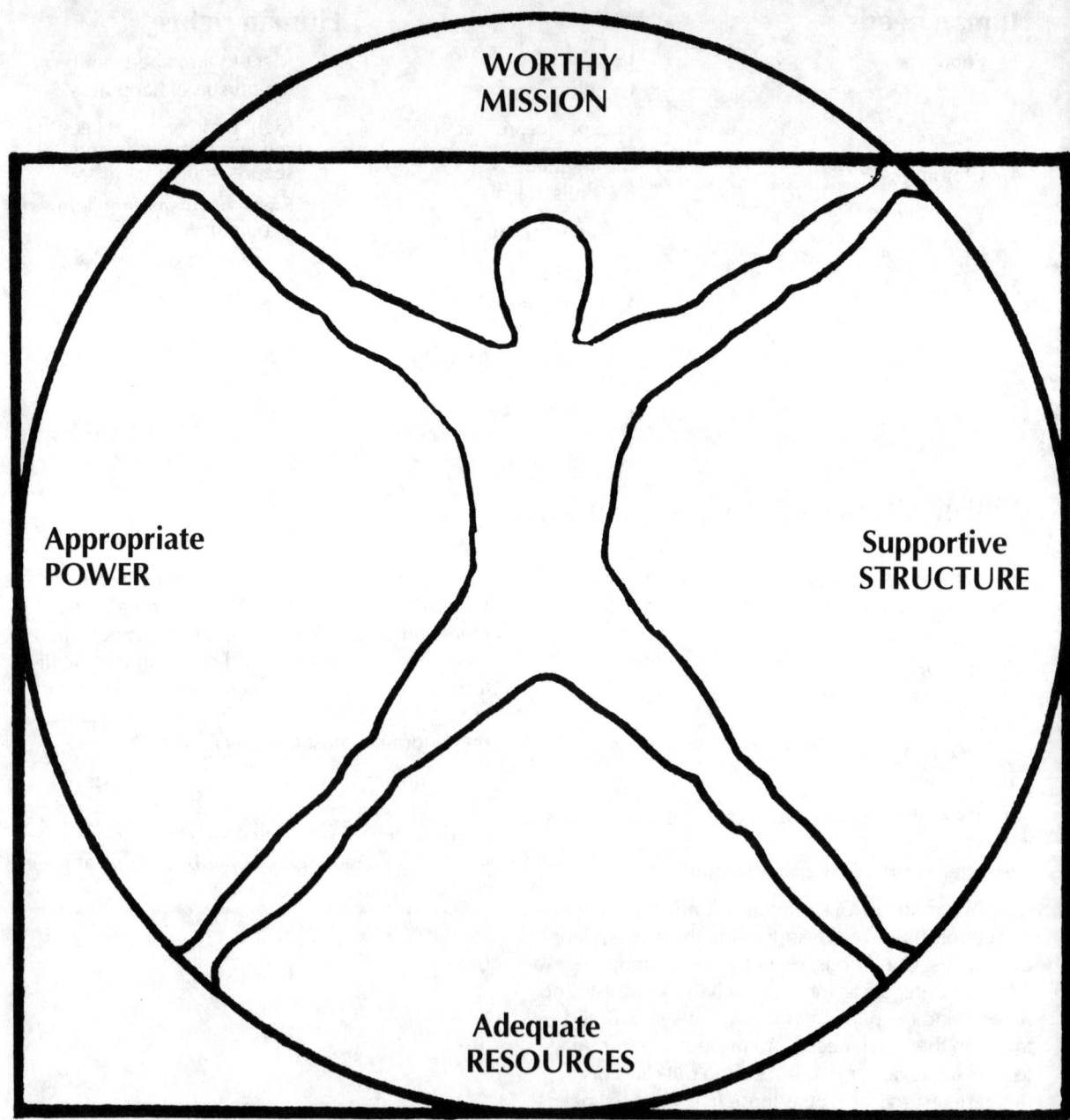

A fully-functioning individual is less frustrated,
less apt to be violent.

Theory by Robert Terry and Jean Alvarez. Chart design by Waring Smith.
©1986, 1990, 1992, 1993, 1994, 1995 PEACE GROWS, Inc., 513 W. Exchange St., Akron, OH 44302 (216)864-5442.

ALTERNATIVES TO VIOLENCE   Session 3 Exercise   27

HOW DO YOU USUALLY HANDLE CONFLICTS?

Without much reflection, please go down this list checking each item as to whether you Always (A), Sometimes (S) or Never (N) do it in a violence/conflict situation:

A	S	N		A	S	N	
__	__	__	Make friends with the enemy	__	__	__	Show your opponent respect & caring. Love your enemy!
__	__	__	Solve the problem together				
__	__	__	Be willing to change your attitude	__	__	__	Be sure all concerned know all the facts
__	__	__	Aim for mutually satisfactory settlement				
__	__	__	Try to overcome opponent's hatred & fear	__	__	__	Show how the change (solution) will be positive
__	__	__	Reject any & all use of violence	__	__	__	Aim for reconciliation for all parties involved
__	__	__	Avoid allowing self or opponent to lose face	__	__	__	Use unexpected, surprise, nonviolent techniques
__	__	__	Allow self & opponent to change position	__	__	__	Be friendly and caring toward the opponent
__	__	__	Hold firmly & calmly to one's goals & values in face of rage or attack	__	__	__	Work with the opponent
				__	__	__	Aim for Win-Win
__	__	__	Create a dilemma in which **any** choice results in solution	__	__	__	Act courageously
				__	__	__	Avoid any harm to opponent
__	__	__	Be willing to suffer oneself but unwilling to cause suffering to opponent	__	__	__	Think & act clearly
				__	__	__	Exercise self-control
__	__	__	Aim for equitable solution acceptable to all parties	__	__	__	Be persistent & patient
				__	__	__	Keep many options open
__	__	__	Realize that equitable, lasting change comes slowly	__	__	__	**TOTAL no. checks each column**
__	__	__	Be dedicated to justice throughout entire process				
__	__	__	Be faithful to the truth at all times/at all costs				
__	__	__	Be helpful. Use your nonviolent training!				
__	__	__	Maintain exemplary conduct. Maintain good public relations				
__	__	__	Create sympathy and understanding on part of public & opponent				
__	__	__	Act with integrity & humility to instill respect & sympathy				
__	__	__	Rely on superior mental, creative, moral resources				

When completed, add up the total number and post where indicated above.

For:

A's multiply that total by 2 = _____

S's multiply that total by 1 = _____

N's receive no points =   0

ADD the TOTAL POINTS. = _____

Total Possible Points are 68. Divide total by 68 to get percentage and mark that percentage at the top of this sheet.

©1986, 1990, 1992, 1993, 1994, 1995 PEACE GROWS, Inc., 513 W. Exchange St., Akron, OH 44302 (216)864-5442.

THINGS TO TRY
when in conflict

Talk to the other person. Be sure no one is being misquoted or misinterpreted.

See the conflict as a joint problem. The aim is to tackle a troublesome issue—not each other.

Collect information—as much as you need.

Note areas of agreement—even if they are minor, it is better to establish early on that you can agree.

Avoid the attitude that something is "only emotional." Feelings count.

List alternate solutions.

Cool down the emotions. In separating the people from the problem, ideally, you will argue about the problem and not attack others or their motives.

Identify the real issue. Focus on the underlying interests, not just on stated positions.

Be imaginative. Together, look for options. Come up with a wide range of possible solutions to benefit all.

Understand basic needs. Try to settle differences in a way that respects the needs we all have for safety, security, love, knowledge, a sense of belonging, esteem, etc.

Be concerned with the common good.

Seek the help of a neutral party when embroiled in a heated conflict, but remember that people are more likely to stick to a solution they had a hand in creating.

Be objective. Depending on the situation, agreements can be reached using "objective criteria" such as fair market value, moral standards, scientific judgment and precedent.

Avoid a contest of wills. ("We'll do it my way or not at all!")

Avoid breaking up relationships. Friends can stop speaking because the "resolution" of their dispute left everyone feeling resentful. Try for a compromise.

Avoid timid compliance. In order to preserve a relationship, one person makes all the concessions.

The above reading was submitted by Sr. Rose Dailey, who learned these things to try at a workshop on conflict management.
©1986, 1990, 1992, 1993, 1994, 1995 PEACE GROWS, Inc., 513 W. Exchange St., Akron, OH 44302 (216)864-5442.

SUMMARY OF CONCEPTS
As related to the subjects listed on worksheet #3

1. *What are my needs?*

    Answers will vary, but words will mean food, clothing, shelter, self-respect and other things listed on page 25.

2. *What are my rights?*

    Answers will vary, but words will mean concepts listed in the Bill of Rights. See page 25.

3. *When have I been deprived of needs and/or rights? How did I feel? How did I respond?*

    Each may relate a different incident. When explaining responses, each will describe frustration and/or anger, resulting in conflict and perhaps violence.

4. *Thinking about when I have been excluded from something I felt I rightfully should be a part of, how did I feel?*

    Answers will describe being deprived, hurt, harmed, etc.

5. *What makes an individual fully-functioning?*

    A person with adequate resources, appropriate power operating within a supportive structure will more likely have positive self-esteem and a secure identity.

Major point to remember:
- Actual or perceived denial of a human need is the main cause of violence.

Session 3
CAUSES OF VIOLENCE
Additional reading

Briggs, Corkille. *Your Child's Self Esteem: The Key To Life.* Garden City, NY: Dolphin Books, 1975.

Healy, Jane M. *Endangered Minds: Why Our Children Don't Think.* NY: Simon and Schuster, 1990.

Hopkins, Susan and Jeffrey Winters. *Discover The World: Empowering Children To Value Themselves, Others And The Earth.* Philadelphia, PA: New Society Pub., 1990.

Kincher, Jonni. *The First Honest Book About Lies.* Minneapolis, MN: Free Spirit Press, 1992.

Mastellone, Flavia Rose. *Finding Peace Through Conflict.* Amherst, MA: National Association for Mediation in Education, 1993.

McGinnis, James B. *Parenting For Peace And Justice: Ten Years Later.* Maryknoll, NY: Orbis Books, 1990.

Packer, Alex J. *Bringing Up Parents: The Teenager's Handbook.* Minneapolis, MN: Free Spirit Pub., 1992.

Rueben, Steven C. *Raising Ethical Children.* Rocklin, CA: Prima Pub., 1994.

Schniedewind, Nancy and Ellen Davidson. *Open Minds To Equality: A Source Book Of Learning Activities To Promote Race, Sex, Class And Age Equity.* Englewood Cliffs, NJ: Prentice Hall.

Schulman, Michael and Eva Mekler. *Bringing Up A Moral Child: A New Approach For Teaching Your Child To Be Kind, Just And Responsible.* NY: Doubleday, 1994.

Tannen, Deborah. *You Just Don't Understand: Women And Men In Conversation.* NY: Ballantine Books, 1990.

Winn, Marie. *Plug-In Drug.* NY: Viking, 1985.

Session 4
RESPONSES TO CONFLICT AND VIOLENCE

Objectives

a. To understand better how we each respond to conflict and violence.

b. To learn the many ways there are to respond.

c. To determine which responses tend to be lose/lose, win/lose and win/win and which this course covers.

WORKSHEET #4

(The following points will be covered in this session. Most points do not have "pat" answers, but the main thing is for you to arrive at an expression of the concepts. These questions are to help you take notes and process the material.)

1. How have I responded to a specific conflict I can remember?

   _____
   _____
   _____
   _____

2. What do I think caused the conflict?

   _____
   _____
   _____

3. What are some nonviolent responses to conflict?

   _____
   _____
   _____

4. How can I learn to respond to conflict in a fair manner to myself as well as the other person (without giving in)?

   _____
   _____
   _____

©1986, 1990, 1992, 1993, 1994, 1995 PEACE GROWS, Inc., 513 W. Exchange St., Akron, OH 44302 (216)864-5442.

Notes or Journal Entry

Assignments:

_____
_____
_____
_____

ALTERNATIVES TO VIOLENCE

WHICH PATH TO TAKE?
Conflict and violence or peaceful resolution

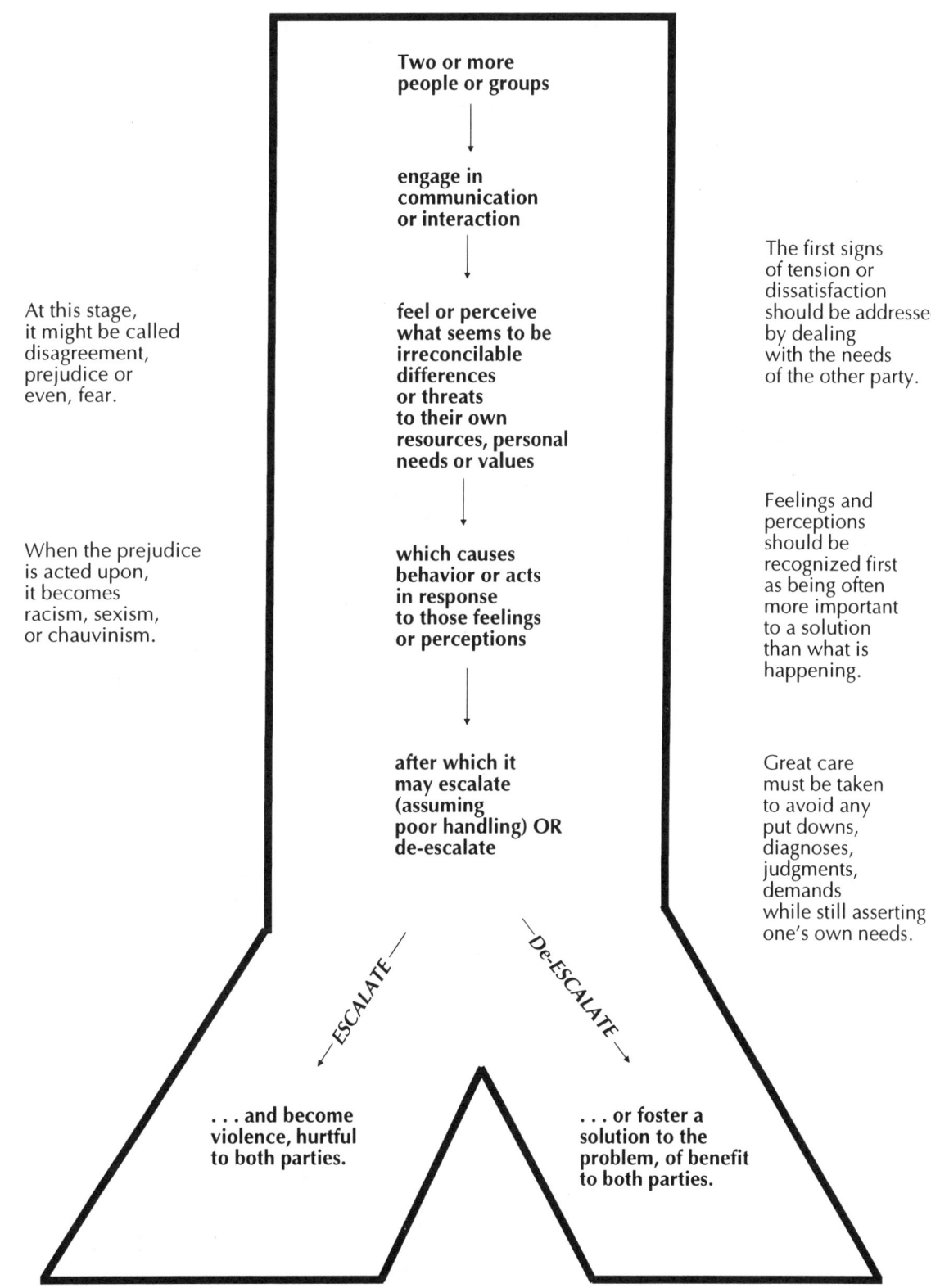

Two or more people or groups

↓

engage in communication or interaction

↓

feel or perceive what seems to be irreconcilable differences or threats to their own resources, personal needs or values

↓

which causes behavior or acts in response to those feelings or perceptions

↓

after which it may escalate (assuming poor handling) OR de-escalate

← ESCALATE   De-ESCALATE →

... and become violence, hurtful to both parties.

... or foster a solution to the problem, of benefit to both parties.

At this stage, it might be called disagreement, prejudice or even, fear.

When the prejudice is acted upon, it becomes racism, sexism, or chauvinism.

The first signs of tension or dissatisfaction should be addressed by dealing with the needs of the other party.

Feelings and perceptions should be recognized first as being often more important to a solution than what is happening.

Great care must be taken to avoid any put downs, diagnoses, judgments, demands while still asserting one's own needs.

The above chart was developed by John Looney.
©1986, 1990, 1992, 1993, 1994, 1995 PEACE GROWS, Inc., 513 W. Exchange St., Akron, OH 44302 (216)864-5442.

WHAT IS CONFLICT RESOLUTION?

Conflict involves opposing ideas and actions; a problem or disagreement.

- Any given conflict has the potential of going in a functional (constructive) path or dysfunctional (destructive) path.

- A functional direction can improve relationships by airing and examining differences and move toward resolving them. This path can be a positive learning experience for life.

- A dysfunctional, destructive direction leaves some feeling victorious while others feel scapegoated or losers; this can escalate into violence.

Resolution includes:

- Learning how to look for alternatives to fighting or fleeing and acting on an alternative.

- Approaching a problem as if both parties could win; thus changing our goals and attitudes.

- Shifting attention away from the participants and onto the problem and how to solve it. (What are those involved doing and what do they hope to accomplish? What do they really need in relation to the conflict?)

To resolve conflicts effectively, we need certain understandings and skills. We will learn these skills in the remaining sessions of this *Alternatives to Violence Workbook*.

Some of the above ideas were adapted from William Kreidler, *Creative Conflict Resolution*, Scott Foresman, 1984, pp. 7-16.
©1986, 1990, 1992, 1993, 1994, 1995 PEACE GROWS, Inc., 513 W. Exchange St., Akron, OH 44302 (216)864-5442.

ALTERNATIVES TO VIOLENCE — Session 4 Chart

RESPONSES TO CONFLICT

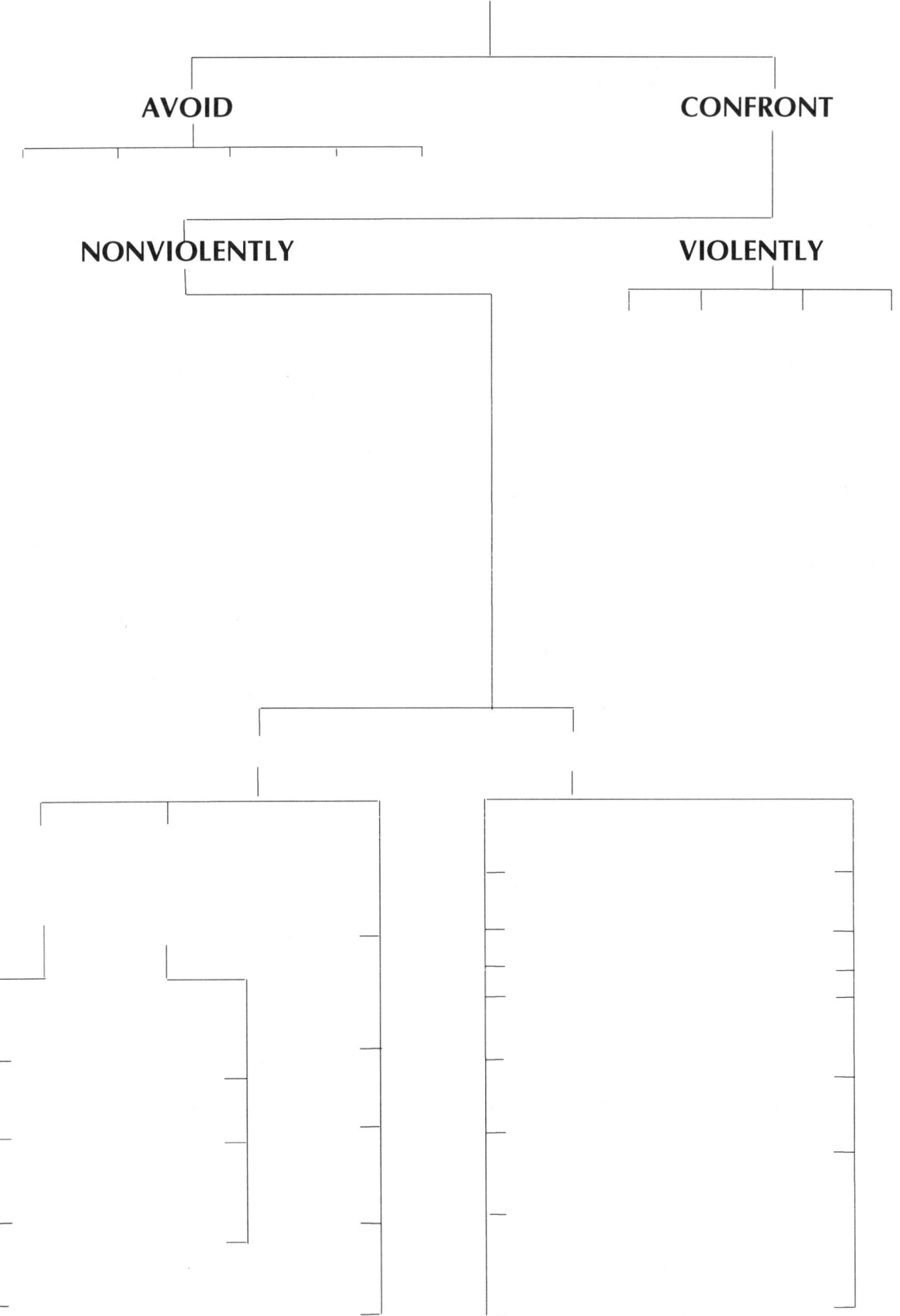

ALTERNATIVES TO VIOLENCE   Session 4 Chart   36

RESPONSES TO CONFLICT

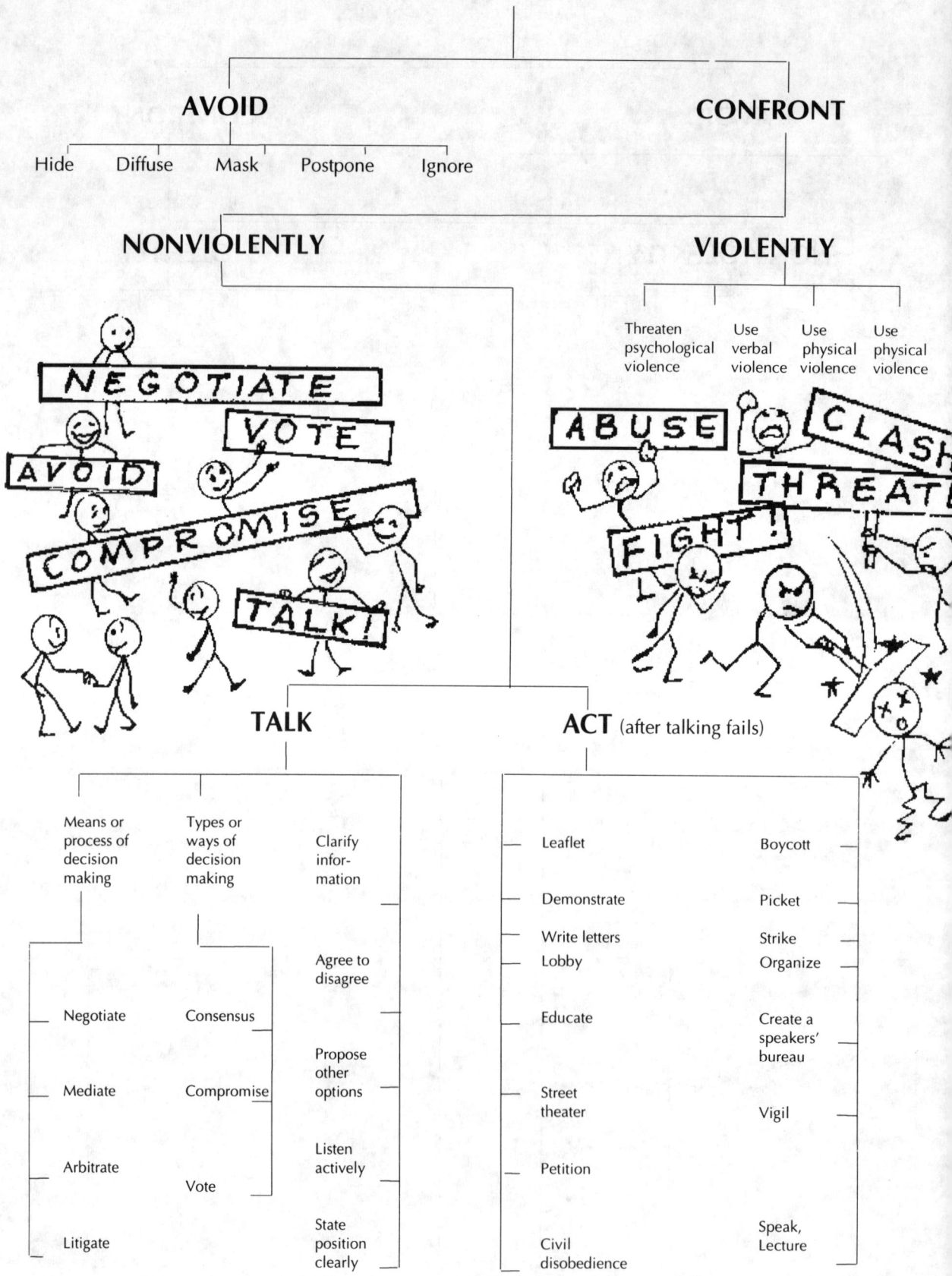

©1986, 1990, 1992, 1993, 1994, 1995 PEACE GROWS, Inc., 513 W. Exchange St., Akron, OH 44302 (216)864-

SUMMARY OF CONCEPTS
As related to the subjects listed on worksheet #4

1. *How have I responded to a specific conflict I can remember?*

   Answers will vary but may include descriptions of the many ways listed in the chart on page 36.

2. *What do I think caused the conflict?*

   See the chart on page 33 for possible causes.

3. *What are some nonviolent responses to conflict?*

   See the chart on page 36.

4. *How can I learn to respond to conflict in a fair manner to myself as well as the other person (without giving in)?*

   If I approach the problem as if both parties could win, I can shift my attention to looking for solutions and away from me and my opponent. I am not going to fight or give in but confront the problem and what we both need.

Major point to remember:
- There are many, many ways to respond to conflict that are effective without either fighting or giving in.

Session 4
RESPONSES TO CONFLICT AND VIOLENCE
Additional reading

Dixon, Dorothy. *Teaching Young Children To Care: 37 Activities For Developing Concern For Others.* Twenty-Third Publications, 1990.

Fugitt, Eva D. *He Hit Me Back First! Creative Visualization Activities For Parenting And Teaching.* CA: Jalmar Press, 1983.

Glenn, H. Steven. *Raising Self-Reliant Children In A Self-Indulgent World: Seven Building Blocks For Developing Capable Young People.* Rocklin, CA: Prima Pub., 1988.

Kaufman, Gershen and Lev Raphael. *Stick Up For Yourself: Every Kid's Guide To Personal Power And Positive Self-Esteem.* Minneapolis, MN: Free Spirit Pub., 1990.

Kottler, Jeffrey A. *Beyond Blame: A New Way Of Resolving Conflicts In Relationships.* San Francisco: Jossey-Bass Publishers, 1994.

Kreidler, William J. *Creative Conflict Resolution: More Than 200 Activities For Keeping Peace In The Classroom, K - 6.* Glenview, IL: Scott, Foresman & Co., 1984.

Levin, Diane E. *Teaching Young Children In Violent Times:* Building A *Peaceable Classroom.* Cambridge, MA: Educators For Social Responsibility, 1994.

McGinnis, Kathleen and Barbara Oehlberg. *Starting Out Right: Nurturing Young Children As Peacemakers.* St. Louis, MO: Meyer-Stone Books, 1988.

Nia-Azariah, Kinshasha, Frances Kern-Crotty and Louise Gomer Bangel. *A Year Of SCRC: 35 Experiential Workshops For The Classroom.* Children's Creative Response To Conflict, 1992.

Nelson, Jane and Lynn Lott. *Positive Discipline For Teenagers.* Rocklin, CA: Prima Pub., 1994.

Prutzman, Priscilla, M. Leonard Burger, Gretchen Bodenhamer and Lee Stern. *The Friendly Classroom For A Small Planet.* Children's Creative Response To Conflict, 1988.

Scholes, Katherine. *Peace Begins With You.* San Francisco, Sierra Club Books, 1989.

Session 5
ALTERNATIVES TO VIOLENCE SKILLS
Listening, stating and getting the facts

Objectives
a. To learn and practice nonviolent listening skills and realize how well I listen to others.

b. To understand the importance of stating things clearly and concisely as an alternative to violence skill.

WORKSHEET #5

(The following points will be covered in this session. Most points do not have "pat" answers, but the main thing is for you to arrive at an expression of the concepts. These questions are to help you take notes and process the material.)

1. Think about a situation in which you have not been listened to. How did you feel?

   _____

   _____

   _____

2. How do you feel when someone listens well to you?

   _____

   _____

   _____

3. What components of good listening do you want to improve?

   _____

   _____

   _____

4. How does the skill of good listening relate to the following statement:

   Resolving human problems nonviolently requires getting the facts which includes all feelings and perceptions as well as what happened.

   _____

   _____

   _____

©1986, 1990, 1992, 1993, 1994, 1995 PEACE GROWS, Inc., 513 W. Exchange St., Akron, OH 44302 (216)864-5442.

Notes or Journal Entry

Assignments:

_____
_____
_____
_____

LISTENING

Violently	**Nonviolently or Actively**
1. Interrupt.	1. Do not interrupt or finish sentences for the speaker.
2. Concentrate on what you are going to say next while the other person is talking.	2. Concentrate on what is being said.
3. Let other things distract you. Do not pay attention to speaker.	3. Focus on speaker.
4. Let your eyes wander.	4. Maintain eye contact with speaker.
5. Do not respond.	5. Ask questions to clarify or obtain more information. Repeat what you feel was said, if not clear to you. Respond by agreeing or disagreeing, by nodding or shaking your head, etc.
6. Put the speaker down and/or emphasize your own knowledge, worth, etc.	6. Never put anyone down. Also, your worth will evidence itself without being pushed.
7. Always make negative attacks on what the other person says.	7. Praise good things said and express agreement whenever you can.

LISTENING VERSUS HEARING

In this fast-paced drive-thru world we live in, the Chinese character for the verb "to listen" takes on an interesting significance. In trying to explain the difference between listening and hearing, nothing does it quite as artistically, poetically, or simplistically as this ancient design.

By integrating representations of not only our ears, but our eyes, our heart, and the selfless act of undivided attention into one holistic character, the Chinese have truly captured the essence of "listening."

ACTIVE LISTENING TECHNIQUES

Statements that help the other person talk

Type of statement	Purpose	To do this	Examples
ENCOURAGING	1. To convey interest 2. To encourage the other person to keep talking	—Don't agree or disagree —Use neutral words —Use varying voice intonations	1. "Can you tell me more . . ." 2. "I wonder if . . ." 3. "Please continue . . ."
CLARIFYING	1. To help you clarify what is said 2. To get more information 3. To help speaker see other points of view	—Ask questions —Restate wrong interpretation to force speaker to explain further	1. "When did this happen?" 2. "What I hear you saying . . ." 3. "What did the other person say?"
RESTATING	1. To show you are listening and understand what is being said 2. To check your meaning and interpretation	—Restate basic ideas, facts	1. "So, you would like your parents to trust you more. Is that right?" 2. "Could this be what's going on, you . . ."
REFLECTING	1. To show that you understand how the person feels 2. To help the person evaluate his/her own feelings after hearing them expressed by someone else	—Reflect the speaker's basic feelings	1. "You seem very upset." 2. "Perhaps you're feeling sad." 3. "You sound angry!"
SUMMARIZING	1. To review progress 2. To pull together important ideas and facts 3. To establish a basis for further discussion	—Restate major ideas expressed including feelings	1. "These seem to be the key ideas you have expressed . . ." 2. "Let me see if I understand, you . . ."

The above reading was submitted by Sr. Rose Dailey, who learned this at a communications workshop sponsored by the Ursuline Sisters of Youngstown. ©1986, 1990, 1992, 1993, 1994, 1995 PEACE GROWS, Inc., 513 W. Exchange St., Akron, OH 44302 (216)864-5442.

ALTERNATIVES TO VIOLENCE Session 5 Reading

COMMUNICATION "LEADS"

Active listening takes much practice. Regularly reviewing this material can help. The following phrases can begin statements that **encourage, clarify, restate, reflect or summarize.**

What I hear you saying . . .

You feel . . .

From your point of view . . .

It seems to you . . .

From where you stand . . .

As you see it . . .

You think . . .

You believe . . .

You're . . . (identify the feeling: for example:
    angry, sad, overjoyed)

I'm picking up that you . . .

Phrases that are useful when you are having some difficulty **perceiving** clearly, or it seems that the disputant might not be **receptive** to your communications:

Could it be that . . .

I wonder if . . .

I'm not sure if I'm with you, but . . .

Would you buy this idea . . .

What I guess I'm hearing is . . .

Correct me if I'm wrong, but . . .

Is it possible that . . .

Does it sound reasonable that you . . .

Could this be what's going on, you . . .

From where I stand you . . .

This is what I think I hear you saying . . .

You appear to be feeling . . .

It appears you . . .

Perhaps you're feeling . . .

I somehow sense that maybe you feel . . .

Is there any chance that you . . .

Maybe you feel . . .

Let me see if I understand: you . . .

Let me see if I'm with you: you . . .

The above reading was submitted by Sr. Rose Dailey, who learned these "leads" at a seminar on resolving conflicts successfully.
©1986, 1990, 1992, 1993, 1994, 1995 PEACE GROWS, Inc., 513 W. Exchange St., Akron, OH 44302 (216)864-5442.

ALTERNATIVES TO VIOLENCE

SUMMARY OF CONCEPTS
As related to the subjects listed on worksheet #5

1. *Think about a situation in which you have not been listened to. How did you feel?*

   Answers will vary but explanations will describe feeling hurt.

2. *How do you feel when someone listens well to you?*

   Answers will vary but explanations will describe feeling respected and may include liking the listener.

3. *What components of good listening do you want to improve?*

   Answers will include any of the seven components of good listening described on page 41.

4. *How does the skill of good listening relate to the following statement: Resolving human problems nonviolently requires getting the facts which includes all feeling and perceptions as well as what happened.*

   Active listening is a way of reflecting back to the speaker what was said. The speaker has an opportunity to confirm or correct the listener's perception. Active listening allows both sides to identify more clearly thoughts and feelings about the conflict.

Major point to remember:
- Good listening is a basic need for practicing nonviolence whereas bad listening, itself, is violent. It hurts the other person.

©1986, 1990, 1992, 1993, 1994, 1995 PEACE GROWS, Inc., 513 W. Exchange St., Akron, OH 44302 (216)864-5442.

Session 5
LISTENING, STATING AND GETTING THE FACTS
Additional reading

Cihak, Mary K. and Barbara Jackson Heron. *Games Children Should Play: Sequential Lessons For Teaching Communication.* Glenview, IL: Scott, Foresman & Co., 1980.

Copeland, Noreen Duffy. *Resolving Conflict: Activities For Children Ages 5 - 8.* Albuquerque, NM: New Mexico Center for Dispute Resolution, 1986.

Dinkmeyer, Don and Gary McKay. *The Parent Handbook: A Systematic Training For Effective Parenting.* Random, 1982.

Drew, Naomi. *Learning The Skills Of Peacemaking: An Activity Guide For Elementary Age Children On Communicating, Cooperating, Resolving Conflict.* Rolling Hills Estate, CA: Jalmar Press, 1987.

Faber, Adele and Elaine Mazlish. *How To Talk So Kids Will Listen & Listen So Kids Will Talk.* NY: Avon Books, 1982.

Lucas, Eileen. *Peace On The Playground: Nonviolent Ways Of Problem-Solving.* NY: Franklin Watts, 1991.

Rosenberg, Marshall B. *A Model For Nonviolent Communication.* Philadelphia, PA: New Society Pub., 1983.

Schmidt, Fran and Alice Friedman. *Creative Conflict Solving For Kids.* Miami Beach, FL: Grace Contrino Abrams Peace Education Foundation, 1989.

Schmidt, Fran and Alice Friedman. *Peacemaking Skills For Little Kids.* Miami Beach, FL: Grace Contrino Abrams Peace Education Foundation, 1988.

Weeks, Dudley. *The Eight Essential Steps To Conflict Resolution: Preserving Relationships At Work, At Home, And In The Community.* Putnam, 1994.

Wichert, Susanne. *Keeping The Peace: Practicing Cooperation And Conflict Resolution With Preschoolers.* Philadelphia: New Society Publishers, 1989.

Session 6
ALTERNATIVES TO VIOLENCE SKILLS
Handling my anger

Objectives

a. To learn how to handle my own anger nonviolently and constructively.

b. To understand better the differences between violent and nonviolent goals, attitudes and tactics.

WORKSHEET #6

(The following points will be covered in this session. Most points do not have "pat" answers, but the main thing is for you to arrive at an expression of the concepts. These questions are to help you take notes and process the material.)

1. When I feel angry I usually . . .

   _____

   _____

   _____

2. What would you like to learn about handling anger?

   _____

   _____

   _____

3. How is handling anger related to conflict resolution?

   _____

   _____

   _____

©1986, 1990, 1992, 1993, 1994, 1995 PEACE GROWS, Inc., 513 W. Exchange St., Akron, OH 44302 (216)864-5442.

Notes or Journal Entry

Assignments:

DEALING WITH OUR ANGER

Anger is a natural emotion that arises from a basic instinct within all of us—aggression. When anger is used properly, it will enhance our lives and strengthen us. When we do not understand the anger within ourselves, it is misdirected; it impedes our emotional growth and we are ultimately weakened.

Ambition or assertion is an example of well-directed and effective aggression. Violence is an example of ineffective and destructive aggression.

In the course of our every-day dealings with others, we encounter aggression in various forms. When we are dealt with unfairly by an unfeeling authority figure, we will feel rage. On the other hand, when we assertively right a wrong, we feel pleasure.

When feeling hostile toward others, greater understanding and dissipation of anger will result if the following rules are followed:

- Do not keep angry feelings to yourself. Find a way to express these feelings to the person who has caused them.
- Be responsible for your feelings. For example, say "I feel angry because . . ." as opposed to "You made me angry."
- Avoid calling the other person names.
- Avoid making statements in the form of a question. For example, say "I feel hurt when you do that" instead of "Do you know how rude you are?"
- Avoid blaming the other person, especially in a humiliating way, such as "It is your fault that we do not have money."
- Say something positive before you criticize. For example, "You are usually a thoughtful person but what you just did made me angry."
- Stick to the argument. Do not discuss other issues.
- Do not silently collect grievances and recite them all at once in an argument. Instead, deal with each issue as it arises.
- Do not try to win an argument by walking away,

reprinted from Fanya Carter
Los Angeles Times Syndicate
Akron Beacon Journal
6-16-85

HANDLING ANGER AND CONFLICT NONVIOLENTLY

1. Listen carefully to oneself to understand as clearly as possible one's own desires and needs in the specific situation.

2. Express those needs to the other person or group, either in conflict or who can help solve the problem. These should be made in clear "I" statements which, mainly, is for handling my anger.

3. Then nonviolently and actively listen to their facts, opinions, perceptions, respond to them and decide how to proceed next.

Note:
Anger, like conflict, is all right. In fact, both are good in themselves. They help get out facts without which problems cannot be solved. The bad only results when they are not handled properly such as violently instead of nonviolently.

Communication Facilitators —DO's

Use "I" statements such as:

- I want . . .
- I need . . .
- I feel . . .
- I like or I don't like . . .

Also use:

- Open-ended questions
- Disarming techniques
    a) Agree with part of an argument
    b) Ask for more specific criticism
    c) List options and choose from them
- Express your own vulnerability
- Express your "dream" solution
  "What I would like to see happen is . . ."
- Request
  "Would you be willing to . . ."

Communication Obstructors —DONT's

Do not use:

- Overlong statements
- Unclear statements
- Put-down statements or questions
- Cut-off statements "You should . . ."
- Commands, demands, threats

Also do not:

- Create triangles
- Overgeneralize
- Assume or diagnose
- Judge or give advice
- Defend oneself
- Deny choices to others

DO's and DONT's submitted by Sr. Rose Dailey, who learned these at a communications workshop sponsored by the Ursuline Sisters of Youngstown. ©1986, 1990, 1992, 1993, 1994, 1995 PEACE GROWS, Inc., 513 W. Exchange St., Akron, OH 44302 (216)864-5442.

ALTERNATIVES TO VIOLENCE
Session 6 Chart

THREE BEHAVIOR STYLES
How do these behaviors relate to handling anger?

Non-assertion . . . . is failing to stand up for oneself, or standing up for oneself in such an ineffectual manner that one's rights are easily violated.

Assertion . . . . is standing up for oneself in such a way that one does not violate the basic rights of another person. It is a direct, honest, and appropriate expression of one's feelings and opinions.

Aggression . . . . . is standing up for oneself in such a way that the rights of the other person are violated in the process. It is an attempt to humiliate or put down the other person.

	Non-assertion	**Assertion**	**Aggression**
Characteristics	Indirect, self-denying, inhibited, hidden bargains, emotional dishonesty double messages	Direct, expressive, levelling, appropriately emotionally honest	Direct, domineering at expense of of another person, cutting off communication, "put-downs"
Your feelings when you engage in this behavior	Hurt, anxious at the time, and possible anger later	Confident, self-respect at the time and later	Righteous, superior, deprecatory of others at the time, and maybe guilty later
The other person's about-self feelings	Guilty or superior	Valued, respected	Hurt, humiliated
The other person's feelings about you	Irritation, pity, disgust	Generally respect	Angry, vengeful

The above chart is by Dr. Patricia Jakubowski-Spector, University of Missouri, St. Louis.
©1986, 1990, 1992, 1993, 1994, 1995 PEACE GROWS, Inc., 513 W. Exchange St., Akron, OH 44302 (216)864-5442.

RHYMING A RESPONSE TO ANGER

This rhyming response to anger is easy to memorize (only four key words) and can easily be brought to mind when we are getting angry.

Name It — I need to name the feeling I am experiencing; to identify it as anger.

Claim It — I say to myself, "Yes, I am angry." I need to own my anger.

Tame It — I ask myself, "What do I want to do with this anger?" Shall I repress it? Shall I express it? How can I express my anger appropriately?

Aim It — I need to direct the anger where it belongs. Instead of mis-placing or dis-placing my anger, I send it to the object, person(s) or situation that deserves it. But, I need to express my anger appropriately and nonviolently.

NAME IT • CLAIM IT • TAME IT • AIM IT

Submitted by Sr. Rose Dailey, who learned this response at a workshop on anger in Seattle, WA.
©1986, 1990, 1992, 1993, 1994, 1995 PEACE GROWS, Inc., 513 W. Exchange St., Akron, OH 44302 (216)864-5442.

SUMMARY OF CONCEPTS
As related to the subjects listed on worksheet #6

1. *When I feel angry I usually . . .*

   Each person will answer in his/her own way. Participants might discuss: Does my response bring out facts of the problem? Does my response lead to seeking solutions? Is my anger dissipated by my response?

2. *What would I like to learn about handling anger?*

   Each person will answer in his/her own way. Answers might describe being able to use "I" statements to clearly state feelings and needs.

3. *How is handling anger related to conflict resolution?*

   By handling anger constructively, I will understand my needs, express myself clearly, gather facts from other(s) and lead myself and other(s) toward solution(s).

Major point to remember:
- Anger can be handled if "I" statements, not put-downs, are used and true respect is shown.

Session 6
HANDLING MY ANGER
Additional reading

Arapakis, Maria. *Softpower: How To Speak Up, Set Limits And Say No Without Losing Your Lover, Your Job Or Your Friends.* NY: Warner Books, 1990.

Beekman, Susan and Jeanne Holmes. *Battles, Hassles, Tantrums and Tears: Strategies For Coping With Conflict And Making Peace At Home.* Hearst Books, 1993.

Covey, Stephen R., A. Roger Merrill and Rebecca R. Merrill. *First Things First: To Live, To Love, To Learn, To Leave A Legacy.* NY: Simon and Schuster, 1994.

Crary, Elizabeth. *Without Spanking Or Spoiling: A Practical Approach To Toddler And Preschool Guidance.* Seattle, WA: Parenting Press, 1993.

Dreher, Diane. *The Tao Of Inner Peace.* NY: Harper Perennial, 1990.

Lerner, Harriet Goldhor. *Dance Of Anger: A Woman's Guide To Changing The Patterns Of Intimate Relationships.* NY: Harper and Row, 1989.

Luhn, Rebecca R. *Managing Anger: Methods For A Happier And Healthier Life.* Los Altos, CA: Crisp Pub., 1992.

Nhat Hanh, Thich. *Peace Is Every Step: The Path Of Mindfulness In Everyday Life.* NY: Bantam Books, 1991.

Sinetar, Marsha. *Elegant Choices, Healing Choices: Finding Grace And Wholeness In Everything We Choose.* Mahwah, NJ: Paulist Press, 1988.

Session 7
ALTERNATIVES TO VIOLENCE SKILLS
Handling anger of others

Objectives

a. To learn principles and skills for handling the anger of another at me.

b. To learn the principles and skills for handling anger between others through third party intervention.

c. To explore some reasons why nonviolence works.

WORKSHEET #7

(The following points will be covered in this session. Most points do not have "pat" answers, but the main thing is for you to arrive at an expression of the concepts. These questions are to help you take notes and process the material.)

1. When someone expresses anger toward me, I usually . . .

   _____

   _____

   _____

2. Have I intervened in a conflict in which I was a third party? What happened and how did I feel?

   _____

   _____

   _____

   _____

3. What happens when a nonviolent response confronts potential or actual violence?

   _____

   _____

   _____

©1986, 1990, 1992, 1993, 1994, 1995 PEACE GROWS, Inc., 513 W. Exchange St., Akron, OH 44302 (216)864-5442.

Notes or Journal Entry

Assignments:

_____
_____
_____
_____

USING THE ANGER OF OTHERS CONSTRUCTIVELY

In Session 6, we learned ways to handle our own anger. By using "I" statements we will not lose our self-control as readily nor will we risk escalation of the hostility by causing the opponent to feel "put down" which makes the person defensive and want to retaliate. We are the authorities on our own feelings and perceptions. Others cannot question our "I" statements and those statements should not attack the opponent in anyway.

In this session we want to learn about two other kinds of anger: 1) anger directed by others at us and 2) anger between two other parties where we may intervene. Often it is not so much what was done that makes us angry as it is how it was done and what perceptions were generated in our mind.

P E R C E I V E

When a person is angry at us that usually means he or she perceives being belittled, ignored, excluded, not respected. In Session 5, we learned one good way to handle this. Through reflective listening we can acknowledge those feelings and perceptions and eventually engage in constructive conversation. We can dialogue ways for addressing the opponent's true needs to relieve the tension and show our concern, kindness and friendship.

To handle anger between two other parties, normally we must start with an effective outside way to distract them from the hostile engagement in which they are involved. Only when the attention of all parties is obtained can problem-solving begin. How to intervene with distraction is what we will be dealing with during this Session 7.

D I S T R A C T

This article was written by John Looney.
©1986, 1990, 1992, 1993, 1994, 1995 PEACE GROWS, Inc., 513 W. Exchange St., Akron, OH 44302 (216)864-5442.

NONVIOLENT THIRD-PARTY INTERVENTION

1. Try to distract or isolate the combatants from each other.

2. Try to isolate the combatants from others who might join in the fray.
   a. By physical separation, as where a march is directed away from a fight.
   b. By mental separation, as when the nature and cares of the conflict are explained so onlookers realize it does not really concern them.

3. Become a mediator or arbitrator who tries to help the combatants solve the problem.

4. Confront the escalation directly, as in pointing out that the fighting will not help and they must stop or by distraction through questions, etc. as escalation threatens.

ALTERNATIVES TO VIOLENCE Session 7 Reading 59

For young people
WHEN OTHERS BOTHER ME
What I can do

1. Talk it out. Ask them "Why?"

2. Ask them to stop.

3. Ignore them. Walk away.

4. Be nice to them.

5. Tell an adult.

6. Threaten to tell.

7. Threaten to harm.

8. Pay them back

} These will probably get **me** into trouble!

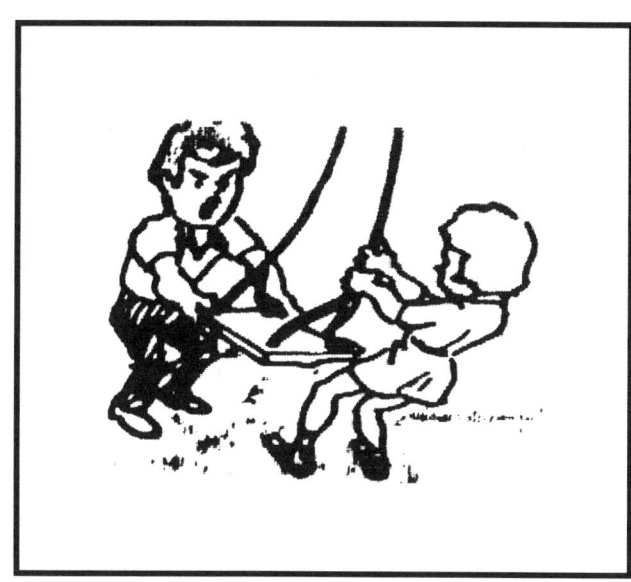

©1986, 1990, 1992, 1993, 1994, 1995 PEACE GROWS, Inc., 513 W. Exchange St., Akron, OH 44302 (216)864-5442.

GUIDELINES FOR FAIR-FIGHTING

- In a fair fight, there is no winner or loser; the aim is a solution.

- In a fair fight, the participants are neither right nor wrong.

- In a fair fight, the participants ask for reasonable specific changes. They do not just complain.

- In a fair fight, feedback is asked for and given on the major points to insure that the information is being heard correctly.

- In a fair fight, feelings are openly expressed and accepted as valid. Feelings are not judged as real or unreal, right or wrong, important or unimportant.

- In a fair fight, issues are discussed one at a time to avoid skipping back and forth between side issues and evading the difficult ones.

- In a fair fight, the original demands are clearly understood and resolved prior to allowing counter-demands to enter the picture.

- In a fair fight, compromise is considered.

- In a fair fight, differences in viewpoints and opinions are tolerated.

- In a fair fight, assumptions and predictions about how another person will react and what he/she will accept or reject are not made.

- In a fair fight, people only speak for themselves by describing their own feelings and thoughts. Assumptions about the other person's thoughts and what they know are not made. They are given ample opportunity to express themselves.

- In a fair fight, sarcasm and labels are inappropriate. Name-calling causes more hurt and defensiveness.

- In a fair fight, only current events are discussed. Past events are not used as weapons.

Guidelines suggested by the DAYTON NEIGHBORHOOD MEDIATION CENTER

From *Mediation Monthly*, January, 1990, Page #3, published by Dayton Neighborhood Mediation Center.
©1986, 1990, 1992, 1993, 1994, 1995 PEACE GROWS, Inc., 513 W. Exchange St., Akron, OH 44302 (216)864-5442.

CONFLICTING PERCEPTIONS

It is said that no two people have the same perception of any event or occurrence. In order to deal with mis-understandings which can lead to anger and hostility, I need to check out my perceptions and compare them to other perceptions. The truth is usually a combination of all perceptions.

The following example is from p. 24, *Getting to Yes*, by Roger Fisher and William Ury.

Tenant's perceptions	Landlady's perceptions
The rent is already too high.	The rent has not been increased for a long time.
With other costs going up, I can't afford to pay more for housing.	With other costs going up, I need more rental income.
The apartment needs painting.	You have given that apartment heavy wear and tear.
I know people who pay less for a comparable apartment.	I know people who pay more for a comparable apartment.
Young people like me can't afford to pay high rents.	Young people like you tend to make noise and to be hard on an apartment.
The rent ought to be low because the neighborhood is run-down.	We landhords should raise rents in order to improve the quality of the neighborhood.
I am a desirable tenant with no dogs or cats.	Your stereo drives me crazy.
I always pay the rent whenever you ask for it.	You never pay the rent until I ask for it.
You're cold and distant; you never ask me how things are.	I am a considerate person who never intrudes on a tenant's privacy.

From GETTING TO YES 2/e by Roger Fisher, William Ury and Bruce Patton. Copyright ©1981, 1991 by Roger Fisher and William Ury. Reprinted by permission of Houghton Mifflin Co. All rights reserved.

EFFECTS: What happens when nonviolence confronts violence?

In his excellent book, *The Power of Nonviolence*, Richard Gregg calls nonviolence moral jiu-jitsu, meaning that nonviolence throws the violent attacker off balance. When the attacker receives a violent response it gives her/him a certain reassurance and moral support. It shows that the intended victim has the same values, fears, and angers s/he has. S/he can predict the victim's next response, plan for it, and use it to her/his advantage.

What if the response is nonviolent? Calm self control is not expected. In the face of blows that are not returned, the intended victim states a belief in truth and justice and asks for an examination of both sides. Resistance is offered but only in nonviolent ways. The acceptance of blows without retaliation proves sincerity. There is no fear or resentment shown. Often, instead, good humor and kindliness is reflected. The endurance of pain is startling. Feelings of curiosity and wonder begin to replace scorn as the aggressor realizes s/he does not face a coward, but rather the opposite. The attacker is unbalanced and, as Gregg says, falls headlong into a new world of values in which s/he feels ignorant and at a considerable disadvantage.

Several factors are at work:

1. The aggressor is surprised and no longer fully in control of the situation. The intended victim, on the other hand, has taken the moral initiative.

2. Prolonged anger is exhausting, whereas training, clearness of purpose, and self-control preserve the nonviolent defender's energy.

3. The attacker's personality becomes divided as her/his more kindly motives are forced to come into conflict with her/his more selfish, violent motives.

4. The aggressor begins to look bad and becomes apprehensive about the effect of her/his aggressiveness on third parties. These third parties are swayed by the clear nonviolence of the resister(s).

5. This new uncertainty about her/his own values and methods and position make the aggressor suggestible to change. Surprise tends to focus her/his attention on that which surprises her/him. The intended victim thus becomes more able to influenc the aggressor than the other way around.

By removing fear, anger, dread of loss, and sense of separateness and substituting feelings of security, sympathy, respect, and good will, nonviolence can overcome cruelty, greed, pride, and bigotry. Nonviolence, even loving one's enemy, proves to be not just idealistic but practical.

SUMMARY OF CONCEPTS
As related to the subjects listed on worksheet #7

1. *When someone expresses anger toward me, I usually . . .*
   Each person will answer in his/her own way.

2. *Have I intervened in a conflict in which I was a third party? What happened and how did I feel?*
   By the end of this session, participants will better understand the strategies on page 58.

3. *What happens when a nonviolent response confronts potential or actual violence?*
   Nonviolence surprises the violent aggressor causing reduced control by the latter and giving moral initiative instead, to the intended victim. The aggressor's kindly motives conflict with selfish, violent ones. The aggressor starts to look bad while the victim gains respect and sympathy from third parties. The former becomes susceptible to influence for change. Nonviolence becomes practical.

Major point to remember:
- Steps for dealing with a conflict between two other people.

Session 7
HANDLING ANGER OF OTHERS
Additional reading

Creighton, Allan. *Helping Teens Stop Violence: A Practical Guide For Educators, Counselors And Parents.* Alameda, CA: Hunter House, 1992.

Jampolsky, Gerald G. *Teach Only Love: The Seven Principles Of Attitudinal Healing.* NY: Bantam, 1983.

Lewis, Barbara A. *Kids With Courage: True Stories About Young People Making A Difference.* Minneapolis, MN: Free Spirit Pub., 1992.

Schmidt, Fran and Alice Friedman. *Fighting Fair For Families.* Miami Beach, FL: Grace Contrino Abrams Peace Foundation, 1989.

Terrell, Ruth Harris. *A Kid's Guide To How To Stop The Violence.* NY: Avon Books, 1992.

Webster-Doyle, Terrence. *Why Is Everybody Always Picking On Me: A Guide To Handling Bullies For Young People.* Middlebury, VT: Atrium Society, 1991.

ALTERNATIVES TO VIOLENCE

Session 8
ALTERNATIVES TO VIOLENCE SKILLS
Negotiation, mediation, arbitration, proposing options

Objectives

a. To define negotiation, mediation, arbitration.

b. To learn the process of negotiation.

c. To develop negotiation skills.

WORKSHEET #8

(The following points will be covered in this session. Most points do not have "pat" answers, but the main thing is for you to arrive at an expression of the concepts. These questions are to help you take notes and process the material.)

1. How do I define the following processes for reaching the final agreement step?

    Negotiation _____

    Mediation _____

    Arbitration _____

2. What other processes are used to conclude the decision or agreement stage?

    _____

    _____

3. What are some nonviolent decision methods?

    _____

    _____

4. What are the steps of negotiation?

    _____

    _____

5. What are the steps of mediation?

    _____

    _____

6. Why are some communities and schools introducing mediation services?

    _____

    _____

©1986, 1990, 1992, 1993, 1994, 1995 PEACE GROWS, Inc., 513 W. Exchange St., Akron, OH 44302 (216)864-5442.

Notes or Journal Entry

Assignments:

_____
_____
_____
_____
_____

NEGOTIATION

Steps toward negotiation

1. **Learn the facts**

    Listen actively and nonviolently. Have positions, perceptions, feelings and facts clearly stated. (Positions, perceptions and feelings are facts.)

2. **Analyze, emphathize**

    Clarify, perceive, differentiate, propose options

3. **Reconcile**

    Integrate positions and ideas
    Find areas of agreement on which to expand
    More integrating
    Test options with parties
    Dialogue to some partial agreements

4. **Reach agreement**

    Compromise, reach consensus,
    specify the solution, agree to the solution

5. **Implement agreement**

    Share power
    List steps needed to put agreement plan into operation
    Fix responsibility for each step
    Establish schedule for completion of each
    Follow this plan to implement the agreed solution
    Establish a schedule for future reviews

6. **Maintain agreement**

    Evaluate results
    Correct where necessary
    Maintain through ongoing communication, evaluation and correction as needed

Facts about negotiation

- Everyone negotiates: families, bosses, workers, teachers, government officials, employers, unemployed.

- Understand the other side's thinking, perceptions, point of view.

- Air and clear up misperceptions, misunderstandings, misinterpretations of each other's intentions.

- Be sure to get all the facts. Organize them. Think about them. Do careful planning about what you will say and do.

- Get rid of assumptions based on fears. Try to minimize, whittle down to bite-size the threatening feeling 'the other' gives us . . . and we give them.

- Don't argue over positions. Try to respond (meet) underlying concerns and interests.

- Separate the people from the issue.

- Recognize the importance of 1) maintaining and furthering relationships, and 2) resolving the issue objectively, fairly.

- Some people's style is hard negotiation; other's is soft negotiation; still other's is merit negotiation.

- The middle way works. Don't be too soft. Don't be too hard. Be assertive, not necessarily aggressive.

- Get rid of good guy-bad guy syndrome.

ALTERNATIVES TO VIOLENCE   Session 8 Reading   68

FLOW CHART
SHOWING MEDIATION PROCESS

The Law and Public Service Magnet High School, Cleveland, Ohio

Mary hears that Louise is saying things about her mother. Mary brings complaint to Mediation Board.

Claire feels that Mrs. Clifton is unfair to her in class. She has met with Mrs. Clifton but still feels unfairly treated. Claire brings complaint.

Incident

Joe has been pushing Clyde around in gym class. Clyde wants to fight. Clyde brings complaint to Mediation Board.

Mrs. Clifton brings complaint against Lou. She has tried meeting with Lou about his behavior in class, but nothing has worked out.

Mediation and alternatives to Mediation will be explained to both parties.

Parties agree to mediate.

Magnet Mediation Board Advocates approach both parties and report on facts of conflict. Advocates schedule panelists for next day.

Mediation scheduled within 48 hours of incident. Time mutually acceptable to parties and panelists.

Mediation is held and results in a signed contract between parties.

Contract filed with Magnet Mediation Board.

Magnet Mediation Board conducts follow-up one month after contract is signed.

If both parties are satisfied with the carrying out of the contract, then file is closed after one month.

Where no agreement to mediate occurs, the regular specified school process is followed. (See *Student Handbook* . . .)

Mediation is held but no agreement is worked out between parties.

If one or both parties are not satisfied, then decision must be made about either moving into regular school process or conducting an additional mediation.

The Law and Public Service Magnet High School, 1651 E. 71st St., Cleveland, OH 44103, Tel.: 216/431-6858; Carole Close, mediation advis
©1986, 1990, 1992, 1993, 1994, 1995 PEACE GROWS, Inc., 513 W. Exchange St., Akron, OH 44302 (216)864-5442.

ALTERNATIVES TO VIOLENCE Session 8 Reading

USING MEDIATION

The Law and Public Service Magnet High School, Cleveland, Ohio

What is mediation?

Mediation is a procedure to get two sides together talking about their problem. It also means that the two parties must begin communicating and finding their own solution. It is a way to help people be responsible for their problems. Most importantly, the problem is solved jointly and nonviolently. Mediation can work anywhere, at home, on the street, at the workplace. It is a peaceful solution to achieving a resolution.

Why mediate?

Mediation is a forum for disputing parties to communicate their feelings. This is a very important concept because no lasting resolution of a conflict is ever possible if there is no full expression or open discussion of the dispute. Once feeelings are expressed, the conflict can be resolved. When conflicts are resolved, peace is created between disputing people.

Who are the mediators?

Each panel will consist of 2 trained students and 1 trained teacher. A panelist acts as a neutral middle person between the disputing parties. A panelist never takes sides or judges which parties are guilty or innocent. The job of the panelist is to try and understand both sides and then help the parties in conflict understand each other's position. Since the panelist is in the middle, he or she can often see both sides more clearly than either of the disputing parties.

The skills needed to become a good mediator are very easy to learn:

1. You must have the ability to focus on what the problem is. Until the key issues are determined, a mediator is usually not going anywhere in solving the dispute.

2. Listening skills are most important because that gives the mediator a tool to help the disputants find a solution.

3. Active listening skills are essential in getting the speaker to talk about the facts and feelings involved. The speaker wants to know they are being listened to. These skills reassure them that they are:

- Facing the speaker squarely.
- Leaning toward them.
- Making eye contact.
- Relaxing and encouraging the speaker to talk.
- The type of questions you ask also help solve the problem faster.
- Open-ended questions which don't require yes or no answers are the best questions to ask for finding out more information.

When to mediate?

Disputes can come to the attention of Magnet Mediation Board in the following ways:

a. Student files complaint;

b. Complaint comes to advocate and advocate pursues;

c. Note is put in specifically designated box in Magnet office;

d. Teacher files complaint.

How does mediation work?

In mediation, there are 6 phases. Each phase helps to make mediation run nice and easy. These phases are:

1. **Introductions** - everyone involved introduces themselves. Panel explains ground rules and procedures.

2. **Telling the story** - each party tells the mediator his/her side of what happened.

3. **Understanding the problem** - parties talk to each other about how each feels.

4. **Alternatives search** - parties think of possible solutions.

5. **Resolutions** - parties together choose solutions that will work and an agreement is written.

6. **Departure** - parties sign agreement and go to next class. (Agreement will be reviewed in one month.)

The Law and Public Service Magnet High School, 1651 E. 71st St., Cleveland, OH 44103, Tel.: 216/431-6858; Carole Close, mediation advisor.
©1986, 1990, 1992, 1993, 1994, 1995 PEACE GROWS, Inc., 513 W. Exchange St., Akron, OH 44302 (216)864-5442.

QUALITY THROUGH NONVIOLENT LEADERSHIP

Traditionally our whole culture and administration style largely has been a violent one. By that is meant that our factories, schools and other organizations often have been controlled from the top down in a largely coercive, fear-laden way with little input from the people below upon whom performance really depends. This has been called "bossism." Priority is given to the needs of the boss and/or the system or organization.

Nonviolent leadership reverses this. Instead of bossing, the nonviolent administrator leads. Workers' confidence replaces fear. Everyone involved has input. Gradually cooperation and collaboration become the norm. Competition, hierarchical authority and wasteful tension, friction and stress become obsolete. In nonviolent leadership, priority is given to the needs of the workers or in the case of schools, the students; if necessary, the system or organization must change.

In World War II, Dr. W. Edwards Deming, a physicist/statistician professor developed some new industrial quality control and management methods based on nonviolent leadership. An attempt was made during the war and after to sell these ideas to American industrial leaders. Such efforts, however, were shunned. "Bossism" was the mode, so "Bossism" would be kept.

As a result of this rejection, Deming presented his ideas to Japan's business leaders. You know the rest. The Deming prize today is the most prestigious award given to any Japanese industry or organization. On entering the lobby of Toyota's administration office, as in many American companies, one is greeted by a large portrait of the founder hanging on the wall to the left. A similar portrait of the present Chief Executive Officer is on the right. But in the middle is an even larger picture of W. Edwards Deming!

After many years of disastrous decline, American industry today is turning to Deming. Though in his early 90's, he is maintaining a full schedule of travelling all over the United States conducting numerous meetings and seminars with American business leaders. Now they are starting to follow his advice eagerly even though fifty years late.

Progress in effective negotiation now is showing tangible results at some American plants. Ford is one. An early article in the *New York Times* describing plans for the new Saturn plant indicated the extent to which the production workers would have input and would be part of the team. Terms of their pioneering labor contract called for workers to be paid salaries instead of hourly wages, and participate in the design and operation of the factory. The agreement stressed consensus decision making and cooperation between management and labor. It called for union members to serve on management committees up to the highest level.

(continued)

This article was written by John Looney.
©1986, 1990, 1992, 1993, 1994, 1995 PEACE GROWS, Inc., 513 W. Exchange St., Akron, OH 44302 (216)864-5442.

Quality from nonviolent leadership and effective negotiation (continued)

Learning of Deming's outstanding accomplishments in industry, William Glasser, the psychiatrist author of *Reality Therapy* asked himself a question: "If the Deming methods work for factories, why not for schools?" *The Quality School, Managing Students Without Coercion* by William Glasser, published in 1990 by Harper & Row, essentially contends that as long as administrators think only of their own needs, such as raising test scores, lowering drop out rates, maintaining a good image in the community to get school levies passed, and do not address the needs of students, they never will achieve quality schools. What needs of students are we talking about? The human needs we discussed in Session 3 are condensed to five:

1. Survival   2. Love   3. Power   4. Freedom and   5. Fun

The growth of social ills in our country through recent decades has denied these five basic needs to many students. With their very survival threatened and love denied at home and in school, with power nil, freedom declining and with wholesome fun and personal satisfaction sparse, it is pretty difficult for them to absorb classroom learning. Everyone wants a quick fix but, in this writer's view, there is no quick fix. Nonviolence, however, is starting to head things in a much more hopeful direction. As many join the effort, progress can escalate rapidly. Also, greater quality of life and growth of self-esteem leads to fuller functioning, empowerment and self actualization. These are very strong preventatives of alcohol and drug abuse.

To help the reader remember what "nonviolent leadership" is, Glasser in his preface inserts the following:

A boss drives. A leader leads.

A boss relies on authority. A leader relies on cooperation.

A boss says 'I.' A leader says 'We.'

A boss creates fear. A leader creates confidence.

A boss knows how. A leader shows how.

A boss creates resentment. A leader breeds enthusiasm.

A boss fixes blame. A leader fixes mistakes.

A boss makes work drudgery. A leader makes work interesting.

For more information on Glasser's work, readers may contact The Institute for Reality Therapy, 7301 Medical Center Drive, Suite 407, Canoga Park, CA 91307. Phone (818) 888-0688.

This article was written by John Looney.
©1986, 1990, 1992, 1993, 1994, 1995 PEACE GROWS, Inc., 513 W. Exchange St., Akron, OH 44302 (216)864-5442.

SUMMARY OF CONCEPTS
As related to the subjects listed on worksheet #8

1. *How do I define the following?*

   Negotiation: the parties carry on a discussion to reach an agreement.
   Mediation: a third party helps the opponent reach agreement.
   Arbitration: the opponents select a third party to make the decision/agreement.

2. *What other processes are used to conclude the decision or agreement stage?*

   Processes include litigation, issuing orders, physically forcing result, voting.

3. *What are some nonviolent decision methods?*

   Nonviolent decision methods include compromise, consensus, agreeing to disagree.

4. *What are the steps of negotiation?*

   There are six steps to good negotiation. See page 67 for an explanation.

5. *What are the steps of mediation?*

   When all the phases described on page 69 are learned and used, mediation works best.

6. *Why are some communities and schools introducing mediation services?*

   Some schools are introducing mediation services in place of certain disciplinary procedures. This is reducing fighting, tension and other discipline problems and improving learning environments. Many communities are starting to have mediation services too. The legal system uses it (called alternatives dispute resolution) in place of court litigation mainly to reduce court docket loads.

Major point to remember:
- Successful, effective negotiation requires active listening and clear stating to get the facts, considering all possible options, and everyone's input with a willingness to share power.

Session 8
NEGOTIATION, MEDIATION, ARBITRATION, PROPOSING OPTIONS
Additional reading

Beer, Jennifer E. *Peacemaking In Your Neighborhood: Reflections On An Experiment In Community Mediation.* Philadelphia, PA: New Society Pub., 1986.

Carter, Artemus and Elisabeth T. Dreyfuss. *Conflict Management And Mediation Handbook.* Cleveland, OH: Cleveland-Marshall College of Law, 1991.

Edelman, Joel and Mary Beth Crain. *The Tao Of Negotiation: How You Can Prevent, Resolve And Transcend Conflict In Work And Everyday Life.* NY: Harper Collins, 1993.

Fisher, Roger, William Ury and Bruce Patton. *Getting To Yes: Negotiating Agreement Without Giving In.* Penguin Books, 1981.

Gerstein, Arnold and James Reagan. *Win-Win: Approaches To Conflict Resolution.* Salt Lake City: Gibbs M. Smith, 1986.

Henriquez, Manti, Meg Holmberg and Gail Sadalla. *Conflict Resolution: A Secondary School Curriculum.* San Francisco: Community Board Program, Inc., 1987.

Kreidler, William J. *Conflict Resolution In The Middle School: A Curriculum And Teaching Guide.* Cambridge, MA: Educators for Social Responsibility, 1994.

Sadalla, Gail, Meg Holmberg and Jim Halligan. *Conflict Resolution: An Elementary School Curriculum.* San Francisco: Community Board Program, Inc., 1990.

Schmidt, Fran, Alice Friedman and Jane Marvel. *Mediation For Kids.* Miami Beach, FL: Grace Contrino Abrams Peace Education Foundation, 1992.

Ury, William. *Getting Past No: Negotiating Your Way From Confrontation To Cooperation.* Bantam Books, 1991.

Woolner, Cate. *Rethinking Mediation: Living Peacefully In A Multi-Cultural World.* Amherst, MA: National Association For Mediation In Education, 1992.

Session 9
ALTERNATIVES TO VIOLENCE SKILLS
Nonviolent personal self-defense

Objectives

a. To examine cases where nonviolent personal self-defense has worked successfully and determine how and why.

b. To develop some basic skills and attitudes for defending ourselves nonviolently.

c. To define nonresistance and distinguish it from noncooperation.

d. To probe the meaning and significance of nonviolence in our lives.

WORKSHEET #9

(The following points will be covered in this session. Most points do not have "pat" answers, but the main thing is for you to arrive at an expression of the concepts. These questions are to help you take notes and process the material.)

1. When and how have I ever responded with nonviolent personal self-defense techniques?

   _____

   _____

   _____

2. From this session I want to remember the following for conveying attitudes important to successful nonviolent self-defense:

   _____

   _____

   _____

3. As other means of active nonviolence, what are nonresistance and noncooperation?

   _____

   _____

   _____

©1986, 1990, 1992, 1993, 1994, 1995 PEACE GROWS, Inc., 513 W. Exchange St., Akron, OH 44302 (216)864-5442.

Notes or Journal Entry

Assignments:

_____
_____
_____
_____
_____

THINKING ABOUT NONVIOLENT PERSONAL SELF-DEFENSE

The topic of Session 9, "Nonviolent Personal Self-defense," is probably the hardest in the course for both teachers and students. Why is this true?

All of us have grown up in a violent, competitive, adversarial, aggressive society. What deluges us, practically from the day we are born, in history books, in newspapers, on television, in sports, from our peers, from our political leaders, from everywhere is that only two responses to conflict and violence exist. A person can fight or run away. But if we run away, we are called a "wimp," which is bad. Therefore, we had better learn how to fight. We have to look after ourselves; no one else will. Even our parents will tell us this.

With this background, we only believe in the practicality of standing up for ourselves. Because we have not been taught it and have not read about it or experienced it, we simply do not believe nonviolence will work in the "real world" where one must be practical. Somehow this continuing emphasis on violence gives people the impression that being a good fighter will always win one's goals, and will always work; conversely, we believe that not fighting will never work. This is unfortunate because both perceptions are wrong.

I remember a woman in one of our classes who was particularly unyielding in her concept that nonviolence would never work, that she would always fight back if attacked. She did not weigh much more than 100 pounds. She only reconsidered when I asked what she would do if there were not one but two assailants. What if each weighed 200 pounds? What if they both were armed and she was not? Would she still fight?

Only then did she think about it more deeply. Finally, she agreed that at times it might be good to have some choices other than fighting. But not knowing these nonviolent alternatives or not having training in the techniques for using them, we are lost. This session is mainly to give us more tools in our self-defense package.

People who use violence can and do lose. People who use nonviolence can and do win. Some have used nonviolent alternatives successfully for centuries all over the globe. We just have never known of all this history. Often we do not even recognize its presence and use in our daily lives. When we do not read about, hear about or see something happening, we "know" it is not true. Yet when we are exposed to a fact five times we believe it, though it may be false.

"Fighters" whether in a war, a boxing ring, a sport or whatever are well trained and disciplined. Without ever having seen a tennis game or taken tennis lessons, who would ever be successful on the court? Yet, we tend to condemn nonviolence as not practical, surrendering, giving in, not doing anything mainly because we do not know about it, understand it, witness it, nor have we been taught the principles and skills to use it effectively. Throughout this course, we are seeking to start making up for all of these generations of ignoring and neglecting the power of nonviolence. This particular session may get to the root of what nonviolence is all about. Ignorance of the principles that are delineated throughout this course, can and do threaten our very survival.

But how might we get started on this particular session? First, let's think about some experience we have had in our life of being either attacked physically or threatened with such attack. We may have to go back to our childhood playground or delve into a more hurtful personal event. (After reading this article, please find a worksheet on page 79 with the following questions:)

. . . . *(continued)*

This article was written by John Looney.
©1986, 1990, 1992, 1993, 1994, 1995 PEACE GROWS, Inc., 513 W. Exchange St., Akron, OH 44302 (216)864-5442.

Thinking about nonviolent personal self-defense (continued)

> **RECALLING AN EXPERIENCE OF PERSONAL ATTACK**
>
> 1. What were the facts of the greatest physical threat in your life, when you suffered or felt the most danger or harm? What happened?
>
> 2. What were your feelings at the time? What was the greatest emotion at the time?
>
> 3. What did you do?
>
> 4. Then what happened?
>
> 5. Were you satisfied with the outcome?
>
> 6. Was there anything you could have done which might have been better?

The greatest emotion felt is fear; fear and violence are closely related. Creating fear in another is doing violence because a person's fear causes violent reactions.

Dr. Gerald Jampolsky, the psychiatrist, has said that human beings have but two emotions. We are born with unconditional love; then we acquire fear. "Love," Jampolsky claims, "is letting go of fear." In fact, this quote is the title of one of his books.

Though usually, we only think of hate and love as opposites, Gandhi claimed that "fear and love are contradictory terms." (see page 97). Is it not true that we cannot really love someone or something we fear? Nor can we fear someone we love. Love implies absolute trust. This faith is part of why true love is so exhilarating because the excitement of finding and experiencing such a relationship tends to be unusual in our culture and enriches so much the entire fabric of our lives.

Perhaps the most impractical application of love is the instruction which Christ gave to "Love your enemies." Imagine, even your enemies! If someone hits your cheek, knocks you down and turns and starts walking away, you are supposed to struggle to your feet and say, "Hey, you forgot something. I have another cheek; come and smack it, too!" What, to most Americans, could seem more ridiculous? Few Christians themselves are comfortable with this instruction of Jesus. Yet this very principle has much to do with applying nonviolent personal self-defense.

That no doubt is why Martin Luther King, Jr. in his sermon on loving your enemy included in the book, *The Strength of Love,* says this is the hardest of all topics. How then, does he handle it? In order to love an enemy, Martin Luther King stresses, first, we must forgive. It is one thing to forgive someone to whom we are related and means much to us, but it is quite another thing to forgive an attacker.

To be successful with nonviolence, we must get ourselves in a frame of mind to forgive an attacker for his/her actions. We must try to understand the causes of those actions. Forgiving will help us to have a clearer mind to deal with the problem. Peace of mind comes from being more ready to forgive than to retaliate. Oscar Arias, former President of Costa Rica, expressed this concept with "no defense is our best defense."

Why does nonviolent self-defense ever work? In our culture so few encounters seem kind and helpful to us or at least we fear so much that we give others little chance to try. When we know someone cares and shows kindness and concern, it is very hard to be mean toward that person.

> *"When we know someone cares and shows kindness and concern, it is very hard to be mean toward t[hat] person."*

True, the message of kindness may not get through to someone whose sensory powers are too dulled by drugs or mental illness. We have said nonviolence does not always work. However, one of our *Alternatives to Violence* graduates who heads a social worker staff in a large, urban mental institution said he felt more than 95% of patients would get the message of kindness. Remember, the situation may be such that nonviolence is the only choice available.

Exactly 300 years ago, in 1692, William Penn explained it this way: "Let us try then what love will do, for if people did once see love, then we should soon find, they would not harm us." In this session of *Alternatives to Violence* we will share cases that might better prepare us for applying nonviolence successfully in actual or threatened personal assault.

This article was written by John Looney.
©1986, 1990, 1992, 1993, 1994, 1995 PEACE GROWS, Inc., 513 W. Exchange St., Akron, OH 44302 (216)864-5442.

RECALLING AN EXPERIENCE OF PERSONAL ATTACK

1. What were the facts of the greatest physical threat in your life, when you suffered or felt the most danger or harm? What happened?

2. What were your feelings at the time? What was the greatest emotion at the time?

3. What did you do?

4. Then what happened?

5. Were you satisfied with the outcome?

6. Was there anything you could have done which might have been better?

©1986, 1990, 1992, 1993, 1994, 1995 PEACE GROWS, Inc., 513 W. Exchange St., Akron, OH 44302 (216)864-5442.

ALTERNATIVES TO VIOLENCE Session 9 Reading

SOME HINTS FOR SUCCESSFUL NONVIOLENT PERSONAL SELF-DEFENSE
How to act confident, never like a victim

- Keep eye contact.

- Care about other and listen actively.

- Ask questions, try to engage in conversation.

- State your needs and feelings in "I" statements.

- Try to respond to the need expressed by the assailant from responses to questions, not the assault.

- Use surprise tactics, which do not frighten.

- Offer options and alternatives.

- Know where to get help.

- Make noise, break and run away, act crazy and shout but do not scream.

- Deeply, emphatically and strongly shout words like "No!" "Stop!" and "Fire!"

- Try to humanize both yourself and your assailant, will surprise and help your control of the situation.

- Never act like a victim.

Nonresistance and Noncooperation

In nonresistance, strive silently to retain one's own dignity.
- Do not look at assailant.
- Do not fight back or protect one's body.
- Physically go limp.
- Do not cooperate in any way.
Examples include harassment, arrest or jail situations.

In noncooperation, a group refuses to help or work with an institution.
- Only used after various other nonviolent skill applications have failed.
- Does not mean giving in.
Examples include conducting a strike or using nonviolent national civil defense.

RAPE
Imagine a robbery victim undergoing the same sort of cross-examination that a rape victim does:

Official: "Mr. Smith, you were held up at gunpoint on First and Main?"

Smith: "Yes."

Official: "Did you struggle with the robber?"

Smith: "No."

Official: "Why not?"

Smith: "He was armed."

Official: "Then you made a conscious decision to comply with his demands rather than resist?"

Smith: "Yes."

Official: "Did you scream? Cry out?"

Smith: "No. I was afraid."

Official: "I see. Have you ever been held up before?"

Smith: "No."

Official: "Have you ever given money away?"

Smith: "Yes, of course."

Official: "And you did so willingly?"

Smith: "What are you getting at?"

Official: "Well, let's put it like this, Mr. Smith. You've given money away in the past. How can we be sure you weren't conniving to have your money taken by force?"

Smith: "Listen, if I wanted . . . "

Official: "Never mind. What time did this holdup take place?"

Smith: "About 11 PM."

Official: "You were out on the street after 11 PM? Doing what?"

Smith: "Just walking."

Official: "Just walking? Weren't you aware that you could have been heldup?"

Smith: "I hadn't thought about it."

Official: "What were you wearing?"

Smith: "Let's see—a suit. Yes. A suit."

Official: "An expensive suit?"

Smith: "Well, yes."

Official: "In other words, Mr. Smith, you were walking around the streets late at night in a suit that practically advertised the fact that you might be a good target for some easy money. Isn't that so? I mean, if we didn't know better, Mr. Smith, we might even think that you were asking for this to happen. Mightn't we?"

From *The Decade of Women: A Ms. History of the Seventies*, Levine & Lyons, eds. Paradon, 1980.
©1986, 1990, 1992, 1993, 1994, 1995 PEACE GROWS, Inc., 513 W. Exchange St., Akron, OH 44302 (216)864-5442.

ALTERNATIVES TO VIOLENCE Session 9 Reading 83

NONVIOLENT SELF-DEFENSE

Some suggestions in no particular order

Have you used any of these actions? On the dotted line to the left of each suggestion, write Y for "Yes" and N for "No."

............Try to overcome the language barrier by nonviolent body language.

............Keep talking in a fairly loud voice.

............While talking, "try" not to comply.

............Try to befriend the assailant.

............Be aware of would-be attacker's fear.

............Consider "laying on of hands."

............Keep talking.

............Try to entice the "other" to fight the battle nonviolently on your terms.

............Try to maintain eye contact with opponent—"do not challenge him."

............Try to diminish the attacker's capacity and desire to be brutal by treating with care, trust, etc.

............Try to persuade the "attacker" to fight the battle on your terms (nonviolently).

............Try to increase the attacker's trust and appreciation of you as a fellow human being . . . having a lot in common.

............Try to plan in **advance** what your objectives and tactics would be if attacked.

............Be clear about your objectives (e.g., not to be hurt; not to inflict hurt).

............Try in some way to communicate (share) your goals and feelings with attacker.

............Move toward your objectives, try not to shift them lest you confuse self or opponent.

............Try not to be frightened—as fear communicates itself instantly to opponent, egging him on. Refuse to act like a victim!

............To minimize fear: breathe deeply; keep talking . . . slowly and in a deep voice.

....(continued)

The above statements can be found in the readings for Session 9 in the first printing of the *Alternatives to Violence Workbook*. Readings will be in the Case Histories. ©1986, 1990, 1992, 1993, 1994, 1995 PEACE GROWS, Inc., 513 W. Exchange St., Akron, OH 44302 (216)864-5442.

Nonviolent self-defense (continued)

............Focus on opponent; encourage him to talk; try to discover where he's at.

............Don't frighten your opponent into hurting you. Move slowly, cautiously.

............Make no abrupt gestures. Tell opponent what you are going to do before you do it.

............Do not be threatening or hostile.

............Don't be afraid to state the obvious and clarify things.

............Don't behave like a victim. But be non-threatening.

............Try to create a scenario new to your opponent

............Seek to befriend your opponent's better nature.

............Try to reach his "spark" of decency; explore it; bring it out.

............Resist as firmly and positively as you can, trying to keep the confrontation on a verbal—intellectual—emotional level—away from the physical level.

............Keep talking. Keep listening. Encourage opponent to talk about what he believes, wishes, fears.

............Keep calm. Talk. Try to outlast him.

............You may, selectively, try laying your hand (palm first) very slowly on opponent's upper arm or chest to drain off anger and calm opponent.

............The active listening you do is more important than what you say.

............There are no guarantees!

The above statements can be found in the readings for Session 9 in the first printing of the *Alternatives to Violence Workbook*. Readings will be in the Case Histories. ©1986, 1990, 1992, 1993, 1994, 1995 PEACE GROWS, Inc., 513 W. Exchange St., Akron, OH 44302 (216)864-

ALTERNATIVES TO VIOLENCE   Session 9 Readinng

NONVIOLENT SKILLS FOR HANDLING CONFLICT CONSTRUCTIVELY

Summary of skills at the personal level

1. **Listen actively**
   - learn facts
   - find truth from other party
   - remember perceptions are facts

2. **State position clearly**
   - express facts as you see them
   - express feelings also
   - use "I" statements

3. **Obtain all facts**
   - go to other sources when necessary
   - clarify what other party says

4. **Develop options**
   - keep mind open to all positions (limiting positions limits possibility of solution)
   - point out mutual advantages of options (may enable opponent to move without losing face)

5. **Handle anger nonviolently**
   - use "I" statements to handle own anger
   - listen actively to handle anger of other

6. **Handling anger of third parties when we are not involved**
   - distract or isolate physically from each other or others not involved
   - distract mentally through questions

7. **Negotiate**
   - continue dialogue for solution(s) on which all agree

8. **Mediate**
   - use third party to help negotiate when parties make no progress

9. **Arbitrate**
   - use third party to make actual decision
   - agree upon by both parties

10. **Nonviolent self-defense**
    - place oneself more on level of attacker (tends to remove one from role of victim)

©1986, 1990, 1992, 1993, 1994, 1995 PEACE GROWS, Inc., 513 W. Exchange St., Akron, OH 44302 (216)864-5442.

SUMMARY OF CONCEPTS
As related to the subjects listed on worksheet #9

1. *When and how have I ever responded with nonviolent personal self-defense techniques?*

    Answers will vary but techniques and skills mentioned on pages 81, 83 and 84 may be described.

2. *From this session, I want to remember the following for conveying attitudes important to successful nonviolent self-defense:*

    Participants will prioritize skills from this session but a few basics should cross all backgrounds—never act like a victim yet do not threaten because it might stimulate defensiveness, close options for backing down without losing face or evoke fear causing more aggression in the other party.

3. *As other means of active nonviolence, what are nonresistance and noncooperation?*

    Nonresistance involves not retaliating or protecting one's self while maintaining one's dignity in silence. Noncooperation is usually a collective refusal to help or work with an institution or group in power.

Major point to remember:
- Never act like a victim.

Session 9
NONVIOLENT PERSONAL SELF-DEFENSE
Additional reading

Forest, Jim. *Making Friends Of Enemies: Reflections On The Teachings Of Jesus.* NY: Crossroad, 1988.

Haskins, James. *Resistance: Profiles In Nonviolence.* NY: Doubleday and Co., 1970.

Levine, Ellen. *Freedom's Children: Young Civil Rights Activists Tell Their Own Story.* NY: Putnam, 1993.

McAllister, Pam. *You Can't Kill The Spirit.* Philadelphia, PA: New Society Pub., 1988.

Nicarthy, Ginny. *Getting Free: You Can End Abuse And Take Back Your Life.* Seattle, WA: Seal Press, 1986.

ALTERNATIVES TO VIOLENCE

Session 10
NONVIOLENCE AS A PHILOSOPHY AND A LIFESTYLE

Objectives

a. To learn about the nonviolent philosophies and lifestyles of other people.

b. To consider how nonviolence relates to and/or is a part of our own philosophies and conduct.

WORKSHEET #10

(The following points will be covered in this session. Most points do not have "pat" answers, but the main thing is for you to arrive at an expression of the concepts. These questions are to help you take notes and process the material.)

1. From the readings in this session on beliefs of nonviolent leaders and religious positions, I found the following significant to me:

   _____
   _____
   _____

2. What is the difference between these two words:

   Pacifism _____

   Passivism _____

3. How can I establish my own position on these issues?

   _____
   _____
   _____

4. When is nonviolence most effective?

   _____
   _____
   _____

©1986, 1990, 1992, 1993, 1994, 1995 PEACE GROWS, Inc., 513 W. Exchange St., Akron, OH 44302 (216)864-5442.

Notes or Journal Entry

Assignments:

_____
_____
_____
_____

WHAT WOULD YOU DO IF?

"OK. You're a pacifist. What would you do if someone were, say, attacking your grandmother?"

"Attacking my poor old grandmother?"

"Yeah. You're in a room with your grandmother and there's this guy about to attack her and you're standing there. What would you do?"

"I'd yell, 'Three cheers for Grandma!' and leave the room."

"No, seriously. Say he had a gun and he was about to shoot her. Would you shoot him first?"

"Do I have a gun?"

"Yes."

"No. I'm a pacifist, I don't have a gun."

"Well, say you do."

"All right. Am I a good shot?"

"Yes."

"I'd shoot the gun out of his hand."

"No, then you're not a good shot."

"I'd be afraid to shoot. Might kill Grandma."

"Come on. OK, look. We'll take another example. Say you're driving a truck. You're on a narrow road with a sheer cliff on your side. There's a little girl standing in the middle of the road. You're going too fast to stop. What would you do?"

"I don't know. What would you do?"

"I'm asking you. You're the pacifist."

"Yes, I know. All right, am I in control of the truck?"

"Yes."

"How about if I honk my horn so she can get out of the way?"

"She's too young to walk. And the horn doesn't work."

"I swerve around to the left of her, since she's not going anywhere."

"No, there's been a landslide."

"Oh. Well, then. I would try to drive the truck over the cliff and save the little girl."

Silence.

"Well, say there's someone else in the truck with you. Then what?"

"What's my decision have to do with my being a pacifist?"

"There's two of you in the truck and only one little girl."

"Someone once said, 'If you have a choice between a real evil and a hypothetical evil, always take the hypothetical one.'"

"Huh?"

"I said why are you so anxious to kill off all the pacifists?"

"I'm not. I just want to know what you'd do if—"

"If I was with a friend in a truck driving very fast on a one-lane road approaching a dangerous impasse where a ten-month-old girl is sitting in the middle of the road with a landslide one side of her and a sheer drop-off on the other."

"That's right."

"I would probably slam on the brakes, thus sending my friend through the front windshield, skid into the landslide, run over the little girl, sail off the cliff and plunge to my own death. No doubt Grandma's house would be at the bottom of the ravine and the truck would crash through her roof and blow up in her living room where she was finally being attacked for the first, and last, time."

"You haven't answered my question. You're just trying to get out of it . . ."

"I'm really trying to say a couple of things. One is that no one knows what he'll do in a moment of crisis. And that hypothetical questions get hypothetical answers. I'm also hinting that you have made it impossible for me to come out of the situation without having killed one or more people. Then you can say 'Pacifism is a nice idea, but it won't work.' But that's not what bothers me."

> "Someone once said, 'If you have a choice between a real evil and a hypothetical evil, always take the hypothetical one.'"

From *Daybreak, An Autobiography* by Joan Baez.

What would you do if? (continued)

"What bothers you?"

"Well, you may not like it because it's not hypothetical. It's real. And it makes the assault on Grandma look like a garden party."

"What's that?"

"I'm thinking about how we put people through a training process so they'll find out the really good, efficient ways of killing. Nothing incidental like trucks and landslides . . . Just the opposite, really. You know, how to growl and yell, kill and crawl and jump out of airplanes . . . Real organized stuff. Hell, you have to be able to run a bayonet through Grandma's middle."

"That's something entirely different."

"Sure. And don't you see that it's so much harder to look at, because it's real and it's going on right now? Look. A general sticks a pin into a map. A week later a bunch of young boys are sweating it out in a jungle somewhere, shooting each other's arms and legs off, crying and praying and losing control of their bowels . . . Doesn't it seem stupid to you?"

"Well you're talking about war."

"Yes, I know. Doesn't it seem stupid?"

"What do you do instead, then? Turn the other cheek, I suppose."

"No. Love thine enemy but confront his evil. Love thine enemy. Thou shalt not kill."

"Yeah and look what happened to him."

"He grew up."

"They hung him on a damn cross is what happened to him. I don't want to get hung on a damn cross."

"You won't."

"Huh?"

"I said you don't get to choose how you're going to die. Or when. You can only decide how you're going to live. Now."

"Well, I'm not going to go letting everybody step all over me, that's for sure."

"Jesus said, 'Resist not evil.' The pacifist says just the opposite. He says to resist evil with all your heart and with all your mind and body until it has been overcome."

"I don't get it."

"Organized nonviolent resistance. Gandhi. He organized the Indians for nonviolent resistance and waged nonviolent war against the British until he'd freed India from the British Empire. Not bad for a first try, don't you think?"

"Yeah, fine, but he was dealing with the British, a civilized people. We're not."

"Not a civilized people?"

"Not dealing with civilized people. You just try some of that stuff on the Russians."

"You mean the Chinese, don't you?"

"Yeah, the Chinese. Try it on the Chinese."

"Oh dear. War was going on long before anybody dreamed up Communism. It's just the latest justification for self-righteousness. The problem isn't Communism. The problem is consensus. There's a consensus out that it's OK to kill when your government decides who to kill. If you kill inside the country, you get in trouble. If you kill outside the country, right time, right season, latest enemy, you get a medal. There are about one hundred and thirty nation-states, and each of them thinks it's a swell idea to bump off all the

> *"I said you don't get to choose how you're going to die. Or when. You can only decide how you're going to live. Now."*

rest because he is more important. The pacifist thinks there is only one tribe. Three billion members. They come first. We think killing any member of the family is a dumb idea. We think there are more decent and intelligent ways of settling differences. And man had better start investigating these other possibilities because if he doesn't, then by mistake or by design, he will probably kill off the whole damn race."

"It's human nature to kill."

"Is it?"

"It's natural. Something you can't change."

From *Daybreak, An Autobiography* by Joan Baez.
©1986, 1990, 1992, 1993, 1994, 1995 PEACE GROWS, Inc., 513 W. Exchange St., Akron, OH 44302 (216)864-5442.

What would you do if? (continued)

"If it's natural to kill why do men have to go into training to learn how? There's violence in human nature, but there's also decency, love, kindness. Man organizes, buys, sells, pushes violence. The nonviolenter wants to organize the opposite side. That's all nonviolence is—organized love."

"You're crazy."

"No doubt. Would you care to tell me the rest of the world is sane? Tell me that violence has been a great success for the past five thousand years, that the world is in fine shape, that wars have brought peace, understanding, brotherhood, democracy, and freedom to mankind and that killing each other has created an atmosphere of trust and hope. That it's grand for one billion people to live off of the other two billion or that even if it hasn't been smooth going all along, we are now at last beginning to see our way through to a better world for all, as soon as we get a few minor wars out of the way."

"I'm doing OK."

"Consider it a lucky accident."

"I believe I should defend America and all that she stands for. Don't you believe in self-defense?"

"No, that's how the Mafia got started. A little band of people who got together to protect peasants. I'll take Gandhi's nonviolent resistance."

"I still don't get the point of nonviolence."

"The point of nonviolence is to build a floor, a strong new floor, beneath which we can no longer sink. A platform which stands a few feet above napalm, torture, exploitation, poison gas, A and H bombs, the works. Give man a decent place to stand. He's been wallowing around in human blood and vomit and burnt flesh screaming how it's going to bring peace to the world. He sticks his head out of the hole for a minute and sees an odd bunch of people gathering material and attempting to build a structure above ground in the fresh air. 'Nice idea but not very practical,' he shouts and slides back into the hole. It was the same kind of thing when man found out the world was round. He fought for years to have it remain flat, with every proof on hand that it was not flat at all. It had no edge to drop off or sea monsters to swallow up his little ship in their gaping jaws."

"How are you going to build this practical structure?"

"From the ground up. By studying, learning about; experimenting with every possible alternative to violence on every level. By learning how to say no to the nation-state, no to war taxes, 'NO' to the draft, 'NO' to killing in general, 'YES' to the brotherhood of man, by starting new institutions which are based on the assumption that murder in any form is ruled out, by making and keeping in touch with nonviolent contacts all over the world, by engaging ourselves at every possible chance in dialogue with people, groups, to try to begin to change the consensus that it's OK to kill."

"It sounds real nice, but I just don't think it can work."

"You are probably right. We probably don't have enough time, so far we've been a glorious flop. The only thing that's been a worse flop than the organization of nonviolence has been the organization of violence."

> **"It was the same kind of thing when man found out the world was round. He fought for years to have it remain flat, with every proof on hand that it was not**

From *Daybreak, An Autobiography* by Joan Baez.
©1986, 1990, 1992, 1993, 1994, 1995 PEACE GROWS, Inc., 513 W. Exchange St., Akron, OH 44302 (216)864-5442.

TO BE NONVIOLENT OR NOT TO BE?

As "What Would You Do If?" indicates, most people are skeptical of the practicality of nonviolence. By this session in this workbook, we have learned that nonviolence has worked not just once, but many times; not just today, but throughout history; not just in America, but all over the globe. Maybe most of us have not tried nonviolence because we have not learned of its successes; only of the victories of military campaigns, and other types of fighting. We have been told little about losses using violent methods.

Nor have we been taught the principles, skills and techniques for using well the power of nonviolence. Could that be why so many do not believe in it and are so skeptical of those who do? This course has tried to offer that learning. But for nonviolence to really work for us, we have to know, understand and practice more than the steps for using it. Nonviolence is a philosophy: a belief system, a value system, a way of life.

Success in nonviolence requires great sensitivity to and caring for other people. For instance, studies show that just learning the steps of mediation and practicing them will not change a person's belief in violence. This writer knows of a skilled high school mediator who resumed fighting and dropped out of mediation. Relationships between the parties, before any mediation steps are taken and after they are completed, determine whether or not there has been conflict resolution. Roger Fisher, co-author of the best seller on negotiation entitled *Getting to Yes* stresses relationships in his newer book *Getting Together*.

The power of nonviolence goes much deeper than following a strategic formula. It is a value system; it is a belief system put into practice. Quakers call it "speaking to that of God in everyone." Demonstrating universal and unconditional concern for the other person, as a keystone of a moral value structure, has the power to transform others. Methods work better when people believe in them and are willing to make referrals and otherwise support the value structure.

There is another significant bonus. In her article "Beyond Self" Angela Tampone states, "New research shows that doing good may be good for your heart, your immune system and your overall vitality." Tampone quotes three mental health experts;* their research indicates that regular volunteer work may dramatically increase life expectancy and that helping others can provide feelings of inner strength aiding us in overcoming our own problems. The research also points out that doing good or witnessing someone doing good may enhance our immune system as well as our nervous system.

---

*David McClelland, psychologist at Harvard; Dr. James House at the University of Michigan, Candace Pert, Johns Hopkins University and the National Institute of Mental Health. Also Angela Tampone, "Beyond Self"; Ross Laboratories, Columbus, Ohio; October, 1990. This article was written by John Looney.
©1986, 1990, 1992, 1993, 1994, 1995 PEACE GROWS, Inc., 513 W. Exchange St., Akron, OH 44302 (216)864-5442.

To be nonviolent or not to be? (continued)

What we are really talking about here is moral development. Dr. Lawrence Kohlberg pioneered work at Harvard on the six stages of moral development. Although few ever reach the top stage, we can improve to a higher stage. This movement, Kohlberg says, cannot happen by expecting someone at stage two to jump immediately to stage five any more than one who has not had arithmetic can jump into calculus. But by association with people in the next highest stage, we can reach for that step.

So where can we begin? In any field do we not learn from the leaders and the foremost institutions? That is why this session is so important. Who are some of these leaders of nonviolence? What have they said? What have they believed? What have they done with their lives? What have the great religions, traditionally the promoters of moral values, said? Let's find out and then let us consider where we stand on these issues.

The 6 stages of moral development are

1. Obedience and punishment
2. Apple polishing
3. Good-boy/nice-girl conformity
4. Rules are rules
5. Social contract and human rights
6. Universal principles.

For more information, read "When Johnny Wants To Do the Right Thing," by Clayton Jones, *The Christian Science Monitor*, August 9, 1978. This article appears in *The Teacher's Guide to the ATV Workbook*, p. 92.

This article was written by John Looney.
©1986, 1990, 1992, 1993, 1994, 1995 PEACE GROWS, Inc., 513 W. Exchange St., Akron, OH 44302 (216)864-5442.

READINGS ON NONVIOLENCE

A QUAKER PROPOSAL

But who, our readers may ask, are we—a handful of Quakers, speaking only for ourselves—to set ourselves up as teachers, with our limited knowledge and experience? The question is a fair one, and we speak humbly, with an acute sense of our limitations. But speak we must. We believe there is an inward teacher, to which through our lives we have tried to listen and to which we believe all people everywhere can attend. By this inward teacher we are convinced that there is a way of death, and a way of life. The way of death is the way of threat and violence, hatred and malevolence, rigid ideology and obsessive nationalism. This way is all too easy to find. The way of life is harder to find; it is uphill, and takes hard work of mind and body and, even more difficult, purification of spirit. Neither rulers, nor parties, nor nations, nor ideologies, nor religions can command the legitimate loyalties of people unless they serve the way of life. Nothing but the truth has divine right. Hard as it is to find, we believe the way of life can and must be found, and we urge all people everywhere to dedicate their lives to its finding.

—from "A New China Policy—Some Quaker Proposals" American Friends Service Committee

ANDREA DWORKIN

In my view, any commitment to nonviolence which is real, which is authentic, must begin in the recognition of the forms and degrees of violence perpetuated against women by the gender class men. Any analysis of violence, or any commitment to act against it, that does not begin there is hollow, meaningless—a sham which will have, as its direct consequence, the perpetuation of our servitude. In my view, any male apostle of so-called nonviolence who is not committed, body and souls, to ending the violence against us is not trustworthy . . . He is someone to whom our lives are invisible.

—from "Redefining Nonviolence" (1975), excerpted by Janey Meyerding, Seattle, Washington

HELEN CALDICOTT, M.D.

We are condemning the future generations to incredible illnesses. Imagine our descendants waking up in the morning with radioactive vats leaking all over the country, the food contaminated, their kids already being born deformed and dying of leukemia and cancer. It is irreversible. I appeal to your sense of goodness, to your love of your children and humanity. We all have that power to do the right thing for the human race.

—stated before the NRC, Boston, Massachusetts, August, 1978 and printed in HANDBOOK FOR WOMEN ON THE NUCLEAR MENTALITY

MOHANDAS K. GANDHI

Whatever may be the result, there is always in me a conscious struggle for following the law of nonviolence deliberately and ceaselessly. Such a struggle leaves one stronger for it. Nonviolence is a weapon of the strong. With the weak it might easily be hypocrisy. Fear and love are contradictory terms. Love is reckless in giving away, oblivious as what it gets in return. Love wrestles with the world as with the self and ultimately gains mastery over all other feelings. My daily experience, as of those who are working with me, is that every problem lends itself to solution if we are determined to make the law of truth and non-violence the law of life. For truth and nonviolence are, to me, faces of the same coin.

The law of love will work, just as the law of gravitation will work, whether we accept it or not. Just as a scientist will work wonders out of various applications of the law of nature, even so a man who applies the law of love with scientific precision can work greater wonders. For the force of nonviolence is infinitely more wonderful and subtle than the material forces of nature, like, for instance, electricity. The men who discovered for us the law of love were greater scientists than any of our modern scientists. Only our explorations have not gone far enough and so it is not possible for everyone to see all its workings. Such, at any rate, is the hallucination, if it is one, under which

Readings on nonviolence (continued)

MOHANDAS K. GANDHI (cont'd.)

I am laboring. The more I work at this law the more I feel the delight in life, the delight in the scheme of this universe. It gives me a peace and a meaning of the mysteries of nature that I have no power to describe.

My experience, daily growing stronger and richer, tells me that there is no peace for individuals or for nations without practicing truth and nonviolence to the uttermost extent possible for 'man.' The policy of retaliation has never succeeded.

—*Young India*, December 15, 1927

BARBARA DEMING

What is it that those who advocate nonviolent revolution believe most essentially? They believe, in the first place, what most Americans supposedly believe—solemnly recited in school, from the Declaration of Independence: That all of us are born with certain inalienable rights. (The text reads "all men," but let us assume that this was meant to stand for all men and women. Or was it—even rhetorically? It was, of course, not meant at that time to apply to black people.) Inalienable rights. Rights, that is, not to be taken from us under any circumstances. Among these rights the right to life, the right to liberty, the right to the pursuit of happiness . . . The advocate of nonviolence believes—and finds an irresistible logic in believing—that the only way to bring such a future into full being is to begin right now as best we can—though this will be at first imperfectly, since we are caught still in the habits of the past—begin nevertheless to act out that respect for one another, right now.

—from "New Men, New Women: Some Notes on Nonviolence" (1971)

CESAR CHAVEZ

Many people feel that an organization that uses nonviolent methods to reach its objectives must continue winning victories one after another in order to remain nonviolent. If that be the case, then a lot of efforts have been miserable failures. There is a great deal more involved than victories. My experience has been that the poor know violence more intimately than most people because it has been a part of their lives, whether the violence of the gun or the violence of want and need.

PETRA KELLY

Because the world's governments are unable to sustain and guarantee peace, the women at Greenham Common formed a living chain around a military weapons base. I call upon women everywhere, young and old, to form a chain around the world, to resist those who say war is inevitable, and to love only those men who are willing to speak out against the violence. We all need to join together—women uncorrupted by male power and men opposed to violence who wish to break out of the rigid patriarchal institutions.

—from THINKING GREEN; chapter one, "Women & Power"

Readings on nonviolence (continued)

RICHARD GREGG

The first signs of a violent society appear in its basic inability to communicate. Words lose their meaning and become hollow. They are twisted and deformed as tools of manipulation and servitude. Noble words such as truth, goodness and love may come to mean despotism, obedience and death. Peace becomes another name for multi-headed war missiles, and nonviolence is wrenched to mean silence, or lack of opposition to thievery, privilege and the status quo.

Violence can be seen as destructive communication. Any adequate definition must include physical, verbal, symbolic, psychological and spiritual displays of hostility and hatred. The definition must include both our acts and our inactions and that which is done directly to people or indirectly to them through what they esteem. Many forms will take on a combination of these characteristics.

Hunger, poverty, squalor, privilege, powerlessness, riches, despair, and vicarious living are forms of violence—forms that a society approves and perpetuates. We have been too willing to discuss violence in terms of ghetto uprisings, student unrest, street thievery and trashing, and have been unwilling to direct our attention to the more pathological types of violence that are acceptable—the types that daily crunch the humanity and life from untold millions of brothers and sisters.

Under the umbrella of violence there reside two distinctively different phenomena. First there is the violence of men and women who act out of frustration, hopelessness and anger in an attempted grasp at life—the act of the slave breaking the chains, which is understandable and inevitable as long as some humans are in bondage. The other type of violence is the violence of the respectable, the violence of the powerful that seeks personal gain and privilege by maintaining inhuman conditions. It is the violence of the board rooms, legislators and jurists—the white collar violence that pours surplus milk down sewers, robs workers of their wages.

RICHARD GREGG (cont'd.)

Nonviolence cannot then be understood as passivity for indifference to the dynamic of life (i.e., communications between men). It is not the posture of removing oneself from conflict that marks the true nonviolent man, but quite on the contrary, it is placing oneself at the heart of the dynamic. *Nonviolence means taking the responsibility for aiding the direction of human communication and brotherhood. Nonviolence means an active opposition to those acts and attitudes that demean and brutalize another, and it means an active support of those values and expressions that foster human solidarity. Nonviolence, in essence, means taking a stand in favor of life and refusing to delegate individual moral responsibility to another person or group; it means taking control of one's life and aiding others in doing likewise. Nonviolence is an attempt to find truth and love even in the midst of hatred, destruction and pride.*

As the means cannot be separated from the desired ends, nonviolence cannot be separated from peace, for it is the value system and the dynamic that makes peace possible.

DOROTHY DAY

If you want to know the kind of politics we seek, you can go to your history books and read about the early years of this country. We would like to see small communities organizing themselves, people talking with people, people caring for people, people coming together in order to make known what they believe and what they would like their nation to do.

—Dorothy Day (about Catholic Worker)
from DOROTHY DAY: A RADICAL
DEVOTION by Robert Coles

Readings on nonviolence (continued)

MARTIN LUTHER KING, JR.

I do not want to give the impression that nonviolence will work miracles overnight. Men are not easily moved from their mental ruts or purged of their prejudiced and irrational feelings. When the underprivileged demand freedom, the privileged first react with bitterness and resistance. Even when the demands are couched in nonviolent terms, the initial response is the same. I am sure that many of our white brothers in Montgomery and across the south are still bitter toward Negro leaders, even though these leaders have sought to follow a way of love and nonviolence. So the nonviolent approach does not immediately change the hearts of the oppressor. It first does something to the hearts and souls of those committed to it. It gives them a new self-respect; it calls up resources of strength and courage that they did not know they had. Finally, it reaches the opponent and so stirs his conscience that reconciliation becomes a reality.

Due to my involvement in the struggle for the freedom of my people, I have known very few quiet days in the last few years. I have been arrested twice. A day seldom passes that my family and I are not the recipients of threats of death. I have been the victim of a near-fatal stabbing. So in a real sense I have been battered by the storms of persecution. I must admit that at times I have felt that I could no longer bear such a heavy burden, and have been tempted to retreat to a more quiet and serene life. But every time such a temptation appeared, something came to strengthen and sustain my determination. I have learned now that the Master's burden is light precisely when we take his yoke upon us.

My personal trials have also taught me the value of unmerited suffering. As my sufferings mounted I soon realized that there were two ways that I could respond to my situation: either to react with bitterness or seek to transform the suffering into a creative force. I decided to follow the latter course. Recognizing the necessity for suffering, I have tried to make of it a virtue. If only to save myself from bitterness, I have attempted to see my personal ordeals as an opportunity to transform myself and heal the people involved in the tragic situation which now obtains. I have lived these last few years with the conviction that unearned suffering is redemptive.

ALTERNATIVES TO VIOLENCE Session 10 Reading 101

WORLD RELIGIOUS POSITIONS

AFRICAN	ISLAM
BAHAI	JAINISM
BUDDHISM	JUDAISM
CHINESE TRADITION	NATIVE AMERICAN
CHISTIANITY	TAOISM
CONFUCIANISM	ZOROASTRIANISM
HINDUISM	

AFRICAN

May peace reign on earth. May the gourd and the pot agree. May their animals live in harmony and all evil worlds be banished into the bush and the vacant forest.
—AFRICAN TRADITIONS
A prayer from Guinea

BAHAI

It is incumbent upon every man of insight and understanding to strive to translate that which hath been written into reality and action.... That one indeed is a man who, today, dedicateth himself to the service of the entire human race.... It is not for him to pride himself who loveth his own country, but rather for him who loveth the whole world. The earth is but one country, and mankind its citizens.
—BAHAI SCRIPTURES
Words of Bahá'u'lláh

The well-being of mankind, its peace and security, are unattainable unless and until its unity is firmly established.
—BAHAI SCRIPTURES
Words of Bahá'u'lláh

Fighting and the employment of force, even for the right cause, will not bring good results.
—'ABDU'L-BAHÁ
Tablets of 'Abdu'l-Bahá, 1909

BAHAI

O Son of Spirit!

The best beloved of all things in My sight is Justice, turn not away therefrom if thou desirest Me, and neglect it not that I may confide in thee. By its aid thou shalt see with thine own eyes and not through the eyes of others, and shalt know of thine own knowledge and not through the knowledge of thy neighbor. Ponder this in thy heart; how it behooveth thee to be. Verily justice is My gift to thee and the sign of My loving-kindness. Set it then before thine eyes.
—BAHAI SCRIPTURES
The Hidden Words of Bahá'u'lláh

O kings of the earth! Compose your differences and reduce your armaments, that the burden of your expenditures may be lightened, and that your minds and hearts may be tranquilized. Heal the dissensions that divide you, and ye will no longer be in need of any armaments except what the protection of your cities and territories demandeth.... We have learned that you are increasing your outlay every year, and are laying the burden... on your subjects. This, verily, is more than they can bear, and is a grievous injustice.
—BAHAI SCRIPTURES
Words of Bahá'u'lláh

©1986, 1990, 1992, 1993, 1994, 1995 PEACE GROWS, Inc., 513 W. Exchange St., Akron, OH 44302 (216)864-5442.

World religious positions (continued)

BUDDHISM

Happily do we live without hate, amongst the hateful. We dwell with hateful men and hate not. . . . Victory begets hatred, and the defeated live in pain. Happily do we live as peaceful beings, renouncing victory and defeat.

There is no fire greater than longing, no greater crime than hate. There is no greater evil than form, and no greater bliss than Peace.
—BUDDHIST SCRIPTURES
The Dhammapada

To dwell in a peaceful land, with right desires in one's heart—

This is the greatest blessing.

Control of self and peaceful speech, and whatever word be well spoken—

This is the greatest blessing.

To live righteously, to give help to kindred, to follow a peaceful calling—

This is the greatest blessing.
—BUDDHIST SCRIPTURES
Words of the Buddha

The fault of others is easily perceived, but that of one's self is difficult to perceive;

A man winnows his neighbor's faults like chaff, but his own fault he hides, as a cheat hides an unlucky cast of the die.

Speak the truth: do not yield to anger; give, if you are asked, even though it be a little: by these three steps you will come near the gods.

Let a man overcome anger by love, let him overcome evil by good; let him overcome the greedy by liberality, the liar by truth.
—DHAMMAPADA 17, 18

For hatred does not cease by hatred at any time;

Hatred ceases by love.
—DHAMMAPADA 8, 15, 1

Let a man leave behind all anger, let him forsake pride, let him overcome all bondage! No suffering befalls a man who is not attached to name and form, and who calls nothing his own.

He who holds back his anger like a rolling chariot, I call him the real driver. Others only hold the reins.

Overcome anger by love; overcome evil by good; overcome greed by generosity; and the lie by truth! Speak the truth and do not yield to anger; give it you are asked, and by these steps you will go near the gods.
—BUDDHIST SCRIPTURES
Pali Texts

A man finds no justice if he carries a dispute to violence. No, he who knows right from wrong, who is learned and guides others—not by violence, but by the same law, being a guardian of the law, who shows intelligence; he is called just.
—BUDDHIST SCRIPTURES
The Dhammapada

All fear violence. All fear death. One should compare oneself to others, and should neither kill nor cause to be killed.

All fear violence. All love life. One should compare oneself to others, and should neither kill nor cause to be killed.

Whoever harms another being, seeking his own happiness, will find no happiness hereafter. But whoever, seeking happiness, harms no other being will find happiness hereafter . . .

He who harms the harmless and defenseless, soon will come to no good: He will suffer pain, disaster, injury, or sickness; loss of mind, oppression, accusation; or loss of loved ones, or loss of wealth, or a ravaging fire that will burn his house. And after death, this foolish man will be reborn in hell.
—BUDDHIST SCRIPTURES
The Dhammapada

©1986, 1990, 1992, 1993, 1994, 1995 PEACE GROWS, Inc., 513 W. Exchange St., Akron, OH 44302 (216)864-

World religious positions (continued)

CHINESE TRADITION

After considerable difficulties, the man collects his powers and overcomes the obstacles to the unity of all men. Sadness gives way to joy.
—CHINESE TRADITIONS
I Ching

Here is a world which condemns a petty wrong and praises the greatest of all wrongs—the attack of one nation on another—and calls it right. Can we say that the world knows the distinction between right and wrong?
—CHINESE TRADITIONS
Words of Mo Ti

Mutual love is righteousness, but warfare is unrighteousness. The former is beneficial to Heaven, spirit, country, and humanity—the latter means destruction to all.
—CHINESE TRADITIONS
Words of Mo Ti

Killing one man constitutes a crime and is punishable by death. Applying the same principle, the killing of ten men makes the crime ten times greater and ten times as punishable; similarly, the killing of a hundred men increases the evil a hundredfold, and makes it that many times as punishable.

All this the people of the world unanimously condemn and pronounce to be wrong. But when they come to judge the greatest of all wrongs—the invasion of one state by another—(which is a hundred thousand times more criminal than the killing of one innocent man) they cannot see that they should condemn it. On the contrary, they praise it and call it right. . . . Indeed, they do not *know* it is wrong.

The man thinks that war against his weaker opponents will bring victory. But lacking in righteousness, he fails in his endeavors. Returning from the path of strife to one of inner harmony with the eternal law, he finds peace and good fortune.
—CHINESE TRADITIONS
I Ching

CHRISTIANITY

I say to you, Do not resist one who is evil. But if any one strikes you on the right cheek, turn to him the other also; and if any one would sue you and take your coat, let him have your cloak as well; and if any one forces you to go one mile, go with him two miles. Give to him who begs from you, and do not refuse him who would borrow from you.
—CHRISTIAN SCRIPTURES
The Gospel of Matthew

Blessed are the peacemakers, for they shall be called sons of God.
—CHRISTIAN SCRIPTURES
The Gospel of Matthew

You have heard that it was said, "You shall love your neighbor and hate your enemy." But I say to you, Love your enemies and pray for those who persecute you, so that you may be sons of your Father who is in heaven; for he makes his sun rise on the evil and on the good, and sends rain on the just and on the unjust. For if you love those who love you, what reward have you? Do not even the tax collectors do the same? And if you salute only your brethren, what more are you doing than others?
—CHRISTIAN SCRIPTURES
The Gospel of Matthew

O Lord, our Christ, may we have thy mind and thy spirit; make us instruments of thy peace; where there is hatred, let us sow love; where there is injury, pardon; where there is discord, union; where there is doubt, faith; where there is despair, hope; where there is darkness, light; and where there is sadness, joy. O divine Master, grant that we may not so much seek to be consoled as to console; to be understood, as to understand; to be loved, as to love; for it is in giving that we receive, it is in pardoning that we are pardoned, and it is in dying that we are born to eternal life. Amen.
—ST. FRANCIS OF ASSISI
Thirteenth Century

World religious positions (continued)

✝ CHRISTIANITY
(continued)

The invincible weapon, always victorious, is the incessant act of love.
—SISTER CONSALATA
Seventeenth Century

Our truth is an ancient one: That love endures and overcomes; that hatred destroys; that what is obtained by love is retained, but what is obtained by hatred proves a burden.
—AMERICAN FRIENDS SERVICE COMMITTEE
Speak Truth To Power

囍 CONFUCIANISM

The superior man is universally minded and no partisan.

When he goes abroad, he behaves toward others as though he were receiving a distinguished guest.

The superior man thinks of his character; the inferior man thinks of his position.

The superior man desires justice; the inferior man desires favor.

The superior man makes demands upon himself; the inferior man makes demands upon others.

The superior man thinks of virtue; the inferior man thinks of comfort.

The superior man thinks of what is right; the inferior man thinks of what will pay.

The superior man regrets not knowing; the inferior man regrets not being known.

The superior man is not concerned that he has no place, but rather how he may fit himself for one.

The superior man ranks the effort above the prize, and worthiness to be known above being known.

Small men never think they are small; great men never think they are great.

The men of old were reserved in speech, lest they should fall short in deed.

Is there any one maxim which ought to be acted upon throughout one's life?

Surely the maxim of loving kindness is such: Do not unto others what you would to have them do unto you.
—THE ANALECTS OF CONFUCIUS

The ancients, when they wished to exemplify illustrious virtue throughout the empire, first brought peace and order to their states. Desiring to bring peace and order to their states, they first brought the same to their families. Wishing to bring peace to their families, they first cultivated themselves. Wishing to cultivate themselves, they first purified their purposes. Wishing to purify their purposes, they first sought to think sincerely. Wishing to think sincerely, they first extended their knowledge as widely as possible. They did this by the investigation of all things.

By investigation of things, their knowledge became extensive; their knowledge being extensive, their thoughts became sincere; their thoughts being sincere, their purposes were rectified; their purposes being rectified, they cultivated themselves; having cultivated themselves, their families were regulated; their families have been regulated, their states were governed rightly; their states being rightly governed, the empire was thereby brought to peace and prosperity.
—CONFUCIAN SCRIPTURES
Words of Confucius

World religious positions (continued)

HINDUISM

Hinduism, generally considered to be the oldest of the world's existing faiths, is the broad term used to designate a large, conglomerate, socio-religious organism to which belong today well over three hundred million Hindus in India proper and some fifteen to twenty million inhabitants of other Asian countries, the West Indies region, and South Africa. An example of active Hinduism outside the geographic boundaries of India was the world-famous nonviolent resistance movement (*Satyagraha*), first set in motion by Mohandas K. Gandhi when a South African resident from 1893 to 1914. As a discriminated-against, though highly successful, emigrant lawyer, Gandhi began in South Africa to develop a classic Indian tent of *ahimsa* (the doctrine of refraining from the harming of others or the taking of life) into an invincible political instrument. After his return home, application of this ancient religious law not only helped free his countrymen from British rule but led them to worship him as a mahatma or Great Soul.

Ahimsa is not merely nonparticipation in destructive activities; it principally manifests itself in constructive activities—services which lead to the upward growth of man. People say that the Goddess of Ahimsa has no weapons; I say that is wrong. The Goddess of Ahimsa has very powerful weapons at her command. They are the weapons of love and are, therefore, creative and not destructive. Yet they do destroy; they destroy hatred, inequity, hunger, and disease. It is true, however, that the weapons of *ahimsa* look small in size and show in action. . .

The light of *ahimsa* cannot be spread by the external and formal mechanism of organizations. History shows that Jesus came alone and the light that he brought pervaded the world—not through church institutions or "Christian" governments, but in spite of them. The light inspires us even today. The same is true of the Buddha. He was a prince but his message could not be spread by the authority of the state. It spread because he threw his kingdom away like a wisp of straw.

After all, what is it that will spread nonviolence? It is not the body that can do it, for the body is an embodiment of violence. *Ahimsa* is assimilated to the extent one rises above one's body. Nonviolence is the natural state of the soul. What *ahimsa*, therefore, needs is the quest of the spirit, the purification of the mind, service of living creatures, love universal and fearlessness.

VINOBA BHAVE
—"The True Nature of Ahimsa and Our Duty," 1949

Whoever sees all beings in himself and himself in all brings does not, by virtue of such realization, hate anyone . . . . . When, to that wise sage, all beings are realized as existing in his own self, then what illusion, what sorrow, can afflict him, perceiving as he does the Unity?

—HINDU SCRIPTURES
Isa Upanishads

When Svetaketu, at his father's bidding, had brought a ripe fruit from the banyan tree, his father said to him,
"Split the fruit in two, dear son."
"Here you are. I have split it in two."
"What do you find there?"
"Innumerable tiny seeds."
"Then take one of the seeds and split it."
"I have split the seed."
"And what do you find there?"
"Why, nothing, nothing at all."

"Ah, dear son, but this great tree cannot possibly come from nothing. Even if you cannot see with your eyes that subtle something in the seed which produces this mighty form, it is present nonetheless. That is the power, that is the spirit unseen, which pervades everywhere and is all things. Have faith! That is the spirit which lies at the root of all existence, and that also art thou, O Svetaketu."

—Chandogya Upanishad

World religious positions (continued)

HINDUISM
(continued)

If you want to see the brave, look at those who can forgive. If you want to see the heroic, look at those who can love in return for hatred.

—HINDU SCRIPTURES
The Bhagavad-Gita

A pacifism which can see the cruelties only of occasional military warfare and is blind to the continuous cruelties of our social system is worthless. Unless our pacifism finds expression in the broad human movement which is seeking not merely the end of war but our equally non-pacifist civilization as a whole, it will be of little account in the onward march of mankind. The spirit of life will sweep on, quite uninfluenced by it.

Immediately after the spirit of exploitation is gone armaments will be felt as a positively unbearable burden. Real disarmament cannot come unless the nations of the world cease to exploit one another.

—Mohandas Gandhi (1869-1948)

War with all its glorification of brute force is essentially a degrading thing. It demoralizes those who are trained for it. It brutalizes men of naturally gentle character. It outrages every beautiful canon of morality. Its path of glory is foul with the passions of lust and red with the blood of murder. This is not the pathway to our goal. The grandest aid to development of strong, pure, beautiful character, which is our aim, is the endurance of suffering, self-restraint, unselfishness, patience, gentleness; these are the flowers which spring beneath the feet of those who accept but refuse to impose suffering.

—Mohandas Gandhi (1869-1948)

ISLAM

Shall I not tell you what is better than prayers and fasting and giving alms to the poor? It is making peace between one another; enmity and malice destroy all virtues.

—ISLAMIC TRADITION
Words of Muhammad

There is no better ruler than Wisdom, no safer guardian than Justice, no stronger sword than Righteousness, no surer ally than Truth

—ISLAMIC TRADITION
Words of Muhammad

Enmity and hatred is cast among them that shall last until the day of Resurrection. But every time they kindle the fire of war, God shall extinguish it. Ever they seek to create disorder on earth; and God loves not those who create disorder.

—ISLAMIC SCRIPTURES
Qu'ran, Sura 5

All of God's creatures are His family. He is most beloved of God who does real good to the members of God's family.

—ISLAMIC TRADITION
Words of Muhammad

JAINISM

This is the quintessence of wisdom: not to kill anything. Know this to be the legitimate conclusion from the principle of reciprocity with regard to nonkilling. He should cease to injure living beings whether they move or not, on high, below, and on earth. For this has been called Nirvana, which consists of peace.

—JAIN SCRIPTURES
The Sutrakritanga

World religious positions (continued)

 ## JUDAISM

More knowledge, more life. More justice, more peace.
—JEWISH TRADITION
The Talmud

Thou shalt not kill.
—JEWISH SCRIPTURES
The Book of Exodus

Whoever can protest against the injustices of his family but refrains from doing so, should be punished for the crimes of his family. Whoever can protest against the injustices of the people of his community, but refrains from doing so, should be punished for the crimes of his community. Whoever is able to protest against the injustices of the entire world but refrains from doing so, should be punished for the crimes of the whole world.
—JEWISH TRADITION
The Talmud

And they shall sit every man under his vine and under his fig tree; and none shall make them afraid.
—Isaiah, Micah; adapted

Grant us peace, Thy most precious gift, O Thou eternal source of peace, and enable Israel to be its messenger unto the peoples of this earth. Strengthen the bonds of friendship and fellow-ship among the inhabitants of all lands. Plant virtue in every soul and may the love of Thy name hallow every heart. Praised be thou, O Lord, our God, giver of peace.
—JEWISH TRADITION
Song of Peace

And he shall judge among the nations, And shall rebuke many people: And they shall beat their swords into plowshares, And their spears into pruning hooks: Nation shall not lift up sword against nation, Neither shall they learn war any more.
—Isaiah 52, 2

 ## NATIVE AMERICAN

The first peace, which is the most important, is that which comes within the souls of men when they realize their relationship, their oneness, with the universe and all its powers, and when they realize that at the center of the universe dwells *Wakan-Tanka*, and that this center is really everywhere, it is within each of us. This is the real Peace, and the others are but reflections of this. The second peace is that which is made between two individuals, and the third is that which is made between two nations. But above all you should understand that there can never be peace between nations until there is first known that true peace which, as I have often said, is within the souls of men.
—NATIVE AMERICAN
Black Elk (Oglala Sioux)
The Sacred Pipe, 1953

The truest and greatest power is the strength of Peace . . . because Peace is the will of the Great Spirit.
—NATIVE AMERICAN
Hopi Declaration of Peace

 ## TAOISM

Even ornamental weapons are not a source of happiness, but of dread. Therefore, the man of Tao will not abide where such things are. A good man at home sets the place of honor at his left hand. But the warrior, on going forth to battle, gives honor to the right hand. For weapons are things of ill omen. The man of enlightenment does not use them except when he cannot help it. His great desire is peace, and he does not take joy in conquest. To joy in conquest is to rejoice at the loss of human life. He who takes joy in bloodshed is not fit to govern the country.
—TAOIST SCRIPTURES
Tao Te Ching

World religious positions (continued)

TAOISM
(continued)

The man of Tao who serves a ruler does not use weapons of force against the people. His acts are those that he would wish rendered to himself. Where armies are quartered, briars and thorns grow. In the wake of great armies, there will follow bad years.
— TAOIST SCRIPTURES
Tao Te Ching

Lao-tzu's viewpoint, born of a time of troubles not unlike the present, seems unusually attractive and appealing just now, for he advocated *wu wei* or "yielding to win," stressed *being* rather than *doing*, and emphasized the good sense, even the unarguable logic, of returning good for evil. What is more, as far back as the sixth century B.C., he was decrying the growing infringement on the rights of individual man by an amorphous entity called the State.

Force and violence are not the way of life; those who do not live by the way of life will soon perish.

The way of life is not the way of actions and assertions.

Yet through the way of life all things achieve their being.

If those who govern the world would follow the way of life, then all things would unfold according to their own nature.

If the people are best by troublesome desires, they should be taught the unnameable simplicity at the core of life.

When men have ceased from covetousness they will become serene.

Among such people peace will come of its own accord.
— TAO-TEH-CHING; paraphrased

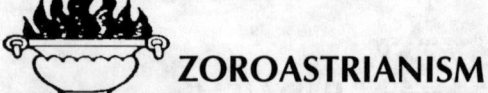

ZOROASTRIANISM

To enjoy the benefits of providence is wisdom; to enable others to enjoy them is virtue. He who is indifferent to the welfare of others does not deserve to be called human. The best way to worship God is to ease the distress of the times and to improve the condition of humanity. This is true religion; to cleanse oneself with pure thoughts, pure words, and pure deeds.
— ZOROASTRIAN SCRIPTURES
The Zend-Avesta

As long as I have will and am physically capable,
 So long will I teach mankind
 To strive for truth, order and peace.
— ZOROASTRIAN SCRIPTURES
The Yasna

We worship the Spirits of the Virtuous to withstand the wrong done by the oppressors who corrupt power and authority; to withstand the wrong done by the dead-in-conscience who forget the social good; and to withstand the wrong done by those yielding to passion, wrath, war, and violence.
— ZOROASTRIAN SCRIPTURES
The Yasht

May wise submission conquer disobedience in this place, and may peace triumph over discord here, and generosity over greed, reverence over blasphemy, truthful speech over lying words. May the Righteous Order gain victory over the lie.
— ZOROASTRIAN SCRIPTURES
The Yasna

WORLD RELIGIOUS POSITIONS

Some Prayers for Peace

ASSISI, Italy, Oct. 27 (AP)– Representatives of 12 major faiths took part here today in the "World Day of Prayer for Peace." Here are excerpts from some of their prayers, as supplied by the Vatican.

BUDDHIST
May all beings everywhere, plagued with sufferings of body and mind, obtain an ocean of happiness and joy.

HINDU
May God protect us; may He nourish us. May we work together with energy. May our studies be fruitful. May we love each other and live in peace.

JAINIST
Peace and universal brotherhood is the essence of the gospel preached by all the enlightened ones of the past and of the future.

MOSLEM
And the servants of the Most Gracious are those who walk on the earth in humility, and when the ignorant address them, they say, "Peace."

SHINTO
Although the people living across the ocean surrounding us, I believe, are all our brothers, why are there constant troubles in this world? Why do winds and waves rise in the ocean surrounding us? I only earnestly wish that the wind will soon puff always all the clouds which are hanging over the tops of the mountains.

AFRICAN ANIMIST
Almighty God, the Great Thumb we cannot evade to tie any knot, the Roaring Thunder that splits mighty trees, the All-Seeing Lord up on high who sees even the footprints of an antelope on a rock mass here on earth: You are the one who does not hesitate to respond to our call. You are the cornerstone of peace.

NATIVE AMERICAN
In smoking the pipe, I invite my family to smoke with me and you, my friends, to pray with me in thanksgiving for this day and for world peace. I will pray that we all may commit ourselves to pray and to work for peace within our families, our tribes, and our nations. I pray for all our brothers and sisters walking our mother earth.

JEWISH
Our God in heaven, the Lord of Peace will have compassion and mercy upon us and upon all the peoples of the earth who implore his mercy and his compassion, asking for peace, seeking peace.

CHRISTIAN
I say to you that hear, love your enemies, do good to those who hate you, bless those who curse you, pray for those who abuse you. To him who strikes you on the cheek, offer the other also; and from him who takes away your cloak do not withhold your coat as well. Give to everyone who begs from you; and of him who takes away your goods do not ask them again. And as you wish that men would do to you, do so to them.

New York Times,
10-28-86

SUMMARY OF CONCEPTS
As related to the subjects listed on worksheet #10

1. *From the readings in this session on the beliefs of nonviolent leaders and religious positions, I found the following significant to me:*
   Each participant may have different responses based on session 10 readings on pages 91-110.

2. *What is the difference between these two words?*
   Pacifism is an active way of living.
   Passivism is being inactive, doing nothing.

3. *How can I establish my own position on these issues?*
   I can establish my own philosophy and lifestyle based on full knowledge of all the possibilities and all the advantages and disadvantages of what I choose. Knowing the beliefs and acts of nonviolent leaders can help me understand nonviolence better.

4. *When is nonviolence most effective?*
   To be nonviolent requires not just knowing tactics but having a clear, firm philosophy, a value or belief system and a nonviolent lifestyle if we are to be most effective.

Major point to remember:
- Nonviolence is a way of life not just strategy; it is belief in and practice of handling disputes without violence. From acts and statements of its leaders, we can learn much to help determine our position.

Session 10
NONVIOLENCE AS A PHILOSOPHY AND A LIFESTYLE
Additional reading

Bacon, Margaret Hope. *The Quiet Rebels: The Story Of The Quakers In America.*
    Philadelphia, PA: New Society Pub., 1985.

Coles, Robert. *The Call Of Service: A Witness To Idealism.* Boston: Houghton Mifflin, 1993.

Fogelman, Eva. *Conscience And Courage: Rescuers Of Jews During The Holocaust.*
    NY: Anchor Books, 1994.

Fox, Matthew. *Creation Spirituality: Liberating Gifts For The Peoples Of The Earth.*
    San Francisco: Harper, 1991.

Gandhi, Mahatma. *The Words Of Gandhi.* NY: Newmarket Press, 1987.

Meltzer, Milton. *Ain't Gonna Study War No More: The Story Of America's Peace Seekers.*
    NY: Harper & Row, 1985.

Muhaiyaddenn, M. R. Bawa. *Islam And World Peace: Explanations Of A Sufi.*
    Philadelphia, PA: Fellowship Press, 1987.

O'Gorman, Angie. *The Universe Bends Toward Justice: A Reader On Christian Nonviolence In The U.S.*
    Philadelphia, PA: New Society Pub., 1990.

Pilgrim, Peace. *Peace Pilgrim: Her Life And Work In Her Own Words.* Santa Fe: Ocean Tree Books, 1982.

Robles, Harold E. *Reverence For Life: The Words Of Albert Schweitzer.* NY: Harper Collins Pub., 1993.

Tolstoy, Leo. *Writings On Civil Disobedience And Nonviolence.* Philadelphia, PA: New Society Pub., 1987.

Vanderhaar, Gerard. *Active Nonviolence: A Way Of Personal Peace.* Mystic, CT: Twenty-Third Pub.

Watley, William D. *Roots Of Resistance: The Nonviolent Ethic Of Martin Luther King, Jr.*
    Valley Forge: Judson Press, 1985.

Session 11
ALTERNATIVES TO VIOLENCE SKILLS
Group participation for problem solving and nonviolent leadership

Objectives

a. To learn the communication problems of participants in group decision making.

b. To develop skills in directing group discussion toward consensus.

c. To understand nonviolent leadership and ourselves as leaders and followers.

d. To explore the nature of power in customary authority roles and in nonviolent roles.

WORKSHEET #11

(The following points will be covered in this session. Most points do not have "pat" answers, but the main thing is for you to arrive at an expression of the concepts. These questions are to help you take notes and process the material.)

1. For a group to solve a problem, what task-oriented roles must be performed?

   _____

   _____

   _____

2. Once initiated, group problem solving requires what maintenance roles?

   _____

   _____

   _____

3. In a group, what blocking or hindering roles have you noticed?

   _____

   _____

   _____

4. What makes a leader nonviolent?

   _____

   _____

   _____

©1986, 1990, 1992, 1993, 1994, 1995 PEACE GROWS, Inc., 513 W. Exchange St., Akron, OH 44302 (216)864-5442.

Notes or Journal Entry

Assignments:

_____
_____
_____
_____
_____

ALTERNATIVES TO VIOLENCE

Session 11 Reading

Power and peacemaking:
COMMUNICATION SKILLS FOR GOOD GROUP CONFLICT RESOLUTION

To use conflict creatively in a group we have to learn communication skills. There are two parts to the process of solving group conflict: (1) the task (2) group maintenance. The roles or skills that help accomplish the task (solve the problem) or maintain the group (nourish relationships) are all important parts of what is often called leadership.

TASK ROLES: use skills that help the group solve the problem

INITIATOR - someone who organizes the group, starts discussion, introduces ideas, raises questions.

INFORMATION SEEKER - clarifies issues, asks for information, asks for definition and goals.

SUMMARIZER - listens well, correlates ideas and suggestions, brings the group up to date by defining where the group stands in solving the problem, indicates areas of agreement and disagreement.

EVALUATOR - keeps the group aware of whether they are attaining their goals.

These four functions are performed by anyone—or several people—in order to keep the group focused on solving the problem.

This article was written by Prill Goldthwait, 1979.
©1986, 1990, 1992, 1993, 1994, 1995 PEACE GROWS, Inc., 513 W. Exchange St., Akron, OH 44302 (216)864-5442.

Maintenance roles nourish individual relationships and strengthen the group life, making it possible for the group to work together well.

MAINTENANCE ROLES: keep the group working

ENCOURAGER - responds acceptingly to others and deals positively with disagreement.

GATE KEEPER - an active listener who makes it possible to hear from others not yet heard from.

COMPROMISER - a good negotiator or mediator, someone who can admit possible error or ignorance on a point, without surrendering her/his viewpoint.

HARMONIZER - reduces tension using humor or by keeping cool, reconciles differences by getting opponents to explore disagreements rather than seeking surrender of one side

The above roles can be performed by anyone or by several people to keep the group feeling good and going strong. Both task roles and maintenance roles work together to facilitate good conflict resolution.

Do you recognize yourself in any of these roles? What happens when nobody does one or more of these jobs in a group?

This article was written by Prill Goldthwait, 1979.
©1986, 1990, 1992, 1993, 1994, 1995 PEACE GROWS, Inc., 513 W. Exchange St., Akron, OH 44302 (216)864-5442.

ALTERNATIVES TO VIOLENCE

Session 11 Reading

We have all been in meetings, classes or discussions where something goes wrong: the business, task, or problem got nowhere. Why? In addition to facilitating (helping) roles, there are also blocking (unhelpful) roles performed in groups.

BLOCKING ROLES: here are five of the most common

COMPETER - an aggressive person who criticizes, blames or puts others down; who feels she/he has to have the "best" idea, or has to be "right."

SELF CONFESSOR who uses the group as a personal sounding board—seeks sympathy for her/his own point of view by telling about personal problems.

BIG TALKER - who never listens to others.

WITHDRAWER - who doodles, daydreams, talks to a neighbor or does not give the whole group the benefit of her/his ideas.

CLOWN - who draws attention to her/himself away from the problem.

The above behaviors are examples of blocking roles which make the process of peacemaking or group conflict resolution more difficult.

So—

If you want to use your person-power for peacemaking use your communication skills and consider which skills you need to learn more about for **conflict resolution**.

This article was written by Prill Goldthwait, 1979.
©1986, 1990, 1992, 1993, 1994, 1995 PEACE GROWS, Inc., 513 W. Exchange St., Akron, OH 44302 (216)864-5442.

POWER AND PEACEMAKING ROLES

Fill in the person's name under the role you think s/he played.

HELPING (FACILITATING) ROLES:

INITIATOR	INFORMATION SEEKER	SUMMARIZER
EVALUATOR	ENCOURAGER	GATE KEEPER
COMPROMISER	HARMONIZER	OTHER

BLOCKING ROLES:

COMPETER	SELF-CONFESSOR	BIG TALKER
CLOWN	WITHDRAWER	OTHER

WHAT GROUP LEADERS, FACILITATORS AND HELPERS CAN DO
WITH PEOPLE WHO TAKE BLOCKING ROLES

[Note: Nonviolence requires that we do not put **anyone** down.]

1. **Clown:** give something to do.

2. **Big Talker:** reflect on something said; thank for input; ask someone who has said little for his/her thoughts; refer to the group's limited time and goal and move on.

3. **Competer:** affirm and recognize, noting the validity of his or her statements and move on (see #2).

4. **Self-confessor:** express interest and concern; acknowledge what has been said but move on (see #2); suggest hearing more during break or after class. (Can apply also to #2 and #3).

5. **Withdrawer:** take aside at break time and do "I" statement if regular gatekeeping requests fail. Person may be uninterested, shy, saboteur, bored or disbelieving.

Keep in mind:

- Helping roles can be assigned, even openly.

- Make it clear that in almost all effective groups these helping roles are being played.

- Keep group, leader and helper objectives in mind.

- Move forward getting people involved in decisionmaking.

- Don't let the discussion get bogged down.

A DIFFERENT "POWER"

Violence and poorly handled conflict and anger in our society originate greatly from our existing cultural concept of power.

Joanna Rogers Macy has a "mini-lecture" on the topic in her book, *Despair and Personal Power in the Nuclear Age*. She contends that western culture has been based on a world-view that reality only consists of clearly definable individual entities or substances like people, trees, atoms, planets, insects, rocks, gases, or liquids. Whole sciences concentrate on identifying, classifying, differentiating those entities.

To Ms. Macy what takes place between entities (actions, communications, relationships, etc.) in our culture is considered less real. Messages, exchanges of energy, feelings like love and hate or perceptions about conditions do not lend themselves to being seen or measured easily. But, through interactions, entities can shove each other around. The stronger can overwhelm the weaker. Therefore, under our western cultural concept, power is defined as domination. Such power can shatter the weaker entity.

Under our western cultural concept, power is defined as domination.

Not wanting to be "wasted" the weaker start building defenses against the stronger. Perhaps some impenetrable shell is created for protection. From this concept power can be defined as invulnerability. The shell is so thick and strong that no reasonable outside impact can be effective or, perhaps, even felt.

From this cultural analysis it becomes apparent that such power indicates an either win/lose or a lose/lose situation, sometimes called a zero-sum game. You win over or you lose out or such disturbance takes place that both lose.

Ms. Macy then points out that, just in this century, scientists have realized that life phenomena and these entities are created and sustained by interconnections. These vital flows of energy, matter, information, cannot be ignored. All life is dynamic, flowing patterns: interrelated, connected, largely co-dependent, like nerve cells, neurons or synapses in a neural net or in the brain.

In this situation, the concept of power becomes entirely different. If defenses are built around a neuron or a synapse to block outside actions and flows of energy or communication, what happens? Does it become more powerful? No, it becomes dysfunctional. Is that not what Alzheimer's disease is all about?

The power of the neuron or synapse depends on its capacity to keep open to messages and its ability to pass on or originate communications. No longer does power relate either to domination or vulnerability. It relates to openness, to cooperation, to collaboration, not to isolation or competition or individual effectiveness.

No longer is "power-over or violent po Instead it ha become "po with" or nor violent powe We only wir we both win we all win.

The old concepts just have not been working for humanity. Day by day our society and world as we know it is being destroyed by violent power; our very survival now depends on moving away from the old concept of power and emphasizing the new.

ALTERNATIVES TO VIOLENCE   Session 11 Reading

NONVIOLENT LEADERSHIP IS MARKED BY:

- Separating feelings about people from feelings about the problem

- Focusing on common needs not differences

- Encouraging multiple solution proposals from which to choose

- Insisting upon a solution fair to all

- Inviting everyone's ideas

- Considering all such ideas carefully

Power is the ability to effect a desired outcome

Violent power is
- Might
- Force
- Strength
- "Bossism"
- Ability to do or act independently of others
- External motivation
- Making people do what you want
- Coercion
- Power exercised **over** others

Nonviolent power is
- Leadership
- Being out in front showing the way
- Motivating people internally
- Inspiring people to follow
- Exercised through seeking consensus
- Power exercised **with** others

©1986, 1990, 1992, 1993, 1994, 1995 PEACE GROWS, Inc., 513 W. Exchange St., Akron, OH 44302 (216)864-5442.

ALTERNATIVES TO VIOLENCE

SUMMARY OF CONCEPTS
As related to the subjects listed on worksheet #11

1. *For a group to solve a problem, what task-oriented roles must be performed?*

    The task-oriented roles to be performed by individual participants are initiator, information seeker, summarizer and evaluator.

2. *Once initiated, group problem solving requires what maintenance roles?*

    The maintenance roles that help the group are encourager, gatekeeper, compromiser and harmonizer.

3. *In a group, what blocking or hindering roles have you noticed?*

    The most common blocking roles to be overcome or limited in their effect are competer, self confessor, big talker, withdrawer and clown.

4. What makes a leader nonviolent?

    The marks of a nonviolent leader are described on page 121.

Major point to remember:
- Never act like a victim.

Session 11
GROUP PARTICIPATION FOR PROBLEM SOLVING AND NONVIOLENT LEADERSHIP
Additional reading

Bobo, Kim, Jackie Kendall and Steve Max. *Organizing For Social Change: A Manual For Activists In The 1990's.* Washington: Seven Locks Press, 1991.

Garfield, Charles. *Second To None: How Our Smartest Companies Put People First.* Homewood, IL: Business One Irwin, 1992.

Haessly, Jacqueline. *Peacemaking: Family Activities For Justice And Peace.* Mahwah, NJ: Paulist Press, 1990.

Peck, M. Scott. *A World Waiting To Be Born: Civility Rediscovered.* NY: Bantam Books, 1993.

Pirtle, Sarah. *Discovery Sessions: How Teachers Create Opportunities To Build Cooperation And Conflict Resolution Skills In Their K - 8 Classrooms.* Amherst, MA: Franklin Mediation Services of University of Massachusetts Mediation Project.

Session 12
ALTERNATIVES TO VIOLENCE SKILLS
Zeroing in on a problem

Objectives

a. To learn a process for focusing a group's attention and energies on solving a problem.

b. To understand how to facilitate a group solution through consensus decision making.

c. To find how to plan the implementation of that solution and put it into operation.

WORKSHEET #12

(The following points will be covered in this session. Most points do not have "pat" answers, but the main thing is for you to arrive at an expression of the concepts. These questions are to help you take notes and process the material.)

1. When have I ever used brainstorming?

   _____

   _____

   _____

   _____

2. Of the six steps explained in this session, I need more practice with . . .

   _____

   _____

   _____

   _____

3. What is consensus? How can I use consensus in my life?

   _____

   _____

   _____

   _____

©1986, 1990, 1992, 1993, 1994, 1995 PEACE GROWS, Inc., 513 W. Exchange St., Akron, OH 44302 (216)864-5442.

Notes or Journal Entry

Assignments:

_____
_____
_____
_____
_____

WHAT IS CONSENSUS?

I used to think that consensus means everyone unanimously votes in favor of an issue. This is not quite accurate. The word "consensus" is derived from the same root as the word "consent."

Therefore, it means not that everyone votes for it or completely approves every little thing about it. Rather, it means that everyone "consents" to it. There may be differences, but those differences are not important enough for the dissenter(s) to block passage. Instead, dissenter(s) willingly "stand aside" and let the action go ahead.

Consensus is a decision-making method in which everyone involved has input to the fullest possible extent. To achieve this, the group facilitation must be nonviolent. As we learned in Session 11, there are ways through helpful and maintenance roles to provide greater assurance that this happens. The blocking roles tend to obstruct consensus decision making.

The consensus process is not something that takes place solely in the meeting. It is an ongoing process between actual meeting times. It necessitates that the disagreeing parties carry on communications in a less formal way outside the meeting situation.

By using the skills of active listening, clear-stating, proposing options, negotiating, mediating, etc. the parties at odds seek to fully understand each other. Feelings and perceptions, word definitions, the detailed areas of disagreement are clarified. Each person seeks to fully understand why the other has taken the position expressed. What are the areas of agreement which can be enlarged upon? What mutual adjustments or improved knowledge or understanding could reduce or eliminate the areas of disagreement? When such progress can be made in narrowing or ending the areas of disagreement then consensus at the next meeting becomes more likely.

Because the term consensus is little understood, many think they have never used it. However presumably when the family selects a movie to go to, it is done by consensus. Jury verdicts are all by consensus. An article in the *New York Times* in 1986 indicated that decision making at the new General Motors Saturn plant would be by consensus. Whenever a group decides to do something that no one objects to, and that seems to happen quite often, that is consensus. All Quaker business meetings have been conducted by consensus for over 350 years. When did you last practice consensus?

This article was written by John Looney.
©1986, 1990, 1992, 1993, 1994, 1995 PEACE GROWS, Inc., 513 W. Exchange St., Akron, OH 44302 (216)864-5442.

MORE ABOUT THE CONSENSUS PROCESS

What is good about consensus?

1. It assures a thorough investigation and study of all facets of the problem.

2. Everyone feels ownership and hence supports the decision. The "losers" do not undermine the program as so often happens when an election is lost.

3. The value of the decision and its effectiveness are greatly enhanced because the knowledge, experience and ideas of everyone involved have contributed.

4. Consensus really is the only decision-making method completely consistent with nonviolence which always seeks a win-win outcome. Compromise, because each side has to give up something, has a mild lose-lose aspect. Voting is clearly win-lose.

What is bad about consensus?

1. It usually takes more time than any of the other decision making processes.

2. It takes more sincere effort on the part of everyone.

3. Not being accustomed to employing it, some people do not understand its operation sufficiently to use consensus well. Either training or considerable experience, or both, in consensus decision making probably is needed for attaining competency in its application.

4. In the case of an emergency, reaching consensus may take too long.

This article was written by John Looney.
©1986, 1990, 1992, 1993, 1994, 1995 PEACE GROWS, Inc., 513 W. Exchange St., Akron, OH 44302 (216)864-5442.

SIX STEP PROBLEM SOLVING

In most cases this procedure has proven very helpful in accelerating group decision making and meaningful action. It focuses on group attention while enabling movement toward consensus.

1. **Brainstorm a list of the problems** facing the group.

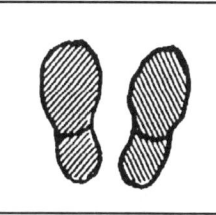

2. **Choose one of those problems.** (Straw votes from time to time, initially with each person voting more than once, will help. Narrow the list. Eventually one problem tends to become clearly the major concern of the group.)

3. **Describe or clarify that problem** so everyone understands it well.

4. **Brainstorm a list of possible solutions.**

5. **Choose the best solution** as in Step #2.

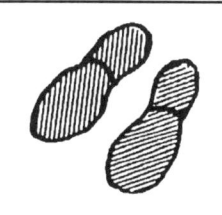

6. **Decide how to implement that solution.** This should include: listing the needed steps, fixing the responsibility and establishing the schedule for performing each step.

Other problems and considerations need not be dropped permanently but can be returned to later if and when appropriate.

SUMMARY OF CONCEPTS
As related to the subjects listed on worksheet #12

1. *When have I ever used brainstorming?*
   Each participant will have a different response.

2. *Of the six steps explained in this session, I need more practice with . . .*
   Answers will vary but each will refer to page 129.

3. *What is consensus? How can I use consensus in my life?*
   Many family decisions use consensus without being conscious about the process. Practice with the steps listed on page 129 could improve win/win outcomes in many areas of my life.

Major point to remember:
- The six steps to zeroing in on a problem.

Session 12
ZEROING IN ON A PROBLEM
Additional reading

Coover, Virginia. *Resource Manual For A Living Revolution.* Philadelphia, PA: New Society Pub., 1985.

Delisle, Jim. *Kid Stories: Biographies Of 20 Young People You'd Like To Know.* Minneapolis, MN: Free Spirit Pub., 1991.

Lawson, James R. and Steven Saint. *Rules For Reaching Consensus: A Modern Approach To Decision Making.* San Diego: Pfeiffer and Co., 1994.

Lewis, Barbara A. *The Kid's Guide To Social Action: How To Solve The Social Problems You Choose And Turn Creative Thinking Into Positive Action.* Minneapolis, MN: Free Spirit Pub., 1991.

Session 13
ALTERNATIVES TO VIOLENCE SKILLS
Applied in the community

Objectives

a. To review alternatives to violence skills for use in personal conflict situations.

b. To learn how the skills apply in community conflicts and examine some actual uses.

c. To understand causes of violence in our communities and the prerequisites for creating nonviolent communities.

WORKSHEET #13

(The following points will be covered in this session. Most points do not have "pat" answers, but the main thing is for you to arrive at an expression of the concepts. These questions are to help you take notes and process the material.)

1. What is a good example of community conflict resolution?

   _____

   _____

   _____

   _____

2. What skills are needed to solve community problems?

   _____

   _____

   _____

3. "Violence is caused when injustices exist in a society." What do I think about this statement?

   _____

   _____

   _____

4. What is required for a society to be just?

   _____

   _____

   _____

   _____

©1986, 1990, 1992, 1993, 1994, 1995 PEACE GROWS, Inc., 513 W. Exchange St., Akron, OH 44302 (216)864-5442

Notes or Journal Entry

Assignments:

_____
_____
_____
_____
_____

APPLYING NONVIOLENCE TO SOLVING COMMUNITY PROBLEMS

Up to this point, we have been looking mainly at interpersonal problems—violence between individuals. We can learn, test and use nonviolent principles and skills most easily with these problems. When it comes to the horrible and growing epidemic of violence in our communities, however, most of us only can wring our hands and avoid or run away from it. Yet there are things we can and must do. This session tries to point the way.

First, we must go back to what we discussed early in the course. We are all one. As Jim Wallis so aptly put it in a January, 1990 *Sojourners Magazine* article called *The Second Reformation Has Begun*: **"What we have yet to understand is that our destinies are all tied together. It is that failure to comprehend our common bond with one another and with the earth that is at the heart of our present crisis. Without that vision, we will surely perish."**

Secondly, our violent, dominating culture seeks to control and contain the symptoms. However, *Alternatives to Violence,* advocating a nonviolent, partnership culture, teaches us that we must address the root causes. Otherwise we can treat the symptoms perpetually. For instance, in just ten years we have doubled the number of prison cells in our "get tough," retaliatory policy. But who feels safer? As far as results are concerned, the violent policy has failed.

Thirdly, at the personal level, the principles and skills learned in this course do address causes. The huge magnitude of our community problems, however, overwhelms us. As with any big problem, solutions must be broken down into short-term, easily-realizable steps. What we need to do, as you can see on page 138, is to recognize that the personal actions have their counterparts at the community level. The main difference is that between two people, the actions of one often can transform the outcome. In the community, effectiveness usually requires working with other people in order to have a sufficient impact.

At the community level, no one can do everything but, and this is the key, everyone can do something. When enough become engaged, then change takes place. Mainly we need the guidelines, the confidence and the will to act. This session seeks to motivate us in that direction.

Fourthly, if we are to address causes, we must know what they are. Referring back to Session 3, we saw that whatever caused the deprival of human needs was the primary cause of violence and that the secondary violence resulting was a retaliatory reaction to the primary. In Session 3 we looked at the fact that an individual to be fully-functioning, and hence nonviolent, requires adequate resources, appropriate power, a flexible, supportive structure (to respond to unanticipated needs) and a clear, worthy mission.

WORTHY MISSION
(Secure identity and some challenge to transcend it)

POWER
(Appropriate)

STRUCTURE or INSTITUTION
(Flexible or supportive)

RESOURCES
(Adequate)

Here we learn that this only can happen in a just society or community. The charts on page 140 should clarify the differences between a society where justice exists and a dysfunctional one where the violence of injustice and its resulting conditions occur.

This article was written by John Looney.
©1986, 1990, 1992, 1993, 1994, 1995 PEACE GROWS, Inc., 513 W. Exchange St., Akron, OH 44302 (216)864-5442.

CONFLICT RESOLUTION ON TWO LEVELS

Personal

(1) Listen actively
(2) State position clearly
(3) Obtain and clarify needed information
(4) Develop alternatives from which to choose

(5) Lead or facilitate solution through group endeavor

(6) Negotiate

(7) Mediate

(8) Arbitrate

(9) Defend oneself nonviolently

(10) Use "active nonviolence"

(11) Use nonresistance

Community

Hearings
Research
Investigative reporting
Discussion of community issues with various people
Awareness of local news
Letters to editors

Legislation
Community organizing
Neighborhood or town meetings
Executive action
Personal witness
Education

Union-Management negotiation
Legislative debates and negotiations
School Board-faculty or parent negotiations

Community mediation centers
School mediation service
Federal labor mediation service

Use of arbitrator like American Arbitration Association person
Use of courts

Organize neighborhood for mutual concern, caring, watching, and nonviolent protection
Obtain outside help such as police or community service before acting violently

Writing letters
Lobbying
Public speaking
Demonstrating
Voting
Doing relief work
Using boycotts
Using strikes
Picketing
Campaigning
Doing civil disobedience
Using "Alternatives to Violence"

Silent, but open, complete noncooperation with community or cultural custom or with regulation felt to be unjust or unfair

©1986, 1990, 1992, 1993, 1994, 1995 PEACE GROWS, Inc., 513 W. Exchange St., Akron, OH 44302 (216)864-5

HOW CAN I UNDERSTAND CAUSES?
and decide what I can do

Page 139 shows a chart which has been developed to help in analyzing given community situations and prescribing treatment. This chart can apply to problems of environmental damage, business management, crime, economic exploitation, inadequate health care, exclusion based on race, sex, age, nationality, religion or any other violent cultural patterns. The cases studied will illustrate ways to resolve conflict and reduce violence at the community level. We must always remember the following prerequisites of a just society (which reduces violence to a minimum), and also work for their implementation:

(1) **A clear identity and worthy mission with cultural and other diversity accepted.**

(2) **Appropriate power sharing.**

(3) **Clearly-defined, flexible, responsive structures and procedures, and**

(4) **Equitably-distributed resources.**

We are not saying this is an easy path to follow. From our earliest years, misinformation, disregarded and slanted history and stereotyping socialize us to reinforce, rather than improve, existing violent cultural patterns.

Our beliefs and perceptions are constantly reinforced by individuals, systems or institutions we know, love and/or trust. These may include our family, our religion, our education, our government and its leaders. The media play a very important, and, too often, unrecognized role.

This socializing to the cultural norm happens to the oppressed as well as to the oppressor. A collusion strengthens the patterns as those in power see the condition as their due while the powerless see the state, in which they find themselves, to be accepted as their lot in life. Thus, the cycle of oppression continues. To reduce violence, the cycle must be broken.

To break the cycle, there are certain key elements which can work to favor our success:

(1) **Human beings have more in common than they do differences.**

(2) **The differences are not inherent. They are culturally learned which means they can be unlearned. New educational and informational approaches become essential.**

(3) **The oppressed, of all kinds, have mutual interests. Those can be used to draw them together to be more empowered for greater impact and effectiveness, and**

(4) **From such an improved power position, the oppressor more easily can be induced to join the oppressors in improving conditions.**

To achieve such results, the principles and skills taught in *Alternatives to Violence* are basic tools. As Arnold Toynbee, the famous historian once said, "The quest for alternatives to violence ought to be given the first place on 'humanity's' crowded agenda. It should come first because it is the most urgent of all and is also the most difficult. It is urgent because . . . violence has become suicidal . . . . "

This article was written by John Looney.
©1986, 1990, 1992, 1993, 1994, 1995 PEACE GROWS, Inc., 513 W. Exchange St., Akron, OH 44302 (216)864-5442.

ALTERNATIVES TO VIOLENCE — Session 13 Chart

WHAT MAKES A SOCIETY JUST?

DYSFUNCTIONAL (violent)

- **STRUCTURE**: rigid, inflexible, unresponsive to people
- **RESOURCES**: inadequate, unfair distribution, not shared, no access
- **POWER**: top heavy, unshared, dictator
- **MISSION**: unclear, confused, ignores diversity, double messages

FULLY FUNCTIONAL (non-violent)

- **STRUCTURE**: flexible, supportive, responds to people's needs
- **RESOURCES**: adequate, shared, equitable distribution
- **POWER**: shared, enabling, empowering
- **MISSION**: clear identity, clear purpose, clear goals, all know it

Theory and diagram by Robert Terry and Jean Alvarez.
©1986, 1990, 1992, 1993, 1994, 1995 PEACE GROWS, Inc., 513 W. Exchange St., Akron, OH 44302 (216)864-5442.

ANALYSIS OF SPECIFIC SITUATIONS

	Situation #1	Situation #2	Situation #3	Situation #4
ACTOR				
MECHANISMS: Mission —				
Power —				
Structure —				
Resources —				
INTENTIONALITY				
PERCEIVED REWARD				
JUSTIFICATION				

Theory and chart model by Robert Terry and Jean Alvarez.
©1986, 1990, 1992, 1993, 1994, 1995 PEACE GROWS, Inc., 513 W. Exchange St., Akron, OH 44302 (216)864-5442.

ALTERNATIVES TO VIOLENCE Session 13 Chart 140

ALTERNATIVE FOR ANALYSIS OF SPECIFIC SITUATIONS

Institutional violence: Violence is when any entity (society, community, institution, group or individual) from a position of power in the entity, intentionally or unintentionally, inequitably distributes resources, maintains inflexible and unresponsive structures, refuses to share power and/or pursues an unclarified and/or unworthy mission while ignoring diversity, for its own supposed benefit and rationalizes its action by blaming or ignoring the victim.

A. Name of institution (or of person using power of institution)	B. Who was (is) being deprived of rights (needs)?	C. What is (was) reaction of sizable segment of society: 1) ignore 2) condone 3) object a) mildly b) vehemently	D. What violent responses could be made in this situation?	E. What nonviolent responses could be utilized to effectively end this institutional violence?
1.				
2.				
3.				

Chart developed by Sr. Rose Dailey, *ATV* trainer.
©1986, 1990, 1992, 1993, 1994, 1995 PEACE GROWS, Inc., 513 W. Exchange St., Akron, OH 44302 (216)864-5442.

ALTERNATIVES TO VIOLENCE

SUMMARY OF CONCEPTS
As related to the subjects listed on worksheet #13

1. *What is a good example of community conflict resolution?*
   Answers will vary of examples of commuity conflict resolution.

2. *What skills are needed to solve community problems?*
   There are many examples on page 136 of skills needed to solve community problems.

3. *"Violence is caused when injustices exist in a society." What do I think about this statement?*
   Each participant will answer in his/her own way.

4. *What is required for a society to be just?*
   Look at the chart on page 138.

Major point to remember:
- Personal skills learned also apply to community problems. Injustice causes community violence.

©1986, 1990, 1992, 1993, 1994, 1995 PEACE GROWS, Inc., 513 W. Exchange St., Akron, OH 44302 (216)864-5442.

Session 13
ALTERNATIVES TO VIOLENCE IN THE COMMUNITY
Additional reading

Albrecht, Lisa and Rose M. Brewer. *Bridges Of Power: Women's Multicultural Alliances.* Philadelphia, PA, 1990.

Berman, Phillip L. *The Courage Of Conviction: Prominent Contemporaries Discuss Their Beliefs And How They Put Them Into Action.* NY: Dodd, 1984.

Berman, Sheldon. *Making History: A Social Studies Curriculum In The Participation Series.* Cambridge, MA: Educators for Social Responsibility, 1984.

Brodkin, Margaret. *Every Kid Counts: 31 Ways To Save Our Children.* San Francisco: Harper Collins, 1993.

Cooney, Robert and Helen Michalowski. *Power Of The People: Active Nonviolence In The United States.* Philadelphia, PA: New Society Pub., 1987.

Coover, Virginia, Ellen Deacon, Charles Esser and Christopher Moore. *Resource Manual For A Living Revolution.* Philadelphia, PA: New Society Pub., 1977.

Fiffer, Steve and Sharon Sloan Fiffer. *50 Ways To Help Your Community: A Handbook For Change.* NY: Doubleday, 1994.

Lappé, Frances Moore and Paul Martin DuBois. *The Quickening Of America: Rebuilding Our Nation, Remaking Our Lives.* San Francisco: Jossey-Bass Pub., 1994.

Susskind, Lawrence and Jeffrey L. Cruikshank. *Breaking The Impasse: Consensual Approaches To Resolving Public Disputes.* NY: Basic Books, 1987.

Session 14
ALTERNATIVES TO VIOLENCE SKILLS
Applied to global problems

Objectives

a. To review alternatives to violence skills for nonviolent conflict resolution at both the personal and community levels.

b. To learn how these skills apply in global conflict situations and consider actual applications.

c. To understand causes of violence in the world and some of the prerequisites for a nonviolent globe.

WORKSHEET #14

(The following points will be covered in this session. Most points do not have "pat" answers, but the main thing is for you to arrive at an expression of the concepts. These questions are to help you take notes and process the material.)

1. What is an example of global violence? What caused it?

   _____

   _____

   _____

2. What does "global family" mean to me?

   _____

   _____

   _____

3. How have any of us shared global responsibility?

   _____

   _____

   _____

4. Which global counterparts to personal/community *Alternatives to Violence* skills would I want to act on?

   _____

   _____

   _____

©1986, 1990, 1992, 1993, 1994, 1995 PEACE GROWS, Inc., 513 W. Exchange St., Akron, OH 44302 (216)864-5442.

Notes or Journal Entry

Assignments:
_____
_____
_____
_____
_____

ALTERNATIVES TO VIOLENCE   Session 14 Reading/Chart 145

BEFORE YOU FINISH EATING BREAKFAST THIS MORNING,

you've depended on more than half the world. This is the way our universe is structured.... We aren't going to have peace on earth until we recognize this basic fact of the interrelated structure of all reality.
—Martin Luther King, Jr.

Tungsten filament from Bolivia. A U.S. child will consume 30-50 times more goods in his/her lifetime than one born in Bolivian highlands.

Clothes from Costa Rica. Workers earn less than 40 cents an hour.

Teak furniture from Honduras. Honduras is the second poorest nation in the western hemisphere. Seventy-five percent of Hondurans live in small, rural villages and earn an average $6 a month.

Baseball and glove from Haiti. Poorest nation in hemisphere, in a village of 6,000, average source of water is two taps. Infant mortality is one-of-five.

Rubber from Thailand. Per capita, Thais make $528 a year.

Assembled in Taiwan. Workers earn less than 25 cents an hour.

Bastnaesite from Burundi. Life expectancy in Burundi is 42 years.

Electricity from coal mined in Clear Fork Valley, KY. About half of the residents live below U.S. poverty line; two-third's have no flush toilets.

Meat, tuna, bananas from Somalia. Somalia exported $90 million in livestock, bananas, meat, tuna, and hides in 1979. The U.S. is one of its three principal trading partners. Somalia has one of the greatest per capital food shortages in the world.

Coffee from Guatemala. Two-thirds of population has annual income of $42.

Pineapples from Philippines. One-half children under four are afflicted by serious deficiency of proteins.

Cocoa and fish from Ecuador 60 percent of children are malnourished.

Sugar from Dominican Republic. Eighty percent of children die before age five.

Other common items supplied by Third World nations: tea from Bangladesh, copper wiring from Chile, aluminum from Jamaica, tin from Malaysia, dog food from fishmeal from Peru, cork (for bulletin board) from Algeria, and natural gas from Mexico.

Illustration by Mac Evans. Poster available from Seeds, 222 East Lake Drive, Decatur, GA 30030. $1.80 each.
©1986, 1990, 1992, 1993, 1994, 1995 PEACE GROWS, Inc., 513 W. Exchange St., Akron, OH 44302 (216)864-5442.

NONVIOLENCE SKILLS APPLIED TO GLOBAL PROBLEMS

The chart on page 145 well illustrates the interdependency of nations and peoples in today's closer-knit world. Yet as those nations and people have come closer in so many ways, during this same twentieth century, wars have destroyed more human lives than in all of previous history combined.

During recent decades as many as thirty or forty full-scale wars have been going on simultaneously all over the earth. But unless our nation is involved, none of these wars are reported well in our media. If we do not read about them or see reports on T.V., we perceive of them as not even taking place.

In every one of those trouble spots we will find that some group or nation is being oppressed and/or excluded from decisionmaking which vitally effects their lives. Albert, in "Guess Who's Coming to Breakfast?," is one example.

The oppression can come from within, as with a dictatorial elite exploiting their own people, or from without, as one more affluent or more aggressive nation seeks to gain improved conditions for itself through use of physical, armed force. Seldom have they seemed to know how to use persuasion and diplomacy in a collaborative way whereby a win/win situation might result. Often, the tragic exploitation of suffering people is both from within and without as the inside leadership and outside nation cooperate for, supposedly, mutual gain.

So the prerequisites for a nonviolent globe really are the same as for a nonviolent community. But because of language, cultural and other barriers, the challenges to overcome existing global violence are greater. Still, the principles, skills, techniques, strategies, philosophy and value system required to solve global problems are no different as you will see in these sessions.

Furthermore, many of us have limited our thoughts of peace and international conflict resolution to war and military tension. Yet all of the other world problems involve conflict too. In many other situations, human suffering and loss can compare to or exceed that from war.

Exploitation, economic competition, environmental and ecological destruction, discrimination, exclusion, inadequate health care and disease, poverty are all spreading at rapid rates, even in highly "developed" countries. In every case, conflict between peoples is involved. These problems, too, require peaceful, fair resolution using the same skills we learned about at the personal and community levels. Yet those skills either have been unknown or unused, while powerful minorities have tried to control and preserve existing conditions which are usually to their short-term benefit.

Hopefully, what we learn in this course will open our minds and our hearts to some new and badly-needed ways of going.

This article was written by John Looney.
©1986, 1990, 1992, 1993, 1994, 1995 PEACE GROWS, Inc., 513 W. Exchange St., Akron, OH 44302 (216)864-5442.

ALTERNATIVES TO VIOLENCE

CONFLICT RESOLUTION ON THREE LEVELS

Personal	Community	Global
(1) Listen actively	Hearings	
(2) State position clearly	Research	
(3) Obtain and clarify needed information	Investigative reporting	
(4) Develop alternatives from which to choose	Discussion of community issues with various people Awareness of local news Letters to editors	
(5) Lead or facilitate solution through group endeavor	Legislation Community organizing Neighborhood or town meetings Executive action Personal witness Education	
(6) Negotiate	Union-Management negotiation Legislative debates and negotiations School Board-faculty or parent negotiations	
(7) Mediate	Community mediation centers School mediation service Federal labor mediation service	
(8) Arbitrate	Use of arbitrator like American Arbitration Association person Use of courts	
(9) Defend oneself nonviolently	Organize neighborhood for mutual concern, caring, watching, and nonviolent protection Obtain outside help such as police or community service before acting violently	
(10) Use "active nonviolence"	Writing letters Lobbying Public speaking Demonstrating Voting Doing relief work Using boycotts Using strikes Picketing Campaigning Doing civil disobedience Using "Alternatives to Violence"	
(11) Use nonresistance	Silent, but open, complete noncooperation with community or cultural custom or with regulation felt to be unjust or unfair	

©1986, 1990, 1992, 1993, 1994, 1995 PEACE GROWS, Inc., 513 W. Exchange St., Akron, OH 44302 (216)864-5442.

ALTERNATIVES TO VIOLENCE

CONFLICT RESOLUTION ON THREE LEVELS

Personal	Community	Global
(1) Listen actively (2) State position clearly (3) Obtain and clarify needed information (4) Develop alternatives from which to choose	Hearings Research Investigative reporting Discussion of community issues with various people Awareness of local news Letters to editors	Travel Study other countries and cultures Host overseas visitors Follow international news Promote and follow international organizations Use appropriate community counterparts as investigative reporting, etc.
(5) Lead or facilitate solution through group endeavor	Legislation Community organizing Neighborhood or town meetings Executive action Personal witness Education	Government leadership Disarmament movements United Nations development, research and action Appropriate technology International organization activists (both government and nongovernment)
(6) Negotiate	Union-Management negotiation Legislative debates and negotiations School Board-faculty or parent negotiations	Diplomacy Trade agreements
(7) Mediate	Community mediation centers School mediation service Federal labor mediation service	UN special sessions and General Assembly meetings
(8) Arbitrate	Use of arbitrator like American Arbitration Association person Use of courts	Arms negotiations Special international mediators
(9) Defend oneself nonviolently	Organize neighborhood for mutual concern, caring, watching, and nonviolent protection Obtain outside help such as police or community service before acting violently	World Court Nonviolent civilian national defense
(10) Use "active nonviolence"	Writing letters Lobbying Public speaking Demonstrating Voting Doing relief work Using boycotts Using strikes Picketing Campaigning Doing civil disobedience Using "Alternatives to Violence"	Boycotts Trade embargoes Relief work Peace Corps Civil disobedience Demonstrations, vigils, etc. Draft and tax resistance
(11) Use nonresistance	Silent, but open, complete noncooperation with community or cultural custom or with regulation felt to be unjust or unfair	Complete noncooperation with government military and/or foreign policies

©1986, 1990, 1992, 1993, 1994, 1995 PEACE GROWS, Inc., 513 W. Exchange St., Akron, OH 44302 (216)864

a briefing about the
NEW INTERNATIONAL ECONOMIC ORDER

What is the new international economic order?

When American audiences are asked if they have ever heard of the New International Economic Order few, if any, have. In the same audience, however, all will know of the Manson murders or the "Son of Sam" murders! Yet, the NIEO is the call of the third world or developing countries, one hundred and twelve of them or two thirds of the world's populations, for specifics of a fairer sharing of world resources. Kurt Waldheim, Secretary-General of the United Nations, says it is "the price of peace among nations." Americans strongly affect the present economic order. In a democracy, citizens are supposed to have knowledge and control. Why do we know nothing about the New International Economic Order but know all about a couple of bizarre murder cases? Does not such ignorance hurt U.S. foreign policy?

How did the NIEO get started?

At the height of the "cold war," developing nations were being pressured to join either the communist or capitalist bloc. In 1955, twenty-four of the "non-aligned" nations met at Bandung, Indonesia, to declare their independence from such commitments and to explore ways of cooperating to better their lot. In 1961, at Belgrade, Yugoslavia, the term "New International Economic Order" was used for the first time when the priorities of disarmament, decolonization, and the elimination of apartheid in South Africa were established. In 1964, at Geneva, the first UN Conference on Trade and Development or UNCTAD I took place. All pleas for help were ignored, but by 1972 even the developed countries were noting instabilities: food and material shortages, the population explosion, unemployment, severe social unrest, environmental damage, inflation, U.S. trade deficits and the devaluation of the dollar which had been the basis of the world's monetary system since World War II. When the OPEC oil embargo in 1973 quadrupled the price of oil, all developing countries supported it, though they were hurt worse than most developed countries. Finally, in 1974 the Sixth Special Session of the United Nations produced the guidelines for the New International Economic Order.

Why is the NIEO needed?

Here are a few of the reasons for the NIEO:

1. Developed countries with 27% of the population have 86% of the gross national product, while the remaining 73% have only 14%. Should countries like ours be overdeveloped while 450,000,000 in the world are starving?

2. 200,000,000 in developing countries are barred from earning a living. There are 350,000 new job seekers in South Asia every week. Of India's urban families, 44% live in only one room.

Latin America has an estimated 44,000,000 squatters.

3. Prices on raw materials sold by developing countries go down while prices from developed countries on manufactured goods they buy go up. In 1960 twenty-five tons of rubber would buy six tractors. Today, this amount will only buy two. Raw material tariffs are low, encouraging competition; manufactured goods have high tariffs to discourage it.

a briefing about the
NEW INTERNATIONAL ECONOMIC ORDER (continued)

4. World food marketing and distribution patterns create hunger:

   - Peruvian peasants have about the worst protein diet deficiency in the world. Peru, however, has one of the worlds's greatest sources of protein. Where does it go? To the United States to be ground into fishmeal for our livestock!

   - Through "plantation economies" large agribusiness multinationals take over third world land to raise coffee, sugar, cocoa, pineapples, beef, bananas, etc. for the developed countries like America. This land is needed to raise food for the local people. Pineapple production is expected to be gone from Hawaii by 1988 with farmworkers there laid off and going on welfare. They became organized to earn $2.65 per hour, no fabulous income, but labor costs in the Philippines are only $ .15 an hour. Filipinos are being pushed off their land and malnutrition is increasing there also.

   - Grain being fed to U.S. livestock to raise beef could very well take care of the world's food shortages, and fertilizers used on our gardens, lawns, and golf courses would cover India's shortage for food production.

   - At $1 billion a day, the world arms race spending increased 600% since 1957, and is equal to or exceeds the total income of the poorest one-half of the world's population. Twenty-five percent of the world's engineers and technicians and forty percent of the research done in the world is devoted to armaments rather than upon the quality of life. That is why the developing countries asked for the UN Special Sessions on Disarmament.

   - Interest payments on the debts of third world countries to the developed world reaches or exceeds economic aid coming to them. So the high foreign aid payments some citizens complain about really may be going to American banks instead of underdeveloped nations.

What does the NIEO call for?

1. Buffer stocks of raw materials are wanted to stabilize prices. In falling markets, stocks can be purchased to hold up prices. In rising markets, they can be sold.

2. Indexation would create a fixed ratio between raw material prices and manufactured goods so they would move up and down together.

3. Local control of resources would enable all governments to take care of the needs of their people first.

4. Some control of the operations of the huge multinational corporations which are more powerful than the governments would help prevent abuses.

5. The formation of producer's cooperatives like OPEC and the International Bauxite Association would increase third world bargaining power to avoid unfair exploitation.

6. Improvement of third world competitiveness with a fairer patent licensing and control of synthetic raw material substitutes would help developing economies.

7. Some form of debt relief is needed.

This article was written by John Looney.
©1986, 1990, 1992, 1993, 1994, 1995 PEACE GROWS, Inc., 513 W. Exchange St., Akron, OH 44302 (216)864-5442.

a briefing about the
NEW INTERNATIONAL ECONOMIC ORDER (continued)

8. Tariff and other adjustments would provide third world countries with better access for their manufactured goods to world markets.

9. Increased economic aid to the extent of 0.7% of the GNP of developed countries is wanted. America now ranks at only 0.26% though it used to be 1%.

10. An end to waste of natural resources such as food, guns, bombers, and oil is requested.

11. Monetary system reform is sought.

12. The right to develop one's own economic system without outside pressure or repression is desired.

Are there any pitfalls to the proposal?

In developed counties like the United States, distribution of wealth among the population is about like this:

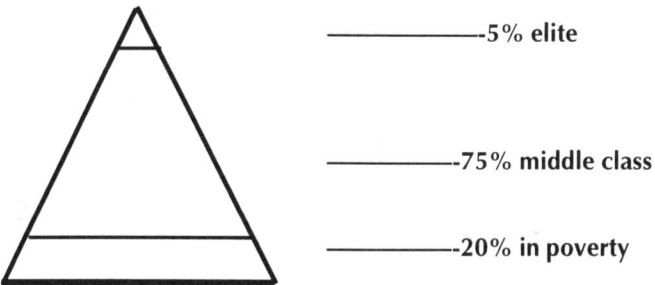

- 5% elite
- 75% middle class
- 20% in poverty

Most of the people benefit from economic improvements. But in underdeveloped countries it is more like this:

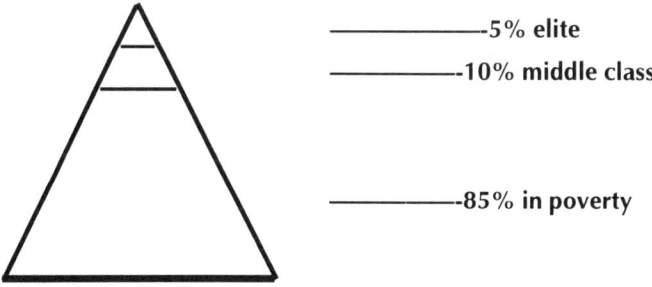

- 5% elite
- 10% middle class
- 85% in poverty

The danger in the NIEO is that the benefits will go to the top 5% and not reach the people. If their basic needs continue to be unmet, the disparity between the rich and the poor will grow, not narrow. Therefore, in most cases, for the NIEO to work properly a new domestic economic order is also needed. If it does not exist, that is the major pitfall of the NIEO.

When help goes only to the elite, as has happened all over the world, including Vietnam, our policies are self-defeating. What the future brings is determined by what is in the hearts and minds of the people today. No policy can be permanently successful which ignores their basic needs.

This article was written by John Looney.
©1986, 1990, 1992, 1993, 1994, 1995 PEACE GROWS, Inc., 513 W. Exchange St., Akron, OH 44302 (216)864-5442.

ALTERNATIVES TO VIOLENCE Session 14 Reading 152

BENEFITS OF THE UNITED NATIONS
Whether you realize it or not, you have been helped in many ways

Here is one thing the UN has done:

The UN has helped keep the peace via mediators, observers and an international police force.

and here are 24 other things the UN has done and is doing . . .

©1986, 1990, 1992, 1993, 1994, 1995 PEACE GROWS, Inc., 513 W. Exchange St., Akron, OH 44302 (216)864

ALTERNATIVES TO VIOLENCE

BENEFITS OF THE UNITED NATIONS
Whether you realize it or not, you have been helped in many ways

2 aided weather forecasting on a global basis for safety of travelers, property, and crops.

3 set forth international rules for air safty.

4 set standard methods of public health and customs immigration at all ports.

5 worked for safety at sea and effective means for shipping and expanding trade.

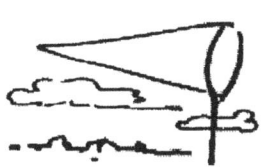   

6 assured the rescue and safe return of astronauts and space vehicles that land in foreign territory.

7 allocated radio and TV frequencies throughout the world to avoid interference.

8 set up international machinery to control movement of narcotics and illegal drugs.

9 worked for population control and family planning.

10 enabled the exchange of over 3 billion pieces of mail between countries yearly.

11 conducted programs to increase industrial output, cut costs, train people and develop new products.

12 fought mass diseases like malaria and tuberculosis.

13 coordinated labor, government & management efforts to increase productivity, protect rights, and improve work conditions.

©1986, 1990, 1992, 1993, 1994, 1995 PEACE GROWS, Inc., 513 W. Exchange St., Akron, OH 44302 (216)864-5442.

BENEFITS OF THE UNITED NATIONS
Whether you realize it or not, you have been helped in many ways

14 promoted private investments to assist economic and social development and reduce the likelihood of war.

15 provided food, shelter and medical supplies for millions of children.

16 taught people to read and trained primary, secondary, and university level teachers.

17 protected the resources of the seabed for the advantage and betterment of all mankind.

18 kept enemies talking to work out their disagreements.

19 helped countries work together on money rates and exchange.

20 lent governments money—about $2 billion a year—for economic growth.

21 helped nations work together on global environment and pollution problems.

 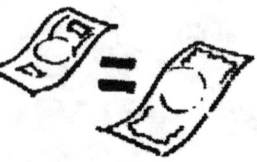  

22 helped nations develop and use new ideas in agriculture, industry, fishing and forestry.

23 helped nearly 1 billion people achieve self-government in the last 25 years.

24 helped hundreds of thousands of refugees who have lived for years in refugee camps.

25 sought continually to limit the spread of nuclear arms and to develop atomic energy for peaceful uses.

 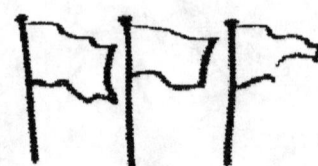  

ALTERNATIVES TO VIOLENCE

SUMMARY OF CONCEPTS
As related to the subjects listed on worksheet #14

1. *What is an example of global violence? What caused it?*
   Each participant will give own example. Causes will be examples of injustice.

2. *What does "global family" mean to me?*
   Because the people of the world have become dependent upon each other, the world's problems do effect our daily lives.

3. *How have any of us shared global responsibility?*
   Each participant will give own example. Some may include ways to share resources and nuture ecology.

4. *Which global counterparts to personal/community Alternatives to Violence skills would I want to act on?*
   See chart on page 148.

Major point to remember:
- Personal and community skills learned also apply to global problems. Injustice causes global violence.

Session 14
GLOBAL PROBLEMS
Additional reading

Bello, Walden. *Dark Victory: The U.S., Structural Adjustment and Global Poverty.*
Oakland, CA: Food First Institute, 1994.

Brown, Lester R. *State Of The World: A Worldwatch Report On Progress Toward A Sustainable Society.*
NY: Norton, 1995.

Erickson, Brad. *Call To Action: Handbook For Ecology, Peace And Justice.*
San Francisco: Sierra Club Books, 1990.

Lappé, Frances Moore and Joseph Collins. *World Hunger: Twelve Myths.* NY: Grove Weidenfeld, 1986.

Lappé, Frances Moore, Rachel Schurman and Kevin Danaher. *Betraying The National Interest.*
NY: Grove Press, 1986.

McGinnis, James. *Educating For Peace And Justice: Global Dimensions.* St. Louis, MO: Institute for Peace and Justice, 1984.

Rodale, Robert and Mike McGrath. *Save Three Lives: A Plan For Famine Prevention.*
San Francisco: Sierra Club Books, 1991.

Session 15
ALTERNATIVES TO VIOLENCE SKILLS
Nonviolent national defense

Objectives

a. To understand better what is happening in the world's trouble spots and envision nonviolent solutions.

b. To examine our own attitudes toward national security.

c. To learn some creative methods for nonviolent national defense.

d. To define nonviolent national defense.

WORKSHEET #15

(The following points will be covered in this session. Most points do not have "pat" answers, but the main thing is for you to arrive at an expression of the concepts. These questions are to help you take notes and process the material.)

1. An example of international violence that troubles me:

   _____

   _____

   _____

2. What caused the above trouble spot?

   _____

   _____

   _____

3. What is the difference between peacekeeping and peacemaking?

   _____

   _____

   _____

4. What is nonviolent civilian national defense?

   _____

   _____

   _____

Notes or Journal Entry

Assignments:

_____
_____
_____
_____
_____

DISREGARDED HISTORY
The power of nonviolent action

American colonial nonviolence, circa 1776

In the 18th century, here in this part of North America, the European settlers used a great deal of violence against indigenous Americans, and then against the Africans who were imported. Nevertheless, the European settlers conducted major campaigns of nonviolent struggle against English controls, particularly for the ten-year period from 1765 to 1775. This was on a scale and significance which may require, when it is more fully researched, a major reinterpretation of American history—which may lead to a reassessment of the relevance and importance of the War of Independence.

There were three separate campaigns, each of which involved economic resistance. It is possible that this is the first major case of international economic sanctions on record.

Daniel Dulany, in the pamphlet he wrote on resistance to the Stamp Act in October of 1765, describes certain basic characteristics of political nonviolent struggle. (Now you'll notice I'm discussing on the political level, not on the religious or moral level.) Dulany said, "Instead of moping and whining to excite compassion, in such a situation we ought with spirit and vigor and alacrity to bid defiance to tyranny by exposing its impotence, by making it as contemptible as it would be detestable." Here is the fundamental conception that you can make tyranny helpless by refusing cooperation with it. So he advocated building up economic production within the colonies to make them self-reliant. They could then sever trade relations with England, which would hurt the English merchants, and consequently this would put leverage on the English government to repeal the Stamp Act.

George Washington, nonviolent strategist

Did you ever think of George Washington as a nonviolent strategist? During this Stamp Act struggle, courts were required to use stamps on official documents. The colonists had decided not to use the stamps. So the question became: "Do the courts remain open without using the stamps, or do the courts close down?" This was in the context of colonists conducting a massive campaign to refuse to pay debts they owed to the English merchants from whom the colonial merchants had purchased their products on credit. Walpole regarded this as the most effective weapon which the colonists wielded. So George Washington advised that they should close down the courts, of course. Obeying the law was impossible. You close the courts, Washington reasoned, because if you close the courts, the courts cannot be used in an effort to collect the money which the colonists were refusing to pay to the English merchants. Therefore, the English merchants would put pressure on their government to repeal the Stamp Act. Very sophisticated nonviolent strategy, calculating effects and counter-effects of specific types of noncooperation.

Thomas Jefferson, faster

Did you know that Thomas Jefferson with his colleagues introduced fasting in the colonial struggle? When the spirit of the resistance was weakening at certain points and people were getting bored, he and his friends (who were known rather as playboys, always going out and dancing) got the very respected and staid chaplain of the Virginia House of Burgesses to propose as his own idea a day of fasting and prayer—for political resistance. It was passed by the House of Burgesses and all of Virginia had a day of fasting and prayer—for political resistance. It wasn't Gandhi who introduced fasting as a political weapon at all.

DISREGARDED HISTORY
The power of nonviolent action (continued)

Later during 1765, Governor Bernard of Massachusetts Bay said: "At this time I have no real authority in this place." And Lieutenant Governor Thomas Hutchinson of Massachusetts Bay said: "in the capital towns of several of the colonies and of this in particular, the authority is in the populace. No law can be carried into execution against their minds." There were cases—significant cases—of the burning of buildings and destruction of property during the Stamp Act resistance. Men who had accepted appointments as stamp distributors were threatened with physical attack and even death and run out of town. But not one person was killed.

During the Townshend resistance, in January 1769, for example, a London newspaper reported that because of the refusal of taxes and the refusal to import British goods, only 3,500 pounds sterling of revenue had been produced in the colonies. The American non-importation and non-consumption campaign was estimated by the same newspaper at that point to have cost British business not a mere 3,500 pounds but 7,250,000 pounds in lost income. Those figures may not have been accurate, but they are significant of the perceptions of the time. The attempt to collect the tax against that kind of opposition was not worth the effort and the futility of trying eventually became apparent.

> **Historically, nonviolence has worked many times.**

Have you ever heard someone argue, "We've tried war. We know that's bad. Now let's try nonviolence. It's never been tried. It's worth a try." Nonsense. There is a vast history of this type of action going back as far as we have records.

The abolition of war does not require an anti-war, anti-military lobby and demonstrations and protest, but the development of effective nonviolent alternatives to military struggle.

As the American movement developed, a radical fringe began to talk the rhetoric of violence. The militia, which the colonies had had for many, many decades, were deliberately developed. Some people began to foresee the movement shifting over to war. But this was not universal, and not preferred by even many radicals. The Suffolk Resolves, passed by the delegates of Suffolk County of Massachusetts Bay in 1774, recognized that violence was possible and the colonists should be ready for violence if it came. However, they recommended instead a different type of struggle—like they had been using: "We would heartily recommend to all persons of this community not to engage in any routs, riots or licentious attacks upon the properties of any persons whatsoever, as being subversive of all order and government; but by a steady, many, uniform, and persevering opposition, to convince our enemies that in a contest so important—in a cause so solemn, our conduct shall be such as to merit the approbation of the wise, and the admiration of the brave and free of every age and of every country."

This article was written by Gene Sharp. Excerpted from an essay by Dr. Sharp in *Fellowship* (May 1976) by Susan D. Hadley, Nyack, NY. ©1986, 1990, 1992, 1993, 1994, 1995 PEACE GROWS, Inc., 513 W. Exchange St., Akron, OH 44302 (216)864-5442.

DISREGARDED HISTORY
The power of nonviolent action (continued)

On the basis of such thought and the Virginia Association, the First Continental Congress developed a sophisticated, phased program of economic and political cooperation. First, it began with a non-importation campaign, to be followed, if necessary, by a non-exportation campaign. The First Continental Congress program of resistance was called the "Continental Association." It was a program of nonviolent resistance and the First Continental Congress was a nonviolent resistance organization. It was a program implemented throughout the colonies, so well developed, so sophisticated, that its equal was probably not seen until Gandhi's work in India. Going along with this was a program of enforcement of these provisions in the colonies with such complete solidarity that the very enforcement organization in many cases gradually became instruments of local government. Development of parallel governmental institutions also occurred on a colony-wide basis, sometimes in deliberate defiance of British-appointed governors. It has been estimated that in 9 or 10 of the 13 colonies, British governmental power had already been effectively and illegally replaced by substitute governments before Lexington and Concord. The Continental Congress was known as "the Congress." Its measures of resistance were known as "laws." British power had de facto collapsed in most of the colonies before a shot was fired. In Maryland, for example, an entire substitute government had taken over.

Considering the de facto independence of most of the colonies by 1775, with the emergence of an inter-colonial confederation-type of government and the experience in the Stamp Act struggles and the Townshend resistance, it is very possible that British power might have totally collapsed de jure short of the eight years which it took for the War of Independence. Rather than the war having speeded up independence, it may very well have postponed it.

Governor Dunmore of Virginia suggested that the "laws of Congress," as he put it, receive from Virginia "Marks of reverence they never bestowed on their legal Government, or the laws preceding from it." He added: "I have discovered no incidence where the interdisposition of Government, in the feeble state to which it is reduced, could serve any other purpose than to suffer the disgrace of a disappointment, and thereby afford matter of great exultation to its enemies and increase their influence over the minds of the people."

At the same time, there was significant support in England for the movement (though not as strong as during the Stamp Act resistance). The extent of the support, and the reasoning for it, should be researched and analyzed. Part of the Continental Association (the program of resistance of the Continental Congress) contained this phrase: " . . . we are of the opinion that a non-importation, non-consumption and non-exportation agreement, faithfully adhered to, will prove the most speedy, effectual, and peaceable measure . . . "

And in Massachusetts, already in early 1774, the Governor, Governor Gage, wrote that "All legislative, as well as all executive power, is gone . . . " Governor Gage made a similar report later in the year. So we must remember that, disregarded as it is in present portrayals of America's Revolution, the American colonials, too, have a highly important place in the history of nonviolent struggle.

Dr. Sharp, Research Fellow of Harvard University's Program for Science and International Affairs, is the author of *The Politics of Nonviolent Action* (Porter Sargent), a massive study of the nature of nonviolent struggle as a social and political technique.

Other books by Dr. Sharp include *Social Power and Political Freedom*, which outlines 20 steps for developing and evaluating nonviolent alternatives and *Gandhi As a Political Strategist*. The latter two are available from Porter Sargent, 11 Beacon Street, Boston, MA 02108.

ELIE WIESEL'S NOBEL PRIZE ADDRESS

It is with a profound sense of humility that I accept the honor you have chosen to bestow upon me. I know: your choice transcends me. This both frightens and pleases me.

It frightens me because I wonder: do I have the right to represent the multitudes who have perished? I do not. That would be presumptuous. No one may speak for the dead, no one may interpret their mutilated dreams and visions.

It pleases me because I may say this honor belongs to all the survivors and their children, and through us, to the Jewish people with whose destiny I have always identified.

I remember: it happened yesterday or eternities ago. A young Jewish boy discovered the kingdom of night. I remember his bewilderment; I remember his anguish. It all happened so fast. The ghetto. The deportation. The sealed cattle car. The fiery altar upon which the history of our people and the future of mankind were meant to be sacrificed.

I remember: he asked his father: "Can this be true? This is the 20th century, not the Middle Ages. Who would allow such crimes to be committed? How could the world remain silent?"

And now the boy is turning to me: "Tell me," he asks, "What have you done with my future? What have you done with your life?"

And I tell him that I have tried. That I have tried to keep memory alive, that I have tried to fight those who would forget. Because if we forget, we are guilty, we are accomplices.

And then I explain to him how naive we were, that the world did know and remained silent. And that is why I swore never to be silent whenever and wherever human beings endure suffering and humiliation. We must always take sides. Neutrality helps the oppressor, never the victim. Silence encourages the tormentor, never the tormented.

Sometimes we must interfere. When human lives are endangered, when human dignity is in jeopardy, National borders and sensitivities become irrelevant. Wherever men or women are persecuted because of their race, religion, or political views, that place must—at that moment—become the center of the universe.

Of course, since I am a Jew profoundly rooted in my people's memory and tradition, my first response is to Jewish tears, Jewish needs, Jewish crises. For I belong to a traumatized generation, one that experienced the abandonment and solitude of our people. It would be unnatural for me not to make Jewish priorities my own: Israel, Soviet Jewry, Jews in Arab lands.

But there are others as important to me. Apartheid is, in my view, as abhorrent as anti-Semitism. To me, Andrei Sakharov's isolation is as much of a disgrace as Iosif Begun's imprisonment. As is the denial of Solidarity and its leader Lech Walesa's right to dissent. And Nelson Mandela's interminable imprisonment.

There is so much injustice and suffering crying out for our attention: victims of hunger, or racism and political persecution, writers and poets, prisoners in so many lands governed by the left and by the right. Human rights are being violated on every continent. More people are oppressed than free.

....(continued)

> "We must always take sides.
> Neutrality helps the oppressor,
> never the victim.
> Silence encourages
> the tormentor,
> never the tormented."

Address by Elie Wiesel, December 10, 1986, Oslo, Norway.
©1986, 1990, 1992, 1993, 1994, 1995 PEACE GROWS, Inc., 513 W. Exchange St., Akron, OH 44302 (216)864-5442.

ELIE WIESEL'S NOBEL PRIZE ADDRESS (continued)

And then, too, there are the Palestinians to whose plight I am sensitive but whose methods I deplore. Violence and terrorism are not the answer. Something must be done about their suffering, and soon. I trust Israel, for I have faith in the Jewish people. Let Israel be given a chance, let hatred and danger be removed from her horizons, and there will be peace in and around the Holy Land.

Yes, I have faith. Faith in God and even in His creation. Without it no actions would be possible. And action is the only remedy to indifference: the most insidious danger of all. Isn't this the meaning of Alfred Nobel's legacy? Wasn't his fear of war a shield against war?

There is much to be done, there is much that can be done. One person—a Raoul Wallenberg, an Albert Schweitzer, one person of integrity—can make a difference, a difference of life and death. As long as one dissident is in prison, our freedom will not be true. As long as one child is hungry, our lives will be filled with anguish and shame.

What all these victims need above all is to know that they are not alone; that we are not forgetting them, that when their voices are stilled we shall lend them ours, that while their freedom depends on ours, the quality of our freedom depends on theirs.

This is what I say to the young Jewish boy wondering what I have done with his years. It is in his name that I speak to you and that I express to you my deepest gratitude. No one is as capable of gratitude as one who has emerged from the kingdom of night.

We know that every moment is a moment of grace, ever hour an offering, not to share them would mean to betray them. Our lives no longer belong to us alone; they belong to all those who need us desperately.

Thank you, Chairman Aarvik. Thank you, members of the Nobel Committee. Thank you, people of Norway, for declaring on this singular occasion that our survival has meaning for mankind.

> *What all these victims need above all is to know that they are not alone; that we are not forgetting them, that when their voices are stilled we shall lend them ours, that while their freedom depends on ours, the quality of our freedom depends on theirs.*

Address by Elie Wiesel, December 10, 1986, Oslo, Norway.
©1986, 1990, 1992, 1993, 1994, 1995 PEACE GROWS, Inc., 513 W. Exchange St., Akron, OH 44302 (216)864-5442.

PERCEPTIONS ARE NOT REALITIES

To learn often requires some unlearning. The use of the Peter Projection map in this session, instead of the Mercator Projection on which we have been raised, contributes to some needed unlearning. When we look at the continents of the world based on actual areas in square miles, we see how much larger the southern hemisphere is than we had perceived. Nor is the United States really the center of the globe.

In this session as we pick out and examine the trouble spots around the world, we note a common thread. In each situation, some group is being excluded, being denied certain needs, being kept from participation in the decision-making process. What have your perceptions been about these trouble spots?

Because we do not read about them, we think they are not taking place, but there are about thirty shooting wars (1,000 or more killed in a year) going on across the globe most of the time. Since the United States sells arms to 142 of the world's 180 governments, no doubt we are playing a role of some kind in most of those conflicts.

As we consider any of the world's trouble spots, we should ask ourselves five questions:

1. What happened?
2. What were the major root causes of the problem(s)?
3. What was done?
4. If violence or war took place, then what might have been done differently? What might have been done nonviolently?
5. If so done, what could have resulted?

The article, *Disregarded History*, beginning on page 161, indicates what could have resulted had the colonists continued nonviolent action against the British instead of going to armed rebellion. Sometime, for an interesting insight to the success of nonviolence in America prior to 1776, look up a biography of Samuel Adams. He played a most important role in organizing the Committees of Correspondence instituting needed communication means throughout the thirteen colonies. These Committees served to move the ideas of Daniel Dulany into effective action.

Actually, there have been many cases of nonviolent, civilian-based defense used successfully against militarily-powerful governments. On page 168 you will find "Historical Examples of Nonviolent Struggle"; on page 169 "Contemporary Examples of Nonviolent Struggle." Along with Session 9, where we studied nonviolent, personal self-defense, course participants are most skeptical of this session on nonviolent national defense. Hopefully, first-time exposure to some of its many successes will begin to break down a bit of the skepticism.

..(continued)

PERCEPTIONS ARE NOT REALITIES (continued)

Though probably most people will say it is idealistic, impractical, "pie-in-the-sky," we should ask ourselves, is nuclear military defense itself really practical, really usable? With all of our fire power, how well have we been handling the world's trouble spots? How can governments start learning more about the new tools we are exploring in this session?

In the 1990 Gulf War against Iraq, we were "successful" in killing up to 200,000 innocent civilians while that government remains intact. The peacemaker treats causes not just symptoms. In the Gulf War, we only addressed symptoms. The peacemaker separates the person from the problem so a cooperative solution can be reached. In Iraq we focused on Saddam Hussein. The peacemaker recognizes that unresolved conflict and violence escalate. We ignored that basic principle. The peacemaker listens and clearly states his or her own needs, goals and purposes. In the Gulf War did we really listen to the negotiation proposals from the other side?

The peacemaker's mind is open to all creative options. They then are pursued with patience and persistence. When war is started, all other options are obliterated. Instead, the true peacemaker uses no violence but relies on creative, mental and moral forces, thoroughly and consistently dedicated to truth and justice.

I believe it was Pete Seegar who once said, "If your only tool is a hammer, then every problem becomes a nail!" If the main tool of a government is military, then every problem seems to become a war.

But humanity now knows how to resolve conflict and solve human problems without violence. Even ruthless dictators have been overcome by nonviolent, civilian-based national defense. No further loss of a single life nor of resources can be justified as long as there is another way. This is the only real, new world order. Every missed opportunity to use nonviolence is at humanity's peril.

> *. . . it was Pete Seegar who once said, "If your only tool is a hammer, then every problem becomes a nail."*
>
> *If the main tool of a government is military, then every problem seems to become a war.*

This article was written by John Looney.
©1986, 1990, 1992, 1993, 1994, 1995 PEACE GROWS, Inc., 513 W. Exchange St., Akron, OH 44302 (216)864-5442.

HISTORICAL EXAMPLES OF NONVIOLENT STRUGGLE

- **494 B.C.** The plebeians of Rome withdrew from the city and refused to work for days in order to correct grievances they had against the Roman consuls.

- **1765-1775 A.D.** The American colonists mounted three major nonviolent resistance campaigns against British rule (against the Stamp Acts of 1765, the Townshend Acts of 1767, and the Coercive Acts of 1774) resulting in *de facto* independence for nine colonies by 1775.

- **1850-1867.** Hungarian nationalists, led by Frances Deak, engaged in nonviolent resistance to Austrian rule, eventually regaining self-governance for Hungary as part of an Austro-Hungarian federation.

- **1905 - 1906.** In Russia, peasants, workers, students, and the intelligentsia engaged in major strikes and other forms of nonviolent action, forcing the Czar to accept the creation of an elected legislature.

- **1917.** The February 1917 Russia Revolution, despite some limited violence, was also predominantly nonviolent and led to the collapse of the czarist system.

- **1913 - 1919.** Demonstrations for woman's suffrage in the United States led to the passage and ratification of the Constitutional amendment guaranteeing women the right to vote.

- **1920.** An attempted *coup d' etat*, led by Wolfgang Kapp against the Weimar Republic of Germany failed when the population went on a general strike, refusing to give its consent and cooperation to the new government.

- **1923.** Despite severe repression, Germans resisted the French and Belgian occupation of the Ruhr, making the occupation so costly politically and economically that the French and Belgian forces finally withdrew.

- **1920s - 1947.** The Indian independence movement led by Mohandas Gandhi is one of the best known examples of nonviolent struggle.

- **1940 - 1945.** There are many examples of nonviolent resistance to Nazi occupation during World War II, especially in Norway, Denmark, and the Netherlands.

- **1944.** Two Central American dictators, Maximiliano Hernandez Martinez (El Salvador) and Jorge Ubico (Guatemala), were ousted as a result of nonviolent civilian insurrections.

- **1953.** A wave of strikes in Soviet prison labor camps led to some limited improvements in living conditions of political prisoners.

- **1955 - 1968.** Using a variety of nonviolent methods, including bus boycotts, economic boycotts, massive demonstrations, marches, sit-ins, and freedom rides, the U.S. civil rights movement won passage of the Civil Rights Act of 1964 and the Voting Rights Act of 1965.

- **1968 - 1969.** Nonviolent resistance to the Soviet invasion of Czechoslovakia enabled the Dubcek regime to stay in power for eight months, far longer than would have been possible with military resistance.

- **1986.** The Philippines "people power" movement brought down the oppressive Marcos dictatorship.

Reading printed with permission from The Albert Einstein Institution, 50 Church Street, Cambridge, MA 02138; 617/876-0311. ©1986, 1990, 1992, 1993, 1994, 1995 PEACE GROWS, Inc., 513 W. Exchange St., Akron, OH 44302 (216)864-5442.

CONTEMPORARY EXAMPLES OF NONVIOLENT STRUGGLE

In countries throughout the world people are joining together to struggle for greater freedom and justice using nonviolent weapons. People are learning that nonviolent struggle can be an effective alternative to both violence and submission. The following is just a short list of the places where nonviolent struggles are being waged today.

CHINA

The brutality of the Beijing Massacre (June 4, 1989) shocked the world. But just as startling to some was the realization that nonviolent struggle could be powerful enough to severely threaten the Chinese government. Armed with an arsenal of nonviolent "weapons," including marches, rallies, fasts, boycotts, blockades, and civil disobedience, the Chinese students effectively undermined the government's legitimacy and galvanized public support for democratic reforms.

POLAND

After martial law was declared in 1981, some skeptics dismissed the nonviolent campaign by Solidarity as a clear failure. Today, however, eight years later, Solidarity is a clear success, having won legal recognition and democratic reforms from the Polish government.

EASTERN EUROPE

In other Eastern European countries, large-scale nonviolent protests have become significant factors in internal conflicts, especially in Czechoslovakia, Hungary, and Yugoslavia.

SOVIET UNION

Nonviolent struggle is being waged by hundreds of thousands, even millions, of people, in Armenia, Georgia, Estonia, Lithuania and Latvia. Even in Moscow itself, advocates of civil rights and democracy are continuing to make their voices heard in these ways. Soviet Jews also are continuing acts of nonviolent resistance—for the right of emigration, for the right to maintain their Jewish identity, and for the legalization of their organizations. They have conducted small public protests, hunger strikes, vigils, and demonstrations in the midst of larger officially-sponsored gatherings.

UNITED STATES

Across the United States, environmentalists, feminists, anti-nuclear activists, labor unionists, human and animal rights activists, and people on both sides of the abortion debate are using a variety of nonviolent methods of struggle to pursue their objectives.

SOUTH AFRICA

Even in South Africa, where many have assumed that only violent revolution can advance the cause of freedom, Africans have been making increasingly effective use of boycotts, strikes, civil disobedience, and stay-at-home actions. These actions often bring together hundreds of thousands of people in nonviolent struggle against the apartheid system.

CHILE

In the 1988 plebiscite on the future of General Pinochet, the successful "NO" campaign sponsored several mass demonstrations that were strictly nonviolent. In one case a million and a half people participated. It seems clear that such popular pressure, combined with other imaginative methods, helped ensure an accurate counting of votes, and a decision by the junta to accept the outcome.

ISRAELI-OCCUPIED TERRITORIES

Despite media attention to the stones and petrol bombs, Palestinians in the Israeli-occupied territories have been using predominantly nonviolent methods of resistance—economic boycotts, commercial strikes, labor strikes, civil disobedience, resignations from certain jobs, tax refusal, etc.—and these are proving their most powerful weapons since the Uprising began in December 1987.

BURMA (Myanmar)

Last year witnessed a remarkable wave of massive demonstrations for the restoration of democracy. These largely nonviolent actions led to the resignations of both General Ne Win, the dictator for 26 years, and General Sein Lwin, his even harsher successor. Recently the resistance has subsided in face of a new military coup, but the democratic opposition remains intact and determined.

In recent years and months, other nonviolent struggles have also been waged by people in **Brazil, South Korea, Mexico, Panama, Pakistan, Taiwan, Haiti, and the Sudan.**

ALTERNATIVES TO VIOLENCE · Session 15 Reading · 168

WHAT REALLY IS NONVIOLENT, CIVILIAN-BASED NATIONAL DEFENSE?
How do we define it and why does it work?

Nonviolent, national defense is: (1) total (2) collective (3) nonviolent resistance or noncooperation with the invading army, occupying force or oppressor. As Gene Sharp, the foremost authority in the field, points out, oppression can only exist with the consent of the oppressed. Remove that consent and the oppressor is helpless.

What the oppressor or invading army relies upon is the fear of the citizens to provide the needed consent. While the resistance of one person can educate or inspire others, it really cannot be enough to disarm the opponent. That is why it has to be total and collective to be effective. Every citizen from all walks of life must come together and act in concert.

What the oppressor or invading army relies upon is the fear of the citizens to provide the needed consent.

An interesting exercise is to envision an invading or oppressive army marching toward your community. What could you and the body of citizens do to defend yourselves, to render the occupying forces ineffective? First, you would need uninterrupted, reliable and secretive means of communication to organize efforts. In Iran, when the Shah was overthrown, audio cassettes were produced, widely distributed and elsewhere, clandestine radio stations were established. Think of other things you would need.

Next, what would the invader require? Directions, reliable street signs, fuel, food, water, etc.? What could you do to deny them to an invader? The cases included with this workbook will give you many ideas, some very unique and surprising.

Why does civilian-based national defense work? Ronald Sider and Richard Taylor in their book *Nuclear Holocaust and Christian Hope* attribute it to four things:

This article was written by John Looney.
©1986, 1990, 1992, 1993, 1994, 1995 PEACE GROWS, Inc., 513 W. Exchange St., Akron, OH 44302 (216)864-5442.

WHAT REALLY IS NONVIOLENT, CIVILIAN-BASED NATIONAL DEFENSE?
How do we define it and why does it work? (continued)

(1) The power of mass involvement.
In ordinary warfare, the actual fighting or resistance is done by a small percentage of the total population. When one side is defeated, the war ends. The enemy can march in and take over a demoralized nation. In CBD, the enemy occupation is considered the beginning, not the end of the battle. The whole population resists young and old, men and women, educated and uneducated, city dweller and rural people.

(2) The power of resistance and non-cooperation.
An occupying army's power is in the fear and obedience of the people because of the enemy's weapons. The people refuse to give in to that fear. Realizing that their consent is required in order for them to be ruled, they determine not to obey. Through thousands of acts they defy the enemy and dramatize public disapproval of the occupation and maintain allegiance to their own way of life.

(3) The power of nonviolence.
Not encountering threat or fear, the occupying soldiers are thrown morally off-balance. The preservation of any society requires at least a minimum respect for human life. No society can function if citizens are free to kill for whim or personal advantage. The kill-or-be-killed atmosphere of war provides the stimulus to overcome this inhibition. The soldiers will find their sense of justification for killing these people undermined. They will begin to doubt the propaganda about the conquered people and may even develop sympathy or respect for them.

(4) The power of good will.
In ordinary warfare, contempt and hatred of the enemy are the fuel that drives the machine, the enemy must be depersonalized. In the practice of CBD, resisters show concern for the enemy as persons. They seek to speak to their antagonists, to forgive those who inflict evil upon them, and even to be ready to heal their enemy's wounds. Christians believe that the power suffering, agape love is ultimately the most powerful force in the universe.

Is this all impractical, far-fetched? Few know that even the Pentagon has provided grant money to Gene Sharp to study ways our government might use these methods!

Do our present military policies provide real security? What is national security? Does it not include political, social, economic health? Do you really feel secure?

Everyone agrees that our country is experiencing serious economic problems. Unemployment, homelessness, poverty all have been growing. Communities are finding it harder and harder to fund such basic needs as good education and health care. It is said we do not have enough money for those things. Is there any logical source for such funding?

This article was written by John Looney.
©1986, 1990, 1992, 1993, 1994, 1995 PEACE GROWS, Inc., 513 W. Exchange St., Akron, OH 44302 (216)864-5442.

WHAT REALLY IS NONVIOLENT, CIVILIAN-BASED NATIONAL DEFENSE?
How do we define it and why does it work? (continued)

Our enemy the Soviet Union has disintegrated. Yet, relying solely on arms for national security, the miliary budget has remained essentially the same. To justify high arms spending we are told other enemies threaten: Iraq, Iran, China, North Korea, Cuba. Let us look at the whole 1991 spending picture:

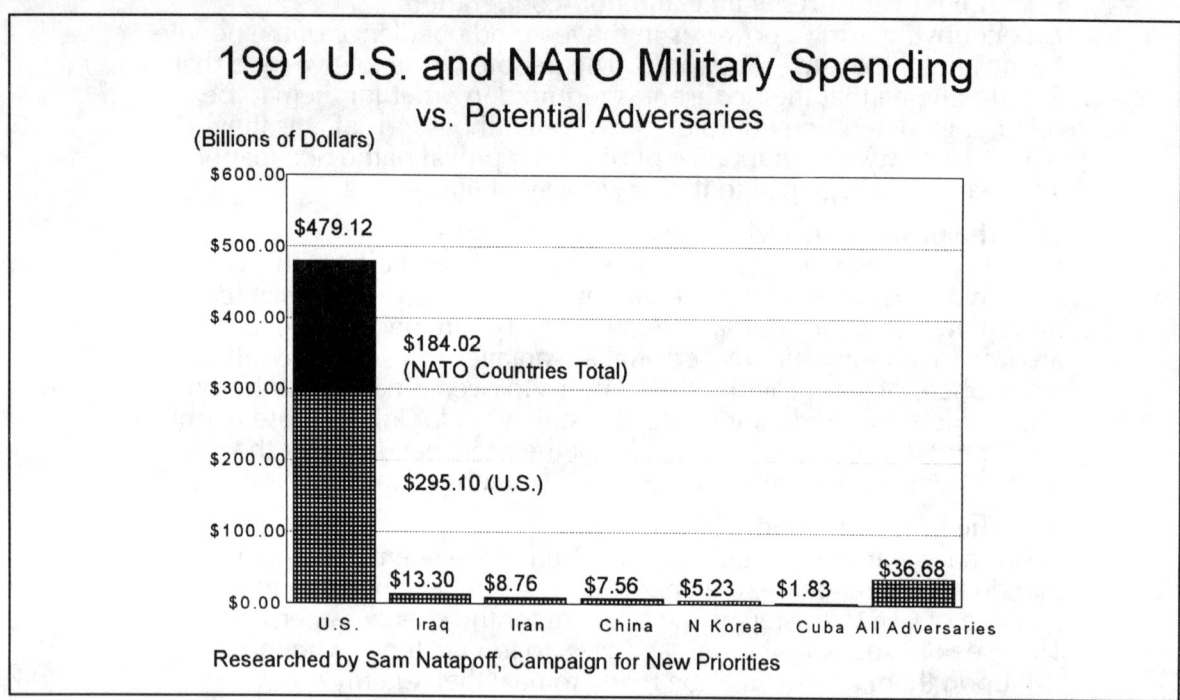

Are we really in danger? Or, somehow, are our hard-earned military tax dollars being wasted? Could they safely be diverted to other needs? Do we really need $479.12 billion to offset a mere $36.68 billion? Is our military program really practical? Because military spending per dollar creates fewer jobs than most other spending, could we not create more jobs rather than lose?

What are we advocating? Not having an army? **All we are advocating, as does this entire course, is that we need to look at all alternatives.** If we have all the facts, if we know all of the options, maybe we could find a better, more practical way of going.

Has there ever been a successful nation, without an army? Maybe. The video, "The Island of Peace" will open our minds further.

SUMMARY OF CONCEPTS
as related to the subjects listed on worksheet #15

1. *An example of international violence that troubles me:*
   Each participant will write own example.

2. *What caused the above trouble spot?*
   Although each will have own reasons, these answers will be cases of people being exploited, excluded and/or denied needs.

3. *What is the difference between peacekeeping and peacemaking?*
   Peacekeeping is preventing fighting but without resolving the conflict. It is often called conflict management.

   Peacemaking is nonviolent intervention to help resolve the conflict. It is often called conflict resolution.

4. *What is nonviolent civilian national defense?*
   Nonviolent civilian national defense is total, collective, non-cooperation with the attacking, invading or occupying forces. Historic cases have demonstrated that it has and can work. They also teach us how.

Major point to remember:
- To resolve international conflict, we must address the causes not just the symptoms.

Session 15
NONVIOLENT NATIONAL DEFENSE
Additional reading

Ackerman, Peter and Christopher Kruegler. *Strategic Nonviolent Conflict: The Dynamics Of People Power In The Twentieth Century.* Westport, CT: Praeger, 1994.

Fahey, Joseph and Richard Armstrong. *A Peace Reader: Essential Readings On War, Justice, Nonviolence, And World Order.* NY: Paulist Press, 1987.

Hedemann, Ed. *War Tax Resistance: A Guide To Withholding Your Support From The Military.* NY: War Resisters League, 1992.

Keen, Sam. *Faces Of The Enemy: Reflections Of The Hostile Imagination.* San Francisco: Harper & Row, 1986.

Laffin, Arthur J. *Swords Into Plowshares: Nonviolent Direct Action For Disarmament.* San Francisco: Harper & Row, 1987.

Thomas, T. M., David R. Conrad and Gertrude F. Langsam. *Global Images Of Peace And Education Transforming The War System.* Ann Arbor, MI: Prakken Pub., 1987.

ALTERNATIVES TO VIOLENCE

Session 16
UNDERSTANDING GLOBAL VIOLENCE
What can we do?

Objectives

a. To review causes of war, violence and terrorism in the world.

b. To learn how world violence relates to the quality of our daily lives.

c. To understand how our lifestyle affects domestic and global violence.

d. To define simple living and see how some are applying it.

WORKSHEET #16

(The following points will be covered in this session. Most points do not have "pat" answers, but the main thing is for you to arrive at an expression of the concepts. These questions are to help you take notes and process the material.)

1. How does world violence relate to the quality of my life?

   _____

   _____

   _____

2. How does my lifestyle affect domestic and/or global violence?

   _____

   _____

   _____

3. What is simple living?

   _____

   _____

   _____

4. What are some ways of applying simple living?

   _____

   _____

   _____

©1986, 1990, 1992, 1993, 1994, 1995 PEACE GROWS, Inc., 513 W. Exchange St., Akron, OH 44302 (216)864-5442.

Notes or Journal Entry

Assignments:

_____
_____
_____
_____
_____

ALTERNATIVES TO VIOLENCE   Session 16 Reading

WHAT IS YOUR ROLE IN THE GLOBAL VILLAGE?

In Session 15 we learned that globally wherever trouble spots with war or strife exist, some group is being denied and excluded. Between nations, within nations, within communities and families it all is much the same.

Session 16 intends to show the nature and magnitude of some of that denial and exclusion through an exercise called the "Global Village Game." When you were born, were you able to select the place? Today in this exercise, you are going to be reborn. You still will have no choice as to where.

As you go through the exercise, think about how it feels to be part of the group to which you belong. How do you feel about the other groups? How much do you think most Americans realize the imbalances shown in this exercise? What does maldistribution mean for the possibility of violence in the world?

Nor is the maldistribution of resources between continents the whole picture. Within continents there can be a great disparity between nations. Asia, for instance, would be much worse were Japan not part of it. Within nations is there equitable distribution? If there were, why would the United States have so many homeless?

What causes global violence, revolution, war and terrorism in the world? Do the "have" nations or peoples ever initiate violence? If so, how? What kinds of violence? Why?

How about the "have-nots?" Do they ever start violence? What kinds? Why?

In Session 2 we learned the major characteristic of violence: it escalates. Internationally and within nations an escalating spiral of violence also takes place when a nation or people is denied human needs, through an oppressive international situation or an oppressive government.'

Those oppressive policies cause either national or international unrest. If and when the unrest reveals itself in active dissent, the oppressor feels threatened. World or government repression is increased, which can lead to active resistance. This stimulates government police action. Then the people or nation may initiate insurgency or terrorist activities. The government feels the need to respond by instituting counter insurgency actions. This can stimulate armed response or revolution. All-out military action or war follows! It is the same old escalation but on a far larger scale.

Enough of us starting to live more simply would enable many others around the globe to simply live!

In today's world, nations are interdependent in many ways and constantly growing more so. Referring to the chart on page 145, we can see how dependent we are on other countries for so many of the material things in our lives. It also shows how, in the countries from which we obtain those things, people are deprived.

This discussion, however, should not end without considering what, if anything, we can do to improve the situation. In Session 18, we will take up ways to work the political system for improvement. Here, the question more is what can we as individuals do to contribute to the more equitable distribution of resources in the world. As North Americans, obviously, we consume more than our share. Is that consumption necessary? Could it be reduced?

Many of us say it could. Enough of us starting to live more simply would enable many others around the globe to simply live! What is advocated is called "simple living."

....(continued)

This article was written by John Looney.
©1986, 1990, 1992, 1993, 1994, 1995 PEACE GROWS, Inc., 513 W. Exchange St., Akron, OH 44302 (216)864-5442.

WHAT IS YOUR ROLE IN THE GLOBAL VILLAGE? (continued)

Simple living means establishing a life style so that we consume no more than we actually need. The following readings will help explain the significance further and suggest many ideas for things we might do to reduce the detrimental effects of our over-consumption.

The economic and environmental forces in conflict over the use of land and resources also need badly to understand and use the principles and skills of win-win conflict resolution.

Some will argue that developing countries need the livelihood our buying from them creates. But releasing land and other resources of third world countries from having to fulfill desires of the developed countries would have just the opposite effect. Those resources then could supply the needs, not now met of third world peoples. Here is an example.

When American pineapple producers came into the Philippines at the invitation of Marcos' government, who had removed native people from the land turned over for pineapple growth, there was a notable increase in malnutrition in the Philippines. That land had been used to grow food for their own people. At the same time, Hawaiian pineapple farm workers went on U.S. welfare in large numbers!

Finally, we must consider the effects of over-consumption on the environment and the damage it does to the ecology. About 100 years too late, we are beginning to look at and respect Native Americans' philosophy toward preserving the earth. Chief Seattle's message on pages 179-180 delineates it so well. The economic and environmental forces in conflict over the use of land and resources also need badly to understand and use the principles and skills of win-win conflict resolution.

To turn things around, we too must realize the tremendously important role we have to play if things are to change. "One American does 20 to 100 times more damage to the planet than one person in the third world and one rich American causes 1,000 times more destruction" according to a report in the *Akron Beacon Journal* of April 6, 1990. This is all due to our much, much greater consumption.

Hopefully, this session will cause us to better understand the way this run-away consumption creates world tensions. They cause us to support expensive military forces to police the world, largely to protect the availability of cheap materials and labor to feed our material needs. Military spending, in turn, causes the higher taxes we so much protest and the lack of money for so many things that really demand higher priority than we are according them. Better education, improved health care, broader drug treatment programs are a few examples. Would they not do much more to improve the quality of our lives than does our obsession with the over-consumption of consumer goods?

John Woolman, about 200 years ago, asked that we look to the clothes we wear, the food we eat, our possession to see "if not the seeds of war are in them!"

ALTERNATIVES TO VIOLENCE

GLOBAL RESOURCE DISTRIBUTION
What would you estimate for income and food?

Continent	Land Area	Population	Per Capita INCOME		Per Capita FOOD	
			Amount	%	# *Tokens* (20 TOTAL)	%
Africa	24%	10%	$			
Asia	35%	59%	$			
Europe	8%	17%	$			
Latin America	17%	8%	$			
North America	16%	6%	$			

(Answers on page 178.)

Source: *World Military and Social Expenditures*, by Ruth Leger Sivard, 1980.
©1986, 1990, 1992, 1993, 1994, 1995 PEACE GROWS, Inc., 513 W. Exchange St., Akron, OH 44302 (216)864-5442.

ALTERNATIVES TO VIOLENCE Session 16 Chart

GLOBAL RESOURCE DISTRIBUTION
What would you estimate for income and food?

Continent	Land Area	Population	Per Capita INCOME Amount	%	Per Capita FOOD # Tokens (20 TOTAL)	%
Africa	24%	10%	$ 250	4%	2	10%
Asia	35%	59%	$ 400	7%	1	5%
Europe	8%	17%	$1300	22%	5	25%
Latin America	17%	8%	$ 500	9%	3	15%
North America	16%	6%	$3400	58%	9	45%

Population distribution for class size

People in Class	Africa (10%)	Asia (59%)	Europe (17%)	Latin America (8%)	North America (6%)
8	1	4	1	1	1
9	1	5	1	1	1
10	1	5	2	1	1
11	1	6	2	1	1
12	1	7	2	1	1
13	1	8	2	1	1
14	1	8	3	1	1
15	2	8	3	1	1
16	2	9	3	1	1
17	2	10	3	1	1
18	2	11	3	1	1
19	2	11	4	1	1
20	2	12	4	1	1
21	2	13	4	1	1
22	2	13	4	2	1
23	2	14	4	2	1
24	3	14	4	2	1
25	3	15	4	2	1
26	3	15	4	2	2
27	3	16	4	2	2
28	3	17	5	2	2
29	3	17	5	2	2
30	3	18	5	2	2

Source: *World Military and Social Expenditures*, by Ruth Leger Sivard, 1980.
©1986, 1990, 1992, 1993, 1994, 1995 PEACE GROWS, Inc., 513 W. Exchange St., Akron, OH 44302 (216)864-5442.

CHIEF SEATTLE'S MESSAGE

In 1854, Chief Seattle, leader of the Suquamish tribe in the Washington territory, delivered this prophetic speech to mark the transferral of ancestral Indian lands to the federal government of the U.S.A.

The Great Chief in Washington sends word that he wishes to buy our land.

The Great Chief also sends us words of friendship and good will. This is kind of him, since we know he has little need of our friendship in return. But we will consider your offer. For we know that if we do not sell, white man may come with guns and take our land. How can you buy or sell the sky, the warmth of the land? The idea is strange to us.

If we do not own the freshness of the air and the sparkle of the water, how can you buy them?

Every part of this earth is sacred to my people. Every shining pine needle, every sandy shore, every mist in the dark woods, every clearing and humming insect is holy in the memory and experience of my people. The sap which courses through the trees carries the memories of the red man.

The white man's dead forget the country of their birth when they go to walk among the stars. Our dead never forget this beautiful earth, for it is the mother of the red man. We are part of the earth and it is part of us. The perfumed flowers are our sisters; the deer, the horse, the great eagle, these are our brothers. The rocky crests, the juices in the meadows, the body heat of the pony, and man—all belong to the same family.

So when the Great Chief in Washington sends word that he wishes to buy our land, he asks much of us.

So, the Great Chief sends word he will reserve us a place so that we can live comfortably to ourselves. He will be our father and we will be his children.

So we will consider your offer to buy our land. But it will not be easy. For this land is sacred to us.

This shining water that moves in the streams and rivers is not just water but the blood of our ancestors. If we sell you land, you must remember that it is sacred, and you must teach your children that it is sacred, and you must teach your children that it is sacred, and that each ghostly reflection in the clear water of the lake tells of events and memories in the life of my people. The water's murmur is the voice of my father's father.

The rivers are our brothers, they quench our thirst. The rivers carry our canoes, and feed our children. If we sell you our land, you must remember, and teach your children, that the rivers are our brothers, and yours, and you must henceforth give the river the kindness you would give any brother.

The red man has always retreated before the advancing white man, as the mist of the mountain runs before the morning sun. But the ashes of our fathers are sacred. Their graves are holy ground, and so these hills, these trees, this portion of earth is consecrated to us. We know that the white man does not understand our ways. One portion of land is the same to him as the next, for he is a stranger who comes in the night and takes from the land whatever he needs. The earth is not his brother, but his enemy, and when he has conquered it, he moves on. He leaves his fathers' graves behind, and he does not care. He kidnaps the earth from his children. He does not care. His fathers' graves and his children's birthright are forgotten. He treats his mother, the earth, and his brother, the sky, as things to be bought, plundered, sold like sheep or bright beads. His appetite will devour the earth and leave behind only a desert.

I do not know. Our ways are different from your ways. The sight of your cities pains the eyes of the red man. But perhaps it is because the red man is a savage and does not understand.

There is no quiet place in the white man's cities. No place to hear the unfurling of leaves in spring or the rustle of insect's wings. But perhaps it is because I am a savage and do not understand. The clatter only seems to insult the ears. And what is there to life if a man cannot hear the lonely cry of the whippoorwill or the arguments of the frogs around a pond at night? I am a red man and do not understand. The Indian prefers the soft sound of the wind darting over the face of a pond, and the smell of the wind itself, cleansed by a midday rain, or scented with the pinon pine.

The air is precious to the red man, for all things share the same breath—the beast, the tree, the man—they all share the same breath. The white man does not seem to notice the air he breathes. Like a man dying for many days, he is numb to the stench. But if we sell you our land, you must remember that the air is precious to us, that the air shares its spirit with all the life it supports. The wind that gave our grandfather his first breath also receives his last sigh. And the wind

CHIEF SEATTLE'S MESSAGE (continued)

must also give our children the spirit of life. And if we sell you our land, you must keep it apart and sacred, as a place where even the white man can go to taste the wind that is sweetened by the meadow's flowers.

So we will consider your offer to buy our land. If we decide to accept, I will make one condition: The white man must treat the beasts of this land as his brothers.

I am a savage and do not understand any other way. I have seen a thousand rotting buffaloes on the prairie, left by the white man who shot them from a passing train. I am a savage and I do not understand how the smoking iron horse can be more important than the buffalo that we kill only to stay alive.

What is man without the beasts? If all the beasts were gone, men would die from a great loneliness of spirit. For whatever happens to the beasts, soon happens to man. All things are connected.

You must teach your children that the ground beneath their feet is the ashes of our grandfathers. So that they will respect the land, tell your children that the earth is rich with the lives of our kin. Teach your children what we have taught our children, that the earth is our mother. Whatever befalls the earth, befalls the sons of the earth. If men spit upon the ground, they spit upon themselves.

This we know. The earth does not belong to man, man belongs to the earth. This we know. All things are connected like the blood which unites one family. All things are connected.

Whatever befalls the earth befalls the sons of the earth. Man did not weave the web of life; he is merely a strand in it. Whatever he does to the web, he does to himself.

But we will consider your offer to go to the reservation you have for my people. We will live apart, and in peace. It matters little where we spend the rest of our days. Our children have seen their fathers humbled in defeat. Our warriors have felt shame, and after defeat they turn their days in idleness and contaminate their bodies with sweet foods and strong drink. It matters little where we pass the rest of our days. They are not many. A few more hours, a few more winters, and none of the children of the great tribes that once lived on this earth or that roam now in small bands in the woods will be left to mourn the graves of a people once as powerful and hopeful as yours. But why should I mourn the passing of my people? Tribes are made of men, nothing more. Men come and go like waves of the sea.

Even the white man, whose God walks and talks with him as friend to friend, cannot be exempt from the common destiny. We may be brothers after all; we shall see. One thing we know, which the white man may one day discover—our God is the same God. You may think now that you own him as you wish to own our land; but you cannot. He is the God of man, and his compassion is equal for the red man and the white. This earth is precious to him, and to harm the earth is to heap contempt on its Creator. The white too shall pass; perhaps sooner than all other tribes. Continue to contaminate your bed, and you will one night suffocate in your own waste.

But in your perishing you will shine brightly, fired by the strength of the God who brought you to this land and for some special purpose gave you dominion over this land and over the red man. That destiny is a mystery to us, for we do not understand when the buffalo are all slaughtered, the wild horses are tamed, the secret corners of the forest heavy with the scent of many men, and the view of the ripe hills blotted by talking wires. Where is the thicket? Gone. Where is the eagle? Gone. And what is it to say goodbye to the swift pony and the hunt? The end of living and the beginning of survival.

So we will consider your offer to buy our land. If we agree, it will be to secure the reservation you have promised. There, perhaps, we may live out our brief days as we wish. When the last red man has vanished from this earth, and his memory is only the shadow of a cloud moving across the prairie, these shores and forests will still hold the spirits of my people. For they love this earth as the newborn loves its mother's heartbeat. So if we sell you our land, love it as we've loved it. Care for it as we've cared for it. Hold in your mind the memory of the land as it is when you take it. And with all your strength, with all your mind, with all your heart preserve it for your children, and love it . . . as God loves us all.

One thing we know. Our God is the same God. This earth is precious to him. Even the white man cannot be exempt from the common destiny. We may be brothers after all. We shall see.

ALTERNATIVES TO VIOLENCE

ON SIMPLE LIVING
"Taking Charge": How you live can make a difference

If the world were a global village of 100 people, one-third of them would be rich or of moderate income, two-thirds would be poor. Of the 100 residents, 47 would be unable to read, and only one would have a college education. About 35 would be suffering from hunger and malnutrition, at least half would be homeless or living in substandard housing.

If the world were a global village of 100 people, 6 of them would be Americans. These 6 would have over a third of the village's income and the other 94 would subsist on the other two-thirds. How could the wealthy 6 live "in peace" with their neighbors? Surely they would be driven to arm themselves against the other 94—perhaps even to spend, as Americans do, about twice as much per person on military defense as the total income of two-thirds of the villagers.

Queries

1. What would an economic system be like that promoted harmony with the environment and the rest of the world family?

2. How can we create economic structures that would reflect our values? What could we do to stop or disengage ourselves from economic structures that go against our values?

3. How far are we willing to go to maintain our standard of living? How closely is the quality of life related to standard of living? What values would you like our economy to embody or protect?

How would our lives change if we were suddenly transformed into members of the victim group in the Third World?

First, take out the furniture; leave just a few old blankets, a kitchen table, one wooden chair (the car went long ago—remember?).

Second, throw out the clothes. Each one may keep the oldest suit or dress, a shirt or blouse. The head of the family has the only pair of shoes.

Third, all kitchen appliances have already gone. Keep a box of matches, a small bag of flour, some sugar and salt, a handful of onions, a dish of dried beans. Rescue those moldy potatoes from the garbage can: those are tonight's meal.

Fourth, dismantle the bathroom, shut off the running water, take out the wiring and the lights and everything that runs by electricity.

Fifth, take away the house and move the family into the toolshed.

Sixth, by now all the other houses in the neighborhood have gone; instead there are shanties—for the fortunate ones.

Seventh, cancel all the newspapers and magazines. Throw out the books. You won't miss them—you are now illiterate. One radio is now left for the whole shantytown.

Eighth, no more postman, fireman, government services. The two-classroom school is 3 miles away, but only half the children go, anyway.

Ninth, no hospital, no doctor. The nearest clinic is now 10 miles away with a midwife in charge. Get there by bus or by bicycle, if you're lucky enough to have one.

Tenth, throw out your bankbooks, stock certificates, pension plans, insurance policies, social security records. You have left a cash hoard of $5.

Eleventh, get out and start cultivating your three acres. Try hard to raise $300 in cash crops because your landlord wants 1/3 and your local moneylender, 10 percent.

Twelfth, find some way for your children to bring in a little extra money so you have something to eat most days. But it won't be enough to keep bodies healthy, so lop off 25 to 30 years of life expectancy.

(Adapted from the FAO magazine *Freedom from Hunger*, based on excerpts from *The Great Ascent* by Robert L. Heilbroner (New York: Harper and Row, 1963).

Readings on Simple Living are from *Taking Charge*, pp. 68-69, published by the American Friends Service Committee, 1978.
©1986, 1990, 1992, 1993, 1994, 1995 PEACE GROWS, Inc., 513 W. Exchange St., Akron, OH 44301 (216)864-5442.

ON SIMPLE LIVING (continued)

Cooperative business

Over fifty million people in the United States belong to some cooperative business: food retailing, repair services, housing, credit unions, farm equipment, and rural electricity, among many others. Cooperatively owned businesses can respond more directly to people's needs than businesses oriented towards profits for the few. There are three types of co-ops: producer cooperatives, worker cooperatives, and consumer cooperatives.

In a producer cooperative, people producing similar things band together to market them. The size of producer co-ops can vary from the immensity of agri-business to small groups of farmers. Small food-growing cooperatives, for example are now their own wholesalers. They have also begun contracting to supply urban food-buying cooperatives. Such guaranteed markets take much of the risk out of farming.

In worker-owner-and-operated cooperatives, workers provide the money to start and run the business and elect the board of directors. Any surplus earnings are distributed as bonuses. Worker-owner cooperatives can take other forms, for example, living communities. In such groups, each person has an equal say in the decision-making process and receives enough money to cover his or her low-consumption needs.

Consumer cooperatives are owned and controlled by their customers, usually through an elected board. Some consumer cooperatives are run as nonprofit businesses that provide workers with an adequate income and consumers with low prices. These can be operated on a direct-charge basis; the Briarpatch Cooperative Market, mentioned elsewhere in this book, is an example. It meets its operating expenses through a monthly charge of fifty cents per member. The initial capital to start the store came from selling membership shares. Co-ops may also return profits to members in the form of patronage refunds, whereby profits are divided and returned to member patrons in proportion to their sales receipts. Some consumer co-ops have workers on their board of directors as well as members. Each member shareholder has one vote, so those with more shares do not have more power.

Cooperatively owned housing

In cooperative housing, all units are financed with single mortgage, which is held by a nonprofit corporation. These units may be houses or apartments or both. The corporation, in turn, is owned by the residents of the housing cooperative through membership shares—one share per residential unit, one vote per share.

Cooperative housing can sometimes be 100-percent financed through federal or local government loans. In this way, the corporation can purchase the housing without having to raise much capital from its members. The only down payment needed to live in the cooperative is the cost of a share, which can be as low as the total of the two months' rent deposit often required on similar housing, with monthly payments equal to, or smaller than, rent on comparable housing. Members can deduct property tax and mortgage interest payments from their state and federal income tax, and they are eligible for the homeowner's property tax exemption in California. When someone moves out, the cooperative buys back the share and resells it to a new resident at no profit. Because the mortgage is held by the cooperative corporation, there is no refinancing cost or 6-percent real estate commission in the transaction. In this way, housing that could normally be

ON SIMPLE LIVING (continued)

afforded only by families with incomes of $14,000 or more a year could be made available to families with incomes as low as $7,500, assuming one-fourth goes to housing.

New York State loaning $234 million to one of the largest cooperatively owned housing complexes in the world, Co-op City in the East Bronx. The monthly payments Co-op City members make are well below prevailing rates in New York City.

Cooperatively owned housing is a good example of how basic needs can be met through cooperation with others. At the present time, most people cannot afford to own their own homes, so they rent. The landlord pays property taxes and his mortgage, for which he gets federal income tax deductions, and he can claim depreciation on the building structure while the value of the land rises. The renter pays all the expenses related to the property through his rent, plus a profit to the landlord for his investment, and his full income taxes. The renter pays more to rent than he would pay if he owned the property he rents. But, separately, most people are unable to qualify for a home loan.

Land trusts

Land trusts present a completely different way of relating to land and to ownership. In a land trust, the land belongs to those who use it. It is not theirs to abuse or sell, but theirs to care for, nurture, and live on as trustees. The trustees use and hold the land for future generations. One group, Landlords End in East Palo Alto, California, did not want to own any land, but did want to settle on some without the expense of renting. Landlords End is an example of land trusting as an alternative to renting. The residents, or trustees, of the land gain no equity in the property and improvements they make. These are retained in the trust. More frequently, in land trust arrangements, only the land is put in trust, with arrangements for residents to recover equity from improvements to buildings or property. One of the Landlords End group put it this way:

> The idea seemed simple. A land trust: the idea of mutuality between people and the land they use; the idea that between people and land there is a caretakership; that land is to be used, but not used up. We would buy the houses we were already living in and put them together into a trust. Making payments would be no more than what we were already paying in rent, and when the past payment was made we would make no more. If any of us left, others would move in and make the payments. Perhaps as we paid off some of the houses we should lower the rents of all, or help others pay off houses. Slowly a rent-free housing zone would emerge. No landlords; people directly responsible for the houses they lived in; buying or taking over empty lots for playgrounds and gardens; perhaps one or two houses for meetings and small stores.

And so we did it. We bought a few houses; scraped up the money from friends—loans of $2,000 here, $5,000 there—friends who knew that the banks invested their savings into war industries but who didn't know what else to do with them; friends who wanted to help an idea get started with little or no interest. And the experiment began. Three years later there are seven houses in close proximity to each other, and between fifteen and twenty people. We didn't wait for a legal formula to do it, we just did it. And now that there is a legal form, it seems important to say, both to ourselves and to others:

The Trust begins in our hearts. It worked out in our lives. The legal form can be used to give clarity. Writing it down seems to lend stability. But don't build trust on a legal system that is guaranteed to set us at each other's throats. The first requisite of Land Trust is a sense of the importance of community and the courage and willingness to struggle.

ALTERNATIVES TO VIOLENCE

ON SIMPLE LIVING (continued)

Voluntary community tax

Often when people work together to meet a common need, a community is formed. These people will have other needs for which they may seek a common solution. One means of supporting groups or funding projects that meet community needs is through a voluntary community tax. Such a tax can give people a choice of whom and what they support. It can be used to make a community more self-sufficient and less dependent on the larger society to meet its needs.

Both the Earthworm Community in Champaign, Illinois, and the cooperative community in Madison, Wisconsin, have experimented with a voluntary community tax. Such a tax is often called a self-tax, because it is self-imposed. In the Earthworm Community, the funds generated from a voluntary 2-percent tax are allocated to various groups and individuals for the purpose of enhancing the quality of community life, promoting community-centered services, or satisfying community needs. Some allocations are made to new and existing member groups as requested, provided they have met the agreed-on criteria. Others are given monthly to service groups such as the Health Center and the Consumer's Union, or to needy workers as income supplements.

The Madison Sustaining Fund collects and allocates that cooperative community's self-taxes to promote and support "a counter-economy which provides goods, services, employment, and a sense of community sharing without profits." Its members include a free medical clinic, a consumer's co-op garage, a theater, a co-op food market, a free high school, a printer, a tenants' union, a restaurant, a bicycle co-op, and legal defense aid, among others. They have initiated a variety of taxes for their purpose and have acted as a planning group for the community.

Voluntary community tax funds are placed in the care of a committee of trustees, or council, who represent everyone and meet regularly to oversee the collection and distribution of the funds. The structure of the committee reflects the political principles of its members; decisions are made by consensus and the chairmanship rotates. Some self-taxes used by these and other communities are:

- Businesses pledge 2 percent of their profit or 4 percent of their gross sales to the community fund.

- Retail businesses ask customers to volunteer a percentage (1 to 3 percent) of their sales price, to be placed in a collection box near the cash register.

- A five-cent mark-up at movie clubs or similar groups is levied.

- Individuals pledge a regular part of their income to the fund.

Your own bank

If you want complete control of your money, including your savings, you will have to start your own credit union or even your own bank. I don't believe in wars and I don't want my money to contribute to them. But what bank can I put my money into and be sure it will not turn around and lend my money to some war industry? None that I know of. And there isn't any way I can check on what a bank does with my money. The small amount of savings I have is in a credit union; that's better than a bank in that I can help set its policies. But I can't write checks on my credit union account. A group associated

ON SIMPLE LIVING (continued)

with the Institute for the Study of Nonviolence tried to go further; they became their own bank for a while.

> We formed our own "peoples bank." We started off with a little box and we wound up with about ninety of us banking in it. The idea was that money should be used and that life should be based around the community. We tried to define community as using one another as resources. Human resources were the wealth and the joy that we had, and we were going to try and take the material parts of that to manifest a sense of small community. We began the bank wanting it to be a no-interest bank, but given an inflationary society where inflation is always eating out from under us, we felt an alternative structure was needed.
>
> We had three different accounts, Fund A, Fund B, and Fund C. Fund A was for saving money; a person could sign in an amount of money and know the money would be kept there and not used by others. Fund B was called the Sharing Fund. This was money that we felt we had in surplus, extra money within our wealth; it could be used back and forth by people.
>
> After toning down and refining, we came up with the idea that anybody in the group could take up to ten percent of the total money in Fund B without asking anybody else. They were to pay it back when they had the money to do so; it was floating money. Fund C was for those of us who were resisting war taxes.
>
> We set aside money that would be used for tax resistance projects. One year we bought a lot of medical supplies and tried to exchange them for bombs at a Navy base in Alameda. We systematically did something similar each year.
>
> Overall though, the operation of the bank was very loose. The bank was totally voluntary, people's roles changed every month, people were busy with other projects. The bank ran for a couple of years, and we were able to loan funds to other land trusts and use the money in ways we wanted.
>
> In the end, we had a problem with a friend who got heavy off into dope and ripped off the money; we lost a thousand and two hundred dollars. Even so, when we assessed ourselves for that loss, it turned out that the amount was basically what it would have cost to have had a bank account; at least the money was not used by the Bank of America.

I came to Palo Alto after the close of the Peoples Bank, but I hope they will try something like it again. One of their key principles in setting up the bank was complete trust. There was no bookkeeper or audit of funds. Everyone was responsible for their own entries. I believe in trusting people, but I also know that I have trouble balancing my own checkbook. I would want at least a monthly, if not weekly, audit of the bank just to catch honest errors. This practice would also have caught any missing funds.

Sharing

Mutual sharing is a satisfying way of meeting our needs and building community. Car pools, potluck dinners, and baby-sitting exchanges are common ways of sharing. Tool sharing, communal kitchens, and many other forms are also becoming more common.

Lee Swenson belongs to one of four households that decided to buy and maintain tools together for everyone's use. Each household contributed five dollars a month toward the purchase of tools. The money accumulated quickly, but they waited for good buys on quality tools before purchasing. Together they bought a power drill, a power sander, a router, a power saw, and a chain saw. Each family paid a minimal amount of money in relation to the number of tools they have access to. The tools are kept at one house, where each family has easy access to them. Each time a tool is used, a quarter is put in an

ON SIMPLE LIVING (continued)

envelope to pay in advance for future repairs. In this way, there is no wait for money for repairs, and the problem of deciding who pays to repair something everyone uses is eliminated. When they allow outsiders to use the tools, two or three dollars are collected to help offset purchase cost and repairs. Occasionally they have more money than needed for repairs so they temporarily stop paying the quarter for each use. This system works very well. The only problem was with the chain saw. It was too hard to maintain. People just seemed to run it into the ground. So there are limits.

In setting up sharing arrangements, Lee cautions that it is very important to clarify things in advance. Trust breaks down when people expect something of each other, but the expectation is never stated or agreed on. "If I borrow your truck for a hundred-mile trip, and it breaks down, do you expect me to pay for the repairs or can I expect you to pay? If I don't do what you expect me to do, you get mad at me. And then I start avoiding you, and the whole thing falls apart. It's usually lack of clarity where trust breaks down, so it is important to set up procedures and work for clarity of assumptions beforehand," Lee emphasizes.

Skill pool

We can also share our skills. In an effort to meet economic needs without the use of money and to build the feeling of community, a group in Monterey, California, has been developing a skill pool. Each member makes his special skills, tools, services, or instructions available to the others. No money changes hands, but a community of concern and sharing has developed. This skill pool includes nurses, electricians, auto mechanics, typists, gardeners, sewers, and many others.

Barter

Barter is a form of exchange in trade without the use of money. We can barter skills and services as well as goods. Our own capabilities can be put to greater and more varied use when we step outside the limits of monetary exchange and meet our needs more directly. My friends and I barter handmade shirts for handmade toys, haircuts for bicycle repairs, artwork for baked goods, garden produce for an auto tune-up, or window repairs for mending. Barter can also be a way of giving different types of work value according to a more human scale. One man bartered with a lawyer to obtain his divorce. He did three hours of construction work for the lawyer to each hour the lawyer worked for him. Normally, the lawyer would have received $50 an hour as his fee, but they were able to get much closer to a human relationship by exchanging their services.

Barter parties can be given where people get together to meet others with whom they can exchange goods and services. Bartering can be facilitated by keeping an open file of people, skills, and goods they wish to barter and the needs or goods they wish to obtain. Bartering can include a chain of people, where three or more people are involved in an exchange. If you can do something for me but I am unable to do what you need, I can still barter with you if I can find someone who can use my services in return for fulfilling your need. This sounds complicated, but it is possible to string out such a trade through five people before everyone's mind gets too boggled.

ON SIMPLE LIVING (continued)

What does it mean to live in the overdeveloped section of a maldeveloped world, as the authors and most of the likely readers of this book do? To us, it means we are surrounded by a gigantic machinery of production and consumption which is set up to keep going and growing at all costs. It means that we are caught up in this machinery in a multitude of ways, more than we even realize. It means that we are the objects of continued and many-leveled pressures aimed at keeping us plugged into this machinery as workers and consumers. Among these pressures are advertising, the credit system and the transformation of gift-giving into "gifting." Let's look more closely at these pressures and the people who benefit from them.

Queries

1.   How often do I buy things because my needs for love, friendship, celebration, job satisfaction, personal recognition, or cultural identity are not being met? How often have I bought someone something instead of showing my friendship or love more directly? Are "gifts" in my family or group things that we do, things that we are, things that we make, or things that we buy?

2.   Of the things that I own, which help me or my family or group to be more active, self-reliant, and involved with each other and others?

3.   Are my freedom of choice and my political and social values restricted by businesses and other institutions whose survival is dependent on high and growing levels of consumption? How?

4.   To what extent are possessions and social status an important part of my self-image based on the things we have and the "quality" of the neighborhood we live in or on who we are as human beings? What education, media, and social messages do we get which reinforce tendencies to evaluate ourselves and others in terms of possessions rather than of personal qualities? How could we change these messages?

5.   Which of my children's demands and expectations are shaped by advertising?

6.   How much of what I spend on consumer goods goes for nonfunctional packaging, needless repairs, needless decoration, advertising, corporate lobbying, market research? Do these contribute anything to quality or use value?

7.   Is my present job dependent on continued growth of a high-consumption economy? Was I thrown out of work by reduced consumption during the economic slump that began in 1973? If not, do I know people who were?

8.   What alternatives to employment based on high and growing consumption do I have? What alternatives should I have? What can I do to help make these alternatives real?

Readings on Simple Living are from *Taking Charge*, pp. 32-33, published by the American Friends Service Committee, 1978.
©1986, 1990, 1992, 1993, 1994, 1995 PEACE GROWS, Inc., 513 W. Exchange St., Akron, OH 44302 (216)864-5442.

ALTERNATIVES TO VIOLENCE

MORE QUESTIONS ABOUT SIMPLE LIVING

Simple living

1. If we could be doing any work we wanted to, would we continue in our present jobs? What kind of work would we prefer? Why?

2. From what sources do we derive our ideas of "the good life"? To what extent do these ideas differ from the way we are now living?

3. To what extent is our recreation either heavily commercialized or basically passive, rather than active?

4. Do we think the "American Way of Life" can be maintained at its present level of resource consumption indefinitely? Who would benefit? Who would suffer? What would be the costs? What can we do about it?

Personal growth

5. What do we know about how the food we eat and the activities we engage in every day affect our health? How do our patterns of consumption and living arrangements affect the health of people in other parts of the world?

6. How many things do we own which cost over $150 (the approximate annual income of the poorest third of the world's population)? What possibilities exist for sharing such resources with others?

7. What are the influences that determine our eating habits and those of our children?

8. How much meat do we eat? Can the amount be reduced? Should it be?

9. Outside school, what three activities involve most of our children's time and energy? Are they passive or active? Are they dependent on things or on other people in order to take place? To what extent do they consume nonreplaceable resources and energy?

10. How could we become more self-reliant this week?

11. What can we do to increase facilities in our neighborhoods for nonconsumerist and cooperative play? Can children be involved in designing and building their own parks and play equipment in our area? In inventing their own games? What could we do to help facilitate this?

Alternative institutions

12. What kinds of human-scale cooperative institutions can we develop to provide products and services for which we now depend on multinational corporations? How can such institutions be structured to encourage community participation and thus help bring people together? Can they be designed to encourage other community-controlled enterprises to develop out of them?

13. How difficult is it to find and purchase unprocessed and organically grown foods in our area, as opposed to processed and perhaps poisoned ones? Are individual or community gardens a viable alternative for us? How about food co-ops or conspiracies?

14. How would we like to see our savings invested? Do banks, insurance companies, pension funds, and the like pursue similar objectives? Do we have any control over these institutions? What alternatives either exist or can be developed?

Redistributing power

15. Do we know which goods and services we use every day would not be available in the absence of cheap labor and raw materials from poor countries? Can we do without or find substitutes for such things? What political and economic measures can we promote to bring about equitable compensation for such resources and the labor involved in their production?

16. What changes are needed in our government policies, business practices, and personal consumption patterns in order for us to consume less energy? How do these changes relate to each other? Is the individual consumer responsible for the bulk of energy consumption in the United States? If not, who is?

Readings on Simple Living are from *Taking Charge*, pp. 26-29, published by the American Friends Service Committee, 1978.
©1986, 1990, 1992, 1993, 1994, 1995 PEACE GROWS, Inc., 513 W. Exchange St., Akron, OH 44302 (216)864-5442.

THE SHAKERTOWN PLEDGE

Many people throughout the country have come to believe that if the world family is to be cared for and fed, the United States must begin wide-scale development. In order for this to happen, they feel American citizens need to adopt new ways of life in which they consume closer to their fair share of the earth's resources. The network of people moving thus to simplify their lives includes individuals and groups from many backgrounds and interests who are committed to bring about a just world standard of living. One such group is the Shakertown Pledge Group, who act out of a religious or spiritual concern. They are united in their desire to struggle to live their commitment and to work for the political, economic, and social change necessary to make global justice a reality.

The Shakertown Pledge was written to express their concern and shared commitment. Several other groups, including nonreligious groups across the country, have created their own pledges or used the Shakertown Pledge as a focus for discussion. We include the Shakertown Pledge and the authors' comments about it as an example of what can be done and encourage you to write your own statement of concern or contact the Shakertown Group.

The Shakertown Pledge

Recognizing that the earth and the fullness thereof is a gift from our gracious God, and that we are called to cherish, nurture, and provide loving stewardship for the earth's resources.

And recognizing that life itself is a gift, and a call to responsibility, joy, and celebration.

I make the following declarations:

1. I declare myself to be a world citizen.
2. I commit myself to lead an ecologically sound life.
3. I commit myself to lead a life of creative simplicity and to share my personal wealth with the world's poor.
4. I commit myself to join with others in reshaping institutions in order to bring about a more just global society in which each person has full access to the needed resources for their physical, emotional, intellectual, and spiritual growth.
5. I commit myself to occupational accountability, and in so doing I will seek to avoid the creation of products which cause harm to others.
6. I affirm the gift of my body, and commit myself to its proper nourishment and physical well-being.
7. I commit myself to examine continually my relations with others, and to attempt to relate honestly, morally, and lovingly to those around me.
8. I commit myself to personal renewal through prayer, meditation and study.
9. I commit myself to responsible participation in a community of faith.

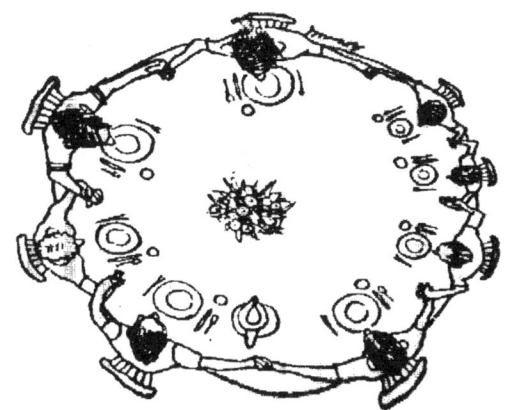

About the Shakertown Pledge

The Shakertown Pledge originated when a group of religious retreat center directors gathered at the site of a restored Shaker village near Harrodsburg, Kentucky. A number of us were personally moved by the global poverty-ecology crisis we saw all around us, and we covenanted together to reduce our levels of consumption, to share our personal wealth with the world's poor, and to work for a new social order in which all people have equal access to the resources they need. We have since been joined by others.

We believe that all people of faith should take this Pledge. We know from the Scriptures that God commands his people to make the cause of the poor and the oppressed their own. If we are truly to practice our faith then we cannot sit idly by while others starve. It's as simple as that.

SUMMARY OF CONCEPTS
as related to the subjects listed on worksheet #16

1. *How does world violence relate to the quality of my life?*
   Each participant will express an answer.

2. *How does my lifestyle affect domestic and/or global violence?*
   Although each participant may refer to an individual example, the group's answers form a pattern. Using more of the world's goods than we need can cause the deprival of human needs elsewhere and, hence, anger, frustration and violence. Terrorism is only a symptom. The real trouble is deprival of human needs and/or respect.

3. *What is simple living?*
   Simple living is reducing one's detrimental effect upon the world and its finite resources.

4. *What are some ways of applying simple living?*
   There are so many ways; on pages 181-188 are a few suggestions and queries about modern living.

Major point to remember:
- The unfair distribution of the world's resources is the major cause of world violence; curbing our wasteful consumption through more "simple living" could help.

Session 16
UNDERSTANDING GLOBAL VIOLENCE
Additional reading

Brill, Jack A. and Alan Reder. *Investing From The Heart: The Guide To Socially Responsible Investments And Money Management.* NY: Crown, 1992.

Cahn, Edgar S. *Time Dollars: The New Currency That Enables Americans To Turn Their Hidden Resource—Time—Into Personal Security And Community Renewal.* Rodale Press, 1992.

Center for Science in the Public Interest. *99 Ways To A Simpler Lifestyle.* Garden City: Anchor Doubleday, 1976.

Dominguez, Joseph R. *Your Money Or Your Life: Transforming Your Relationship With Money And Achieving Financial Independence.* NY: Viking, 1992.

Elgin, Duane. *Voluntary Simplicity: Toward A Way Of Life That Is Outwardly Simple, Inwardly Rich.* NY: William Morrow, 1993.

Marlin, Alice Tepper. *Shopping For A Better World: A Quick And Easy Guide To Socially Responsible Supermarket Shopping.* NY: Ballantine Books, 1992.

Needleman, Jacob. *Money And The Meaning Of Life.* NY: Doubleday, 1991.

Robbins, John. *Diet For A New America.* Walpole, NH: Stillpoint, 1987.

Robinson, Jo. *Unplug The Christmas Machine: A Complete Guide To Putting Love And Joy Back Into The Season.* NY: Quill, 1991.

Shannon-Thornberry, Milo. *The Alternative Celebrations Catalogue.* NY: Pilgrim Press, 1982.

Simple Living Collective. *Taking Charge: Achieving Personal And Political Change Through Simple Living.* NY: Bantam Books, 1977.

Voran, Marilyn Helmuth. *Add Justice To Your Shopping List.* Scottdale, PA: Herald Press, 1986.

ALTERNATIVES TO VIOLENCE

Session 17
ALTERNATIVES TO VIOLENCE SKILLS
Applied to current events

Objectives

a. To apply our alternatives to violence skills learning to interpret and/or resolve both violent and nonviolent situations and events as reported in our daily newspapers or on radio and TV news broadcasts.

b. To gain more insight into the vast need for these problem-solving skills in society and the world.

c. To better understand how well the media reports the news and how that affects the prevalence of violence and serves our needs as citizens of a democracy.

d. To learn the effect of technology's growth on violence's impact and magnitude.

WORKSHEET #17

(The following points will be covered in this session. Most points do not have "pat" answers, but the main thing is for you to arrive at an expression of the concepts. These questions are to help you take notes and process the material.)

1. The violence that permeates our homes through the media makes me feel . . .

   _____

   _____

   _____

   _____

2. What example of conflict resolution or nonviolence can you remember reported about recently?

   _____

   _____

   _____

   _____

3. What do you think about this statement: "The media is misleading often not so much for what it says but for what it does not say or what emphasis it gives various kinds of stories."?

   _____

   _____

   _____

   _____

©1986, 1990, 1992, 1993, 1994, 1995 PEACE GROWS, Inc., 513 W. Exchange St., Akron, OH 44302 (216)864-5442.

Notes or Journal Entry

Assignments:

_____
_____
_____
_____

ALTERNATIVES TO VIOLENCE — Session 17

CURRENT EVENTS WORKSHEET

1. **State the facts:**

   a. What violence occurred in your article? What **typ**e of violence was this?

   b. What nonviolence occurred? What nonviolence principles and techniques (what **type**s of nonviolence) were used?

   c. What was the initial conflict about (why did the violence occur)?

2. **How could this problem be solved?**

   a. How do you think the **initial conflict** could have been confronted and resolved nonviolently?

©1986, 1990, 1992, 1993, 1994, 1995 PEACE GROWS, Inc., 513 W. Exchange St., Akron, OH 44302 (216)864-5442

CURRENT EVENTS WORKSHEET (continued)

2. **How could this problem be solved?** (continued)

   b. How do you think nonviolence could be used **now** (or at the time the article was printed) to resolve or improve the situation?

   c. If you were in a position of power (tell what this position would be) in this situation, how would **you** choose to handle the present conflict situation?

3. **Anything else you learned from this case study:**

OUR SKILLS APPLIED TO CURRENT EVENTS

After reviewing the cases and proposed scenarios suggested by the newspaper articles you gathered for this session, it seems appropriate to ask ourselves a very important question: Does the media contribute in any way to the growth of violence in our society and, if so, how?

The answer seems to center around two other questions:

(1) How is the news reported?

(2) How is the news not reported?

When you were looking for articles on violence and on nonviolence, what were the easiest to find? Why is violence so predominant in media coverage both in the print media and on the electronic? Both in news and in "entertainment?"

Is it because more violence takes place? No, undoubtedly far more human problems and conflicts are handled nonviolently or we would all be dead! Just as history texts largely have been purveyors of violent military history, the mass media in America has been obsessed with glamorizing violence and sensationalism.

It has been said that if we read about or hear about something five times, we know it is true. If we do not read or hear about it, then we know it is not happening. Consequently, the type of reporting going on is causing citizens to be more fearful and hence to have greater tendencies toward violence. A good example comes from a study made by Washington's Center for Media and Public Affairs. Although government tallies found no substantial increase in crime or in violent crime rates in 1993, that year the number of crime news stories doubled on ABC, CBS, and NBC evening news shows, from 830 to 1,698, with murders tripling from 104 to 329.

When nonviolent events are not covered, the public does not think they are happening. Furthermore, they learn nothing of the principles, skills, techniques and strategies involved in forging successful, nonviolent solutions. Perhaps even more importantly, they learn little of organization, working on promoting and leading nonviolence which, if properly informed, they might join and help strengthen.

But there may be a still more negative role which the media plays. Not only is there violence reporting overkill and nonviolence reporting neglect, but there also is factual distortion.

Like I assume many of you did, I grew up believing we in America were blessed with an open, free, and truthful press making us the best-informed citizens of any country in the world. I would like to relate a few personal experiences which shattered that illusion for me.

"... undoubtedly far more human problems and conflicts are handled nonviolently or we would all be dead!"

The first experience took place shortly after I graduated from college. Giving away my age, I will tell you that this took place on the eve of our participation in World War II. Two organizations were advocating opposing positions regarding American involvement: The Committee to Defend America by Aiding the Allies was opposed to the America First position to try to stay out of Europe.

Charles Lindbergh, a real hero to the younger generation of that day, had visited Germany and witnessed the armaments build up there. America First invited him to Chicago to address a rally warning against our involvement. Mainly out of curiosity, a friend and I decided to go the event which was being held at Soldiers Field. That stadium seated over 100,000. About 35,000 or 40,000 must have attended because the stadium was about a third full. The same week, I believe the Committee to Defend America by Aiding the Allies held a rally at the former Chicago Coliseum.

This article was written by John Looney.
©1986, 1990, 1992, 1993, 1994, 1995 PEACE GROWS, Inc., 513 W. Exchange St., Akron, OH 44302 (216)864-5442.

OUR SKILLS APPLIED TO CURRENT EVENTS (continued)

Later the old *Life* magazine, with their photographic journalism, covered the two events. The empty end of Soldiers Field was pictured indicating very low attendance. On the other hand, photos of the Coliseum showed a crowded hall and several hundred outside who could not even get in. Certainly, this was a very popular event? But the Coliseum only housed about 8,000 people!

In this way, a crowd of, at the most, 9,000, was made to look much bigger than one of perhaps 40,000. That was the day I lost my confidence in the reliability of the American media.

In the early 1980s the nuclear weapons freeze resolution was the largest single initiative on ballots across the country. However, election night you could have twisted your dial all night long and never have heard a report on any of that voting. The nuclear freeze resolution passed the city councils of Cleveland, Youngstown, and Akron, Ohio. All such meetings are covered by reporters from the three daily newspapers in these cities. However, not a one of those three papers reported on the resolution passage.

Later I received a letter from a woman, whose brother-in-law, visited Taipei, Taiwan. She sent me a letter in which she said she thought I would like to read the enclosed clipping he had sent her. It was from the *China Daily News*, evidently an English language newspaper there. What do you think the article said? "The nuclear weapons freeze resolution passed the Cleveland City Council!" Thereafter I started telling people they would have to subscribe to Far Eastern newspapers to keep posted on their town's events.

Why do we have the situation we do? One managing editor told a group of us who had called on him to discuss such things that if we thought the role of the newspaper was to work on reform, institute more justice, etc., we were dead wrong. Instead, he said, the newspaper is a business (as are radio and TV). Its purpose is to make money!

This means less investigative reporting for one thing. Investigation costs money. It is much cheaper to use press releases from the government and other organizations.

One time I read that the White House public relations budget was double that of CBS, NBC, ABC news, Associated Press and the then UPI Wire Services, the ten largest newspapers and *Time, Newsweek,* and *U.S. News* combined—double all of that!! In addition, the corporations have their huge public relation budgets. Why is this so important? Is any administration, public or private, going to put out a release saying we are doing a lousy job, or, there is a lot of corruption and waste in our organization or, even, we have been wrong in our stand?

"But what can individuals do? There are always three steps to social improvement of any kind. First is awareness."

Money governs the media as it does many things. Organizations working for peace, justice, nonviolence, have very, very meager resources. But what can individuals do? There are always three steps to social improvement of any kind. First is awareness. Unless citizens and that includes you and me, know something is happening, certain people are suffering, whatever, absolutely nothing is going to change. Here are some suggestions for building awareness.

Over the next year, try to get fully acquainted with an alternative news source presently unknown to you and not a part of the mass media. *The Nation, The Progressive, Sojourners, In These Times* are suggestions. Compare reporting in it with your usual mass media source. Some books to look into might include: *The Media Monopoly* by Ben Bagdikian; *Manufacturing Consent* by Herman and Chomsky; *The Powers That Be* by David Haberstam; *Unreliable Sources* by Lee Martin and Norman Solomon; *Inventing Reality* by Michael Parenti; *Make-Believe Media* by Michael Parenti; *Telecommunications, Mass*

This article was written by John Looney.
©1986, 1990, 1992, 1993, 1994, 1995 PEACE GROWS, Inc., 513 W. Exchange St., Akron, OH 44302 (216)864-5442.

OUR SKILLS APPLIED TO CURRENT EVENTS (continued)

Media and Democracy by Robert McChesnt; and *The Media's Social Responsibility* by John Looney.

The second step to improvement is concern. Citizens can be very informed but unless that information leads them to a deep and abiding concern about the problems which they have uncovered, again nothing is going to change. Here, contact with those who are suffering from the situation and/or those who are working on the problem will do the most to develop concern as long as there is, in the first place, a value system which cares about others. Joining an activist group will do much. Concern is essential because without a concern, no person is going to act and without action, again there will be no change.

Thirdly, action means doing something about it. What are some things one might do? Being alone in a concern can makes one feel powerless. However, even one person can critique the media and write letters to the editor, call into radio talk shows, or visit media offices, pointing out what they have learned. FAIR, Fairness and Accuracy In Reporting, 130 West 25th Street, New York, NY 10001, phone (213)633-6700, is doing a good job. Their publication, *EXTRA!*, P.O. Box 911, Pearl River, NY 10965-0911, ($20 for students, seniors and low income). PROPAGANDA Review, Media Alliance, Fort Mason Center, Bldg. D, San Francisco, CA 94123, phone (915)386-4902 is another recommended source of information.

Regardless of the position one may hold on any issue, the purpose of this article is to stress the importance to democracy, to justice and to violence reduction and prevention, for the mass media, somehow, to begin presenting **all** sides of every issue. Name calling as well, should be dropped. "Liberal," "conservative," "radical" tend to eliminate real, essential dialogue. They wave flags in some people's minds which prevent further listening and shut off further communication and worthy analysis. Only when citizens have all of the facts can human problems be solved and violence be reduced. It is the responsibility of the media to see that this happens. Only then can current events really be dealt with effectively and constructively.

> *"The second step to improvement is concern. . . . Thirdly, action means doing something about it."*

This article was written by John Looney.
©1986, 1990, 1992, 1993, 1994, 1995 PEACE GROWS, Inc., 513 W. Exchange St., Akron, OH 44302 (216)864-5442.

WHAT IS OPPRESSION?

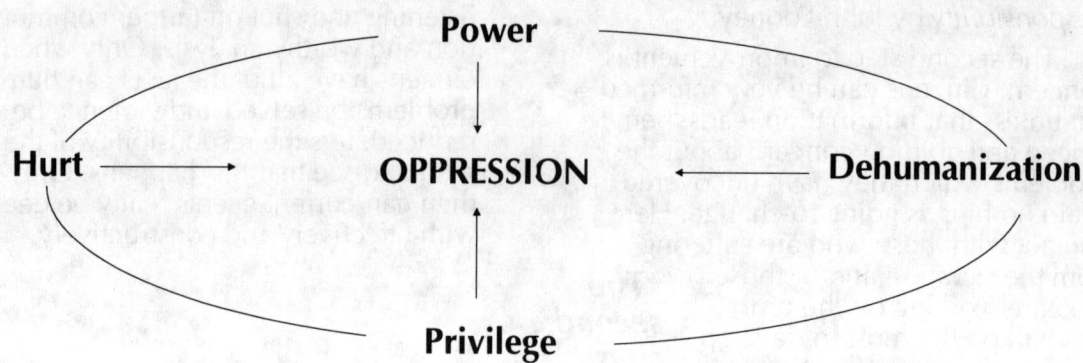

- The systematic subjugation of one (relatively less powerful) social group by another (relatively more powerful) social group which is sanctioned by cultural beliefs and institutions the results of which benefit one group at the expense of the other.

- A systematic social phenomenon in which a person in a dominant social group holds a set of negative beliefs and acts on these beliefs toward people in a subordinate social group. These beliefs and actions result in a privileged existence for the dominant social group, a limited existence for the subordinate social group, and the dehumanization of both.

- Prejudice + power.

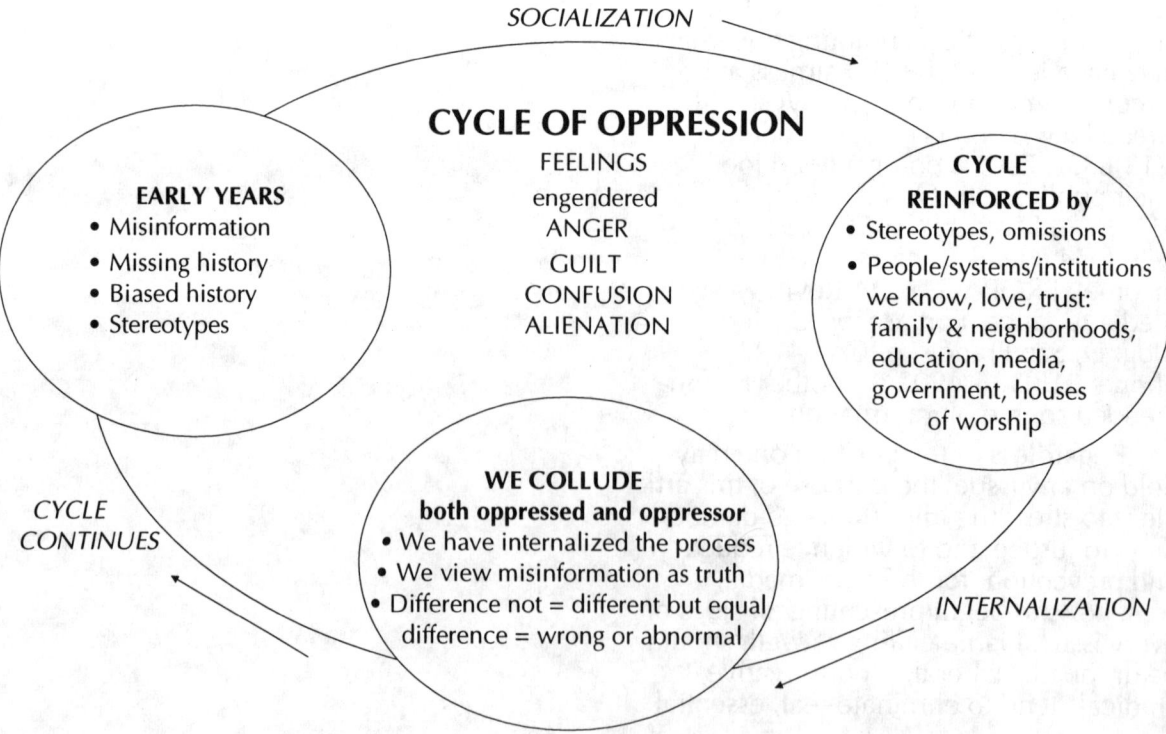

Adapted from Sr. Shelia Maria Tobbe, *ATV* trainer.
©1986, 1990, 1992, 1993, 1994, 1995 PEACE GROWS, Inc., 513 W. Exchange St., Akron, OH 44302 (216)864-5442.

GUIDELINES FOR INTERRUPTING OPPRESSION
(Racism, Sexism, Classism, Etc.)

1. **Own it.** Use "I statements" and let others know that you are personally offended.

2. **Don't "beat up" the person(s) involved.** People will be much more likely to be open to new information and to your feedback if you do not personally attack them!

3. **Provide accurate information**, which may directly contradict a stereotype or misinformation. Do your homework so that you can educate the person(s) involved.

4. **Sometimes the best way to interrupt oppression is to remove yourself from the situation.** This may be for safety or just the most effective way of interrupting.

5. **Don't wait for a member of a target group to speak up** when issues affecting that group are raised, or stereotypes perpetuated, etc. Expecting members of target groups to be spokespersons for their group, or take responsibility for interrupting racism, sexism, classism, anti-Semitism, or other forms of oppression contradicts a strong ally position and puts an additional burden on members of that group.

6. **Frequently ask the question** "Who's not at the table?" and raise issues which would be important to person not represented in your group. Noticing who may be "invisible" in a discussion is a powerful interruption to oppression (e.g., are Latino, Native American, and Asian-American perspectives visible or being considered?).

7. **Understand that silence, or failing to interrupt racism and other forms of oppression, is collusion** (you're either part of the solution or part of the problem).

8. **Continue to interrogate or self-examine your unearned privileges and power.** Being honest with yourself and others about ways in which you have benefits from such privileges is an important step in being a stronger ally!

9. **Remember that we are all both perpetrators and victims (or targets) of oppression**, that racism hurts everybody and can be unlearned.

10. **Remember, too, that allies are part of reciprocal relationships** and are not "rescuers," "missionaries," or members of a "Wanna-Be Nation." We go the distance—together.

SUMMARY OF CONCEPTS
as related to the subjects listed on worksheet #17

1. *The violence that permeates our homes through the media makes me feel . . .*

   Each participant will have own response.

2. *What example of conflict resolution or nonviolence can you remember reported about recently?*

   Each participant will have own response.

3. *What do you think about this statement: "The media is misleading often not so much for what it says but for what it does not say or what emphasis it gives various kinds of stories."?*

   Each participant will have own response.

Major point to remember:
- International violence can be reduced by a greater implementation of justice with which the media could and should help more. Newer technology greatly increases both the impact and the danger of violence in our world.

Session 17
CURRENT EVENTS AND MEDIA
Additional reading

Jensen, Carl and Project Censored. *Censored: The News That Didn't Make The News And Why.*
NY: Four Walls Eight Windows, 1994.

Lee, Martin A. and Norman Soloman. *Unreliable Sources: A Guide To Detecting Bias In News Media.*
NY: Carol Publishing Group, 1992.

Parenti, Michael. *Inventing Reality: The Politics Of News Media.* NY: St. Martins Press, 1993.

Postman, Neil. *Amusing Ourselves To Death: Public Discourse In The Age Of Show Business.*
NY: Viking, 1985.

Session 18
ALTERNATIVES TO VIOLENCE SKILLS
Working the system

Objectives

a. To examine if, when, why and how we should get involved actively in seeking nonviolent social and/or political change.

b. To learn other ways of working in the United States for nonviolent improvements when alternatives to violence talking skills fail to get results.

c. To understand those methods better and how their use is encouraged under the provisions of the U.S. Constitution.

d. To practice at least one of these methods.

Worksheet #18

(The following points will be covered in this session. Most points do not have "pat" answers, but the main thing is for you to arrive at an expression of the concepts. These questions are to help you take notes and process the material.)

1. What are some responsibilities of citizens in a democracy like the United States?

   _____

   _____

   _____

2. What are some ways community and national affairs affect our personal lives?

   _____

   _____

   _____

3. Why should I get involved?

   _____

   _____

   _____

4. How can I get involved?

   _____

   _____

   _____

ALTERNATIVES TO VIOLENCE

Notes or Journal Entry

Assignments:

_____
_____
_____
_____
_____

WORKING THE DEMOCRATIC SYSTEM

In Session 17 we examined the need for us to be fully informed in order to be able to address the problems of violence in our society. But becoming informed is only the first step. Though not necessarily in the mass media, all kinds of information is available. Thousands of studies have been made, books published, papers read, research projects initiated, speeches presented, documentary films produced, alternative media distributed, workshops conducted, studies commissioned, bills passed. Still violence remains largely uncurbed. Why?

Educating ourselves and others truly is the necessary first step. Education is a very important form of action. However, if we should possess all of that mass of information and it just remains inside our heads never used or applied then of what good is it? Until we act on that information for improving the sources of violence in ourselves, our families, our homes, our neighborhoods, our communities, our workplaces, our nation, all of our world, nothing can change. This session introduces us to the topic of working and acting to reduce violence without which the whole preceding part of the course seems of little or no avail.

Frances Moore Lappé, author of the famous *Diet for a Small Planet*, and Paul Martin DuBois, have formed an organization called The Institute for the Arts of Democracy/Building Citizen Democracy. Their descriptive flyer points out how we think of democracy as something we "have," something we fight for or achieve. However, they say democracy is not what we "have" but what we "do." Democracy is a "way of life built on the capacities of ordinary citizens and drawing forth our passion and participation." The reduction of violence requires our passion and participation.

What can one person do? No one can do everything but everyone can do something. Outstanding examples pointed out by a War Resister's League flyer include Mary Dryer's preaching of Quakerism on the Boston Commons whose resulting hanging shamed the Massachusetts Bay and other colonies into adapting greater religious tolerance; or Henry David Thoreau's one night in jail protesting the Mexican War and his book *On Civil Disobedience* inspired leaders as widely apart as Leo Tolstoy in Russia and Mohandas Gandhi in India and, through them, Martin Luther King Jr. in the United States. It was Rosa Parks' persistence in sitting in the "whites only" section of a Montgomery bus which triggered the whole Civil Rights Movement and first involved Martin Luther King, Jr. We may never even know how our statements or acts may spread and inspire or motivate others to action.

Besides informing ourselves, such things are urged as writing editors; phoning call-in shows; just talking with people and sharing literature with them; selecting a socially responsible job; doing volunteer work which helps overcome oppression, injustice and/or violence; making the most out of elections; contacting elected officials and leaders in private organizations involved; determining whether or not your buying supports the breeding of violence; participating in school and neighborhood activities; taking and teaching this course; investing responsibly; working against all forms of oppression; organize, join and/or financially supporting organization working against oppression and violence and for peace, justice and the relief of suffering. (See a list of organizations in the appendix for starters.) Also, use the form on page 211 to survey and perhaps publish a directory of local organizations to help promote them.

Even talking with others sometimes takes courage. Having the class share their activities might both reveal that they are involved in more than is realized. It might give those who are not involved some ideas. Most religious institutions, for instance, are working on issues or social services which need help.

Have you heard the story of *The One-Hundredth Monkey*? It is the title of a small book authored by Ken Keyes. The book tells of some research done with monkeys on islands near Japan. Apparently these monkeys liked sweet potatoes. The researchers buried some in the sands along the shore. Initially, the monkeys dug them up and ate them, sand and all. Then the researchers showed just one monkey how to wash off the sand. That monkey showed others and the teaching spread as both the cleaning method and the improved taste were learned. Suddenly, according to the report, when the one-hundredth monkey learned and began the washing process, all of the monkeys on the island followed suit. The new approach even spread to other islands.

This article was written by John Looney.
©1986, 1990, 1992, 1993, 1994, 1995 PEACE GROWS, Inc., 513 W. Exchange St., Akron, OH 44302 (216)864-5442.

WORKING THE DEMOCRATIC SYSTEM (continued)

What this proposes is that, maybe, you will be that hundredth monkey in the process of changing our society and world. Everyone, as we said, can do something. One person alone can do little to reduce social violence. However, when enough individual efforts join, things will change. The challenge is to alter our culture from a violent, often dangerous, competitive one, to a more caring one. A culture is made up of the attitudes, values, behaviors, etc. of the individuals who make up that culture. As the changed total patterns grow from person to person, our goals will be achieved. Violence can be reduced or even eliminated.

One other caveat is necessary as we discuss working the democratic system. We must be sophisticated enough to know quite a bit about that system. For instance we have suggested making the most out of elections. Much more than just voting or working for the candidate of your choice is required. For instance, unless we understand the existing methods of campaign financing and work against it, just supporting a good candidate of our choice, which is a worthwhile action, still cannot be enough where offices, in reality, go to the highest bidder. What we think is an election too often can become an auction.

You may be trying to influence radio or TV programming to be more balanced not realizing that instituted fairness regulations were repealed in the 1980s. New legislation may be needed.

Writing a letter to your Congressperson is highly recommended. Normally, you should receive a letter back. If it agrees with you, you may feel your mission is well accomplished.

Over ten years ago I was in a Congresswoman's office and told her how confused I was about another congressperson's view versus vote on an issue. She smiled and said, "Oh, didn't you ever hear of the *Washington Monthly* survey?" It seems that magazine had written two letters purporting to be from two different constituents and advocating opposite sides of a given issue. Close to half of the congressional recipients replied answering favorably to both sides. Really, only the voting record and/or overwhelming visible support for a given position are what counts!

This little article can only hint at things to do. Surely, however, this has given you some ideas. Still, you may say, what about things like drive by shootings and other random acts of violence? It really is too late, after the fact, to do anything. But so much could be done before the fact, which we are not doing as this course points out. Have you heard of the movement to promote random acts of kindness instead? Who could not join and gain satisfaction from it?

But we are talking here about working on community, national and global problems. How can we affect them? Why should one? There are so many problems and concerns in daily life.

But if the status quo is what satisfies the majority, why should I speak out? John Stuart Mills' essay "On Liberty" says it is important because if the idea is no good, no one else will pay attention. But, if it is good, and speaking out is denied, then the action will be deprived of that good idea which might well take root and grow to the benefit of all. Furthermore, everyone should be included. Exclusion, inattentiveness to anyone is a major form of violence, as we have learned.

Again, if it is so hard to change government that the normal actions of talking, letter writing, lobbying, working in campaigns fail, what else can be one? Direct nonviolence may have to be invoked: marches, demonstrations, petitions, boycotts, etc. even civil disobedience. But are these not un-American? Why do we think they would ever work?

Very little social improvement has taken place in U.S. history through normal legislative channels. People worked on anti-slavery actions for decades. Women seeking the right to vote marched, lay down in the streets, went to prison. Labor organizations demonstrated, leafletted, occupied factories where they just sat down. The list is long. The successes are many. Civil disobedience played a prominent role. These actions rather than being Un American are guaranteed by the U.S. Constitution in our Bill of Rights. They really are "as American as motherhood and apple pie" as the saying goes.

By knowing not just what to do but how to do it, we can change our society. We can reduce violence. We can create a more caring nation. It is never too soon to get started.

This article was written by John Looney.
©1986, 1990, 1992, 1993, 1994, 1995 PEACE GROWS, Inc., 513 W. Exchange St., Akron, OH 44302 (216)864-5442.

ALTERNATIVES TO VIOLENCE

CONFLICT RESOLUTION ON THREE LEVELS

(1)	Listen actively	Hearings	Travel
(2)	State position clearly	Research	Study other countries and cultures
(3)	Obtain and clarify needed information	Investigative reporting	Host overseas visitors
(4)	Develop alternatives from which to choose	Discussion of community issues with various people Awareness of local news Letters to editors	Follow international news Promote and follow international organizations Use appropriate community counterparts as investigative reporting, etc.
(5)	Lead or facilitate solution through group endeavor	Legislation Community organizing Neighborhood or town meetings Executive action Personal witness Education	Government leadership Disarmament movements United Nations development, research and action Appropriate technology International organization activists (both government and nongovernment)
(6)	Negotiate	Union-Management negotiation Legislative debates and negotiations School Board-faculty or parent negotiations	Diplomacy Trade agreements
(7)	Mediate	Community mediation centers School mediation service Federal labor mediation service	UN special sessions and General Assembly meetings
(8)	Arbitrate	Use of arbitrator like American Arbitration Association person Use of courts	Arms negotiations Special international mediators

©1986, 1990, 1992, 1993, 1994, 1995 PEACE GROWS, Inc., 513 W. Exchange St., Akron, OH 44302 (216)864-5442.

CONFLICT RESOLUTION ON THREE LEVELS

(9) Defend oneself nonviolently	Organize neighborhood for mutual concern, caring, watching, and nonviolent protection Obtain outside help such as police or community service before acting violently	World Court Nonviolent civilian national defense
(10) Use "active nonviolence"	Writing letters Lobbying Public speaking Demonstrating Voting Doing relief work Using boycotts Using strikes Picketing Campaigning Doing civil disobedience Using "Alternatives to Violence"	Boycotts Trade embargoes Relief work Peace Corps Civil disobedience Demonstrations, vigils, etc. Draft and tax resistance
(11) Use nonresistance	Silent, but open, complete noncooperation with community or cultural custom or with regulation felt to be unjust or unfair	Complete noncooperation with government military and/or foreign policies

ALTERNATIVES TO VIOLENCE

LOCAL GROUP SURVEY FORM

Name of group _____

Address _____

City and state_____ ZIP _____

Title, if any_____ Phone _____

Meeting time and place _____
_____

How many attend?_____ On mailing list? _____

Issues covered _____
_____
_____

Major activities _____
_____
_____

Resources (speakers, literature, films, newsletter, etc.) _____
_____
_____
_____

Other groups suggested? (name, phone numbers)

Surveyed by: _____ Date _____

©1986, 1990, 1992, 1993, 1994, 1995 PEACE GROWS, Inc., 513 W. Exchange St., Akron, OH 44302 (216)864-5442.

HOW-TO-WRITE MEMBERS OF CONGRESS AND THE PRESIDENT

Letters to Members of Congress, the President and other officials influence public policy.

"But does my letter **really** do any good?" The answer is "Yes." Letters from home are one important way public officials gauge reaction to pending legislation, new policy decisions and announcements.

Members of Congress often say they are encouraged to introduce or support legislation because of the mail they receive. Favorable mail can help members take a more courageous stand. Adverse mail can discourage them from voting for legislation they might otherwise support.

> **YOUR VOTE COUNTS MORE**
>
> I think letters have an effect on members of Congress. Everybody's vote counts in America, but those who sit down and write letters make their votes count more times. . . . Nothing is more effective than a letter that reflects both an understanding of the question involved and a sincere expression of a personal viewpoint based on that understanding.
> —Comment by John F. Kennedy, August, 1963, to editors of national women's magazines.

One Representative attributed his change in attitude toward the Arms Control and Disarmament Agency to consistent efforts and correspondence of one constituent whom he respected. A senator said he voted for an anti-war amendment because of constituent pressure from back home.

> **INSTANT RESPONSE**
>
> The President and the White House staff are especially interested in the immediate public response to Presidential speeches and decisions on policy before an organized campaign may develop. **Why not make it a habit to send a telegram to the President giving your reaction within six hours after a major statement is made.**

In writing your letter:

1. Spell names correctly, write legibly.

Address Senators:

Senator ....
Senate Office Building
Washington, DC 20510
Dear Senator ....

Address Representatives:

Representative ....
House Office Building
Washington, DC 20515
Dear Rep. ....

Address the President:

President ....
The White House
Washington, DC 20501
Dear President ....

2. Be as brief as possible.

3. Begin with commendation for a vote or a speech where possible. Support a courageous stand and encourage continued leadership.

4. Come to the point quickly, clearly and concisely. Where possible. give the bill number or title of the legislation.

5. Give reasons for your stand in your own words. Draw on your own personal experience. You may wish to enclose a newspaper article, an editorial, a letter to the editor from your local paper, or other information.

6. Raise questions. A well formulated question can express a viewpoint and encourage response.

7. Write about only one subject in a letter. The legislator's reply may give occasion to raise another issue. How often should you write? Think of your relationship as personal. Don't become a pest; but recognize that you have not fulfilled your citizenship responsibility with one letter a year. How often might you write a friend about these issues?

HOW-TO-WRITE MEMBERS OF CONGRESS (continued)

8. Make your letter timely. Action Bulletins and suggestions from FCNL give up-to-the-minute information and supply names of key Members who will be making the decisions. A letter to your own legislators soon after a bill is introduced can alert them to a bill in which you are interested. Letters to members of the Committee considering the bill are most important. Congress does most of its work in the Committee. It has been estimated that 90% of the bills pass on the floor as they come from the Committee. If you write a Member of Congress other than the one who represents you, little attention may be paid to your letter unless you say why you are writing to someone in a different state or district.

9. Ask to be put on the mailing list for the legislator's newsletter. Most members now distribute newsletters and often send questionnaires soliciting constituents' opinions.

How does a member of Congress handle mail?

Former Representative Byron L. Johnson, Colorado, wrote in *Fellowship*, July 1962:

A Representative gets 100 to 300 pieces of mail a day. A Senator gets many more, especially if from a large state. . . .

A staff member will open it, and assign it to whichever aide can best deal with it. The elected official will only be given those that concern him personally, for whatever reasons, and the ones that he has asked to handle directly. . . .

Except for a few Senators, every member reads and signs his outgoing mail, whether he dictated it, or had it prepared by a staff aide in accordance with his instructions. Any new topic, or new argument, requires a new decision as to the form of reply. Your letter, if routine, will get routine treatment. But if it is special for whatever reason, it will deserve, and get special treatment. For you are presumed to be a voting constituent and no member wants to alienate a voting constituent . . . .

The Congressmen and the executive officers both ask for a mail count, by subject and attitude, from time to time.

Your letters aren't enough. Listen to former Representative Byron Johnson:

But having written him, your job really is not over. If he votes with you he must come home and defend his vote before those who may think differently. You must help create a public climate of opinion that agrees with you . . .

This will require, not only letter writing, but calls, meetings, conferences, round tables, seminars, discussions, and every other form of public discussions, education and conversion. If you have the audacity to tell your elected representative what he should do, and why, surely you can discuss these with your fellow citizens.

WHAT ABOUT . . .

- **petitions?** They count for very little in Washington.
- **postcards?** A letter is better.
- **telegrams?** An attention getter and especially useful just before a vote. It is also easy. Just lift your phone and send a 15-word Public opinion message. Earlier in the legislative process a well-written letter can give your views more effectively.
- **phone calls?** Person to person calls, especially if you have had previous contact with the Member, sometimes get through. Phone 202/224-3121 and ask for the Member by name.
- **personal visits?** Best of all; require more preparation on issues. Read FCNL's *How to Visit Your Congressman*.
- the legislator who pays no attention: Read FCNL's *How-to-Work in Politics* and *How-to-Work for the Congressional Candidate of Your Choice*.

Friends Committee on National Legislation, 245 Second Street, N.E., Washington, DC 20002.
©1986, 1990, 1992, 1993, 1994, 1995 PEACE GROWS, Inc., 513 W. Exchange St., Akron, OH 44302 (216)864-5442.

HOW-TO-WRITE A LETTER TO THE EDITOR

"**Americans are writing more letters to newspapers than ever before and newspapers are publishing more letters in ever-expanding letters columns.**" (*The Masthead*, National Conference of Editorial Writers [NCEW]. Fall 1980) In a special report of the NCEW, 84% of those newspapers surveyed said that letters volume has increased in the last ten years. A majority described the increase as substantial.

Editors are well aware that they are receiving more letters than ever before. In an effort to keep pace with the increased load, many newspapers have increased the size of their open forums. Some editors attribute the recent development and spread of op-editorial pages to the fact that letters from readers overflow the editorial pages.

Studies show that letters from readers are among the most widely read features in daily newspapers. **When a letter of yours appears on the editorial page, you probably have the largest audience you will ever address.** It is possible to estimate its size. A small town weekly have may have a circulation of one or two thousand. A metropolitan daily may have as many as one or two million. According to the NCEW, more than one-third of the newspaper's audience are regular readers of the editorial and opinion pages in their daily newspaper, and almost three-fourths usually read those pages. A letter to the editor is a good way to express ideas about timely subjects of general concern.

Here are some suggestions which can help you to write the kind of letter that is most likely to receive favorable consideration on the editorial desk:

1. If possible, **use a typewriter** and double-space the lines. Write on only one side of the paper. If you have no typewriter, write plainly and neatly with ink. Do not crowd words or lines.

2. **Plan your first sentence carefully.** Try to make it short and interesting. If you begin with a reference to a news item, editorial or letter in the paper addressed, your letter immediately has added interest for the editor. However, this is not always feasible nor absolutely necessary.

   Encourage and support writers who had the courage to express an opinion that will elicit floods of disagreement. Positive feedback encourages more good articles.

   If you write to criticize, **begin with a word of appreciation, agreement or praise.** Don't be merely critical; make constructive suggestions.

3. **Deal with only one topic in a letter.** It should be timely and newsworthy. Be sure your meaning is clear. Use simple and short words, short sentences and paragraphs. Your letter will be easier to read.

   Express your thoughts as clearly and considerately as possible. Check your local paper for the average length of a letter and try not to exceed it. In addition to considering what will be accepted, you must consider what will be read.

5. **Avoid violent language or sarcasm.** A calm, constructive presentation of your thought is more persuasive than ranting. It is possible to be both frank and friendly.

6. **Help supply facts** that may be omitted or slanted in presentation of the news or editorials. You can render a valuable service to the public by presenting views that may ordinarily be given little or no attention by the press. (The *Newsletter* and other publications of the Friends Committee on National Legislation are valuable resources.)

7. **Don't hesitate to use a relevant personal experience** to illustrate a point. When presented well, it can be persuasive.

8. **Bring moral judgments to bear** upon issues confronting the nation and the world. Appeal to readers' sense of fair play, justice and mercy. Challenge them to respond to the issue.

9. **Try to be hopeful and practical.** Out of fear and despair, people may avoid the most pressing issues of the day. But they may take action when given a possible response and reason to believe that there is hope for a solution.

Friends Committee on National Legislation, 245 Second Street, N.E., Washington, DC 20002.
©1986, 1990, 1992, 1993, 1994, 1995 PEACE GROWS, Inc., 513 W. Exchange St., Akron, OH 44302 (216)864-5442.

HOW-TO-WRITE A LETTER TO THE EDITOR (continued)

> **The editorial and opinion pages are the intellectual dessert of the daily newspaper. While the items on these pages may not top the list of readers' interests, the editorial and opinion pages fill a key niche in the total package of content deliverd each day by the newspaper.** (*The Masthead,* National Conference of Editorial Wroters, Winter 1980-81).
>
> *The Masthead* also reports that editorial cartoons and letters from readers are the best read items on the editorial and opinion pages. They are followed in popularity by the newspaper's own editorial position. Columnists have the smallest readership base.
>
> In a readership survey, the strongest motivation for reading the editorial and opinion pages was "to feel I am participating in current events." This was followed by "to keep up with the latest events.," "to determine what is important," "to use in discussions with my friends," "to help me make decisions on issues," "to strengthen my arguments on issues," and "to help me form opinions about things going on around me." The fact that reading the editorial page can be considered a form of participation in current events indicates its value as a forum for the public expression of ideas.

10. You can make appropriate changes in your letter and **send it to editors of newspapers in other cities.** When doing so, always send first copies, never carbons or photocopies. As a rule, do not send exactly the same letter to different papers in the same city. (The *New York Times* and a number of other papers have a policy against publishing letters which are also sent to other papers.)

11. **Always sign your name** and give your address and telephone number. You can use a pen name or initials for publication, but the editor must know the source of the letter. According to the NCEW, letters are most frequently rejected for lack of identification. Don't be timid about signing your name. The times call for a fearless witness for peace and justice.

12. Don't give up looking for your letter too soon. It may not appear for ten days or even longer. **Don't be discouraged if your letter is not printed.** You have given the editor the benefit of your thinking. There may have been too many letters to print ours. Try again. If one letter in ten is accepted, you have reached an audience large enough to make your effort worthwhile. (But your score will probably be better than that!)

13. If the editorial policy of your local newspaper is consistently at odds with your views on some major issues, remember that it is possible to **meet with and "lobby" an editorial board j**ust as you would a legislator. Arrange a meeting along with several community leaders (to indicate the breadth of concern and agreement with your point of view) and come prepared with materials and names of local experts to enable the paper to write more balanced stories in the future.

FREEDOM OF SPEECH
The viewpoint of John Stuart Mill

". . . speaking generally, it is not, in constitutional countries, to be apprehended that the government, whether completely responsible to the people or not, will often attempt to control the expression of opinion, except when in doing so it makes itself the organ of the general intolerance of the public. Let us suppose, therefore, that the government is entirely at one with the people, and never thinks of exerting any power of coercion unless in agreement with what it conceives to be their voice. But I deny the right of the people to exercise such coercion, either by themselves or by their government. The power itself is illegitimate. The best government has no more title to it than the worst. It is as noxious, or more noxious, when exerted in accordance with public opinion than when in opposition to it. If all mankind minus one were of one opinion, mankind would no more be justified in silencing that one person than he, if he had the power, would be justified in silencing mankind . . . the peculiar evil of silencing the expression of an opinion is that it is robbing the (human) race, posterity as well as the existing generation—those who dissent from the opinion, still more than those who hold it. If the opinion is right, they are deprived of the opportunity of exchanging error for truth; if wrong, they lose, what is almost as great a benefit, the clearer perception and livelier impression of truth produced by the collision with error . . . "

" . . . the opinion which it is attempted to suppress by authority may possibly be true. Those who desire to suppress it, of course, deny its truth; but they are not infallible. They have no authority to decide the question for all mankind and exclude every other person from the means of judging. To refuse a hearing to an opinion because they are sure it is false is to assume that **their** certainty is the same as **absolute** certainty. All silencing of discussion is an assumption of infallibility. Its condemnation may be allowed to rest on this common argument, not the worse for being common."

from *On Liberty* by John Stuart Mill, Chapter II *Of the Liberty of Thought and Discussion.*
©1986, 1990, 1992, 1993, 1994, 1995 PEACE GROWS, Inc., 513 W. Exchange St., Akron, OH 44302 (216)864-5442.

AMENDMENTS TO THE CONSTITUTION

Amendment 1

Congress shall make no law respecting an establishment of religion, or prohibiting the free exercise thereof; or abridging the freedom of speech, or of the press; or the right of the people peaceably to assemble, and to petition the Government for a redress of grievances.

Amendment 2

A well regulated Militia, being necessary to the security of a free State, the right of the people to keep and bear Arms, shall not be infringed.

Amendment 3

No Soldier shall, in time of peace be quartered in any house, without the consent of the Owner, nor in time of war, but in a manner to be prescribed by law.

Amendment 4

The right of the people to be secure in their persons, houses, papers, and effects, against unreasonable searches and seizures, shall not be violated, and no Warrants shall issue, but upon probably cause, supported by Oath or affirmation, and particularly describing the place to be searched, and the persons or things to be seized.

Amendment 5

No person shall be held to answer for a capital, or other infamous crime, unless on a presentment or indictment of a Grand Jury, except in cases arising in the land or naval forces, or in the Militia, when in actual service in time of War or public danger; nor shall any person be subject for the same offence to be twice put in jeopardy of life or limb; nor shall be compelled in any criminal case to be a witness against himself, nor be deprived of life, liberty, or property, without due process of law; nor shall private property be taken for public use, without just compensation.

Amendment 6

In all criminal prosecutions, the accused shall enjoy the right to a speedy and public trial, by an impartial jury of the State and district wherein the crime shall have been committed, which district shall have been previously ascertained by law, and to be informed of the nature and cause of the accusation; to be confronted with the witnesses against him; to have compulsory process for obtaining witnesses in his favor, and to have the Assistance of Counsel for his defense.

Amendment 7

In suits at common law, where the value in controversy shall exceed twenty dollars, the right of trial by jury shall be preserved, and no fact tried by a jury, shall be otherwise re-examined in any Court of the United States, than according to the rules of the common law.

Amendment 8

Excessive bail shall not be required, nor excessive fines imposed, nor cruel and unusual punishments inflicted.

Amendment 9

The enumeration in the Constitution, of certain rights, shall not be construed to deny or disparage others retained by the people.

Amendment 10

The powers not delegated to the United States by the Constitution, nor prohibited by it to the States, are reserved to the States respectively, or to the people.

ALTERNATIVES TO VIOLENCE

SUMMARY OF CONCEPTS
As related to the subjects listed on worksheet #18

1. *What are some responsibilities of citizens in a democracy like the United States?*

    Answers will vary but most examples will point toward special responsibility for the operation of democracy. Citizens need to learn and use effective ways to make their wishes known.

2. *What are some ways community and national affairs affect our personal lives?*

    Answers will vary.

3. *Why should I get involved?*

    By working to make our government just, we reduce violence, both overt and less obvious.

4. *How can I get involved?*

    See chart on pages 209 and 210.

Major point to remember:
- In a democracy, citizens are responsible for what their government does, much of which really affects their lives. There are many ways they can and should get involved.

Session 18
WORKING THE SYSTEM
Additional reading

Caldicott, Helen. *Nuclear Madness: What You Can Do.* NY: W.W. Norton & Co., 1994.

Carter, Jimmy. *Talking Peace: A Vision For The Next Generation.* NY: Dutton Children's Books, 1993.

Harris, Sam. *Reclaiming Our Democracy: Healing The Break Between People And Government.* Philadelphia, PA: Camino Books, 1993.

Lappé, Frances Moore and Paul Martin DuBois. *The Quickening Of America: Rebuilding Our Nation, Remaking Our Lives.* San Francisco: Jossey-Bass Pub., 1994.

MacEachern, Diane. *Enough Is Enough: The Hellraiser's Guide To Community Activism.* NY: Avon Books, 1994.

Schorr, Lisbeth B. *Within Our Reach: Breaking The Cycle Of Disadvantage.* NY: Doubleday, 1988.

Walls, David. *The Activist's Almanac: The Concerned Citizen's Guide To The Leading Advocacy Organizations In America.* NY: Simon and Schuster, 1993.

Zimmerman, Richard. *What Can I Do To Make A Difference? A Positive Action Sourcebook.* NY: Penguin, 1991.

ALTERNATIVES TO VIOLENCE

Session 19
ALTERNATIVES TO VIOLENCE SKILLS
Imaging a better world

Objectives

a. To envision and feel what it would be like if there were no violence and no weapons, only nonviolent conduct in whatever framework we wish to examine (classroom, home, workplace, school, athletic field, neighborhood, community, nation, world).

b. To determine the needed steps and time schedule to get there (i.e., to a world without weapons, a school without corporal punishment, etc.).

c. To realize how clearly envisioning a goal helps us get there.

Worksheet # 19

(The following points will be covered in this session. Most points do not have "pat" answers, but the main thing is for you to arrive at an expression of the concepts. These questions are to help you take notes and process the material.)

1. What conditions would I like to see improved?

    at home: _____

    at work: _____

    in my community: _____

    in my country: _____

2. Do I have a vision with clear objectives?

    _____
    _____
    _____
    _____

3. What do you think about: **A major obstacle to improving conditions anywhere is the difficulty in developing nonviolent power sharing.**

    _____
    _____
    _____
    _____

©1986, 1990, 1992, 1993, 1994, 1995 PEACE GROWS, Inc., 513 W. Exchange St., Akron, OH 44302 (216)864-5442.

Notes or Journal Entry

Assignments:

_____
_____
_____
_____
_____

ALTERNATIVES TO VIOLENCE

IMAGING A NONVIOLENT COMMUNITY OR WORLD
How we got there in 30 years

"Community" can be a family, school, neighborhood, business or whatever selected for relevance to class.

A "nonviolent world" is one without weapons.

The time span (30 years) and its breakdowns should be reduced where appropriate; e.g., establishing a nonviolent school or classroom should be possible, say, in two years, not 30.

What is it like now? List things that are different. (Assume we are in the 30th year of this new age.)
Actual years:

What happened 15 to 25 years ago? List. (Back from the 30th year.)
Actual years:

What happened up to 15 years ago? List. (Back from the 30th year.)
Actual years:

25 to 30 years ago? List. (Back from the 30th year.)
Actual years:

©1986, 1990, 1992, 1993, 1994, 1995 PEACE GROWS, Inc., 513 W. Exchange St., Akron, OH 44302 (216)864-5442.

ASSURING NONVIOLENCE

This session is intended to give course participants both hope and direction. If only we might have a true vision, a real understanding, of a school, a community, a world actually practicing peace and justice. In such a paradise everyone is concerned about and cares for each other. If we could just experience this, how much all would be inspired.

Therefore, Session 19 asks that we each create an image in our mind to put ourself into that more perfect life. It may be a world without weapons, a school or a community without violence, whatever we are seeking to attain together as a group.

How? First we become "futurists." Now we live in this wonderful new situation with caring and concern for one another. We "experience" how great this new community of human beings really is. Then, we brainstorm as big a list as we can of what is so enjoyably different from all we endured and suffered back in 1995. We write a list of those items in the upper lefthand column of page 223.

Next, we become "historians." Looking back from our veritable paradise, we try to recall how we arrived where we are from those horrible old times. What was done? When? Those are written into the other appropriate sections on page 223. The group's responses should be posted for all to see.

Our historic research can cover many areas: education, health care, economic practices, violence, environmental and ecological issues, military operation, status of hunger and homeless problems, crime, budget priorities, etc., etc.

As the data from the group are posted, you will see a plan for reducing or ending violence or helping whatever else we are trying to improve in our organization or world. The specific, incremental steps for reaching our goals need to be defined. Business calls this imaging process; management by objectives.

However, is not something most important still lacking? People throughout history have had marvelous plans. Yet too often they remained just that—plans. Most are never implemented. Why? How can we avoid the same tragic experience here?

For the motivation formula, I go back to the late Charles Wells. He was a professional journalist. After working for the mainstream media, he began publishing a little newsletter called *Between the Lines*. It influenced thousands of people in very constructive ways.

The first requirement, he said, is information or awareness. If you do not know something is happening, you cannot be concerned about it. Concern is the second requirement. If you are not concerned about it, you will never do anything about it. Action is the third requirement. If there is no action by the needed numbers of people, there will be no change. From information and awareness comes concern. From deep enough concern comes action. Only from proper action by enough "grass roots" people comes change.

All social change has been slow. History books tend to have us believe that the Civil War, and only the Civil War, ended slavery. Actually John Woolman, Case No. 10-A in this *Workbook*, began organizing against slavery in the late 1700s. Anti-Slavery Leagues formed. Public opinion in opposition gradually grew over decades until the political climate would support the change. The movement to reduce or eliminate violence is born and growing in the same way. Keep your eyes and ears on the developments and join the bandwagon. Your whole life will change and, eventually, so will schools, communities, nations and world!

This article was written by John Looney.
©1986, 1990, 1992, 1993, 1994, 1995 PEACE GROWS, Inc., 513 W. Exchange St., Akron, OH 44302 (216)864-5442.

SPECIFIC CHANGES IN MY UNDERSTANDING OR ATTITUDES SINCE TAKING THIS CLASS

(To be filled out and kept in this *Workbook* as a record of personal growth you may experience while taking this course. After the course, as you experiment with the precepts you have learned, you may wish to add to this list.)

SPECIFIC THINGS I PLAN TO DO TO WORK FOR NONVIOLENCE/PEACE

(Please record here, for your personal use and future references, specific things you are doing or plan to do as a result of what you have learned during this course. These might cover personal conduct or actions. They might also include supporting groups you have started to or plan to work with for achieving a better, less violent community, society and world.)

What I have learned: **How I am applying it or plan to apply it:**

ALTERNATIVES TO VIOLENCE

OFFER OF HELP

(Please fill out wherever applicable and turn in to the facilitator.)

_____ Yes, I'd like to help more people learn about *Alternatives to Violence.*

_____ I would like to have someone come and speak to my group about the course.

_____ Please explain how I can get the course started in my _____ school
_____ religious institution
_____ community organization.

_____ I would be willing to serve on a committee to help promote and administer efforts in my area.

_____ I would be interested in finding out how to become a teacher/facilitator.

_____ Someday, I might even consider recruiting and helping train new teachers.

_____ I hope our class people can get together some in the future.

_____ I would suggest you contact this person who, I believe, might be interested in sponsoring a course.

Name_____ Phone _____
Address _____
City & State _____ ZIP _____

Regarding the possibility of offering a course at: _____
_____ Please see back of this sheet for other names.
_____ Sorry, but I do not know how I can help right now.

Name_____ Phone _____
Address _____
City & State _____ ZIP _____

Space for further comments:

©1986, 1990, 1992, 1993, 1994, 1995 PEACE GROWS, Inc., 513 W. Exchange St., Akron, OH 44302 (216)864-5442.

SUMMARY OF CONCEPTS
As related to the subjects listed on worksheet #19

1. *What conditions would I like to see improved?*
   at home:
   at work:
   in my community:
   in my country:
   Examples will vary.

2. *Do I have a vision with clear objectives?*

   Management by objective, in which we define where we want to go and then plan and implement the steps to get there, applies to improving the world as well as a business or other enterprise.

3. *What do you think about:*
   A major obstacle to improving conditions anywhere is the difficulty in developing nonviolent power sharing.

   A requirement of a just society is the sharing of power. Collectively, we have the ability to improve conditions.

Major point to remember:
- Improving conditions is possible. Working together, with real dedication and a clear vision of our objectives, we can accomplish most anything.

Session 19
IMAGING A BETTER WORLD
Additional reading

Harman, Willis and John Hormann. *Creative Work: The Constructive Role Of Business In A Transforming Society.* Indianapolis: Knowledge Systems, Inc., 1990.

Knudsen-Hoffman, Gene. *Ways Out: The Book Of Changes For Peace.* Santa Barbara, CA: J. Daniels, 1988.

Macy, Joanna Rogers. *Despair And Personal Power In The Nuclear Age.* Philadelphia, PA: New Society Pub., 1983.

Macy, Joanna Rogers. *World As Lover, World As Self.* Berkeley, CA: Parallax Press, 1991.

Nhat Hanh, Thich. *For A Future To Be Possible: Commentaries On The 5 Wonderful Precepts.* Berkeley, CA: Parallax Press, 1993.

True, Michael. *Ordinary People: Family Life And Global Values.* Maryknoll, NY: Orbis Books, 1991.

Weisbord, Marvin R. *Discovering Common Ground: How Future Search Conferences Bring People Together To Achieve Breakthrough Innovation, Empowerment, Shared Vision And Collaborative Action.* San Francisco: Berrett-Koehler Pub., 1992.

Williamson, Marianne. *Illuminata: Thoughts, Prayers, Rites Of Passage.* NY: Random House, 1994.

ALTERNATIVES TO VIOLENCE

Session 20
REFLECTION AND CELEBRATION

Objectives

a. To reflect on our learning experience together.

b. To show our appreciation to and thanks for each other.

c. To evaluate the course by pointing out both what seemed good about it and what seems to need improvement.

d. To celebrate our friendship and growth.

e. To determine, by sharing our future plans, how we can grow further in understanding and involvement.

f. To have some fun together!

Worksheet # 20

(The following points will be covered in this session. Most points do not have "pat" answers, but the main thing is for you to arrive at an expression of the concepts. These questions are to help you take notes and process the material.)

1. What are some things I have learned I can do?

   _____

   _____

   _____

   _____

2. About what would I like to learn?

   _____

   _____

   _____

   _____

3. How can we celebrate growth?

   _____

   _____

   _____

   _____

©1986, 1990, 1992, 1993, 1994, 1995 PEACE GROWS, Inc., 513 W. Exchange St., Akron, OH 44302 (216)864-5442.

Notes or Journal Entry

REFLECT AND CELEBRATE

Many participants tell us that this course has opened their minds and hearts to new ideas and stimulated some new commitments. Think about and list on page 225 changes in understanding and attitudes. Also, think about some things you plan to do as a result of these changes and write your plans on page 226. During Session 20, sharing these changes and plans should create an interesting and rewarding class experience.

During Session 20 your completion of the Evaluation Sheet on page 235 will provide significant feedback for improving this material and course.

We have much to celebrate; we have found each other. The directions on page 233 help us think about one another and provide a memento to take home from the course.

Quaker faith is based on the belief that there is "that of God" in every person. All great religions, as we saw in Session 10, seek to enhance the quality of life through promoting respect and caring for everyone. The expression and sharing of feelings and beliefs has provided insight into the astounding sanctity of each life.

The amazing divine nature of human beings recognized, spoken to, respected and revered is what will bring us to our goals. This revelation applied will change our own lives, the lives of those we know and the world around us. What greater could there be to celebrate?

ALTERNATIVES TO VIOLENCE

AN AFFIRMATION

Please insert your name here. Then pass the sheet to the person next to you until it returns to you, with everyone's comments, for you to keep.

NAME _____

Please write only positive things on here about the above person, and then pass to person next to you to do the same. This exercise also may be done by posting a sheet for each person on the wall during the last few sessions and encouraging insertions. Having colored felt markers (water soluble to prevent bleeding through the paper or newsprint) on hand and encouraging multicolored comments and even artwork can produce quite an attractive momento of the class for each participant to take home.

ALTERNATIVES TO VIOLENCE EVALUATION SHEET

1. A friend learns of your taking this course and asks your advice for someone else about taking it. What would you say?

2. How have your attitudes changed toward violence and nonviolence since this course began and why? What in particular have you learned?

3. What did you like best about the course (what specific exercises, readings, etc.) and why?

4. What topics were not covered enough or would you like to see added?

5. What would you most like to see changed in the course and why?

6. Other comments or new ideas:

7. What have you done already or do you plan to do in the future about applying what you have learned in this course to your life and/or a certain specific problem or problems?

8. Have you been able to keep the journal as assigned? Why or why not? (Your insight is needed.)

9. Location of course and name of teacher/facilitator(s):

If necessary, use the back and/or another sheet for your comments.
Please fill out and turn in or return to:
Alternatives to Violence, **Peace GROWS, Inc., 513 West Exchange Street, Akron, OH 44302.**

©1986, 1990, 1992, 1993, 1994, 1995 PEACE GROWS, Inc., 513 W. Exchange St., Akron, OH 44302 (216)864-

ALTERNATIVES TO VIOLENCE

REPORT OF ONGOING EXPERIENCES

Record of experiences, personal observations and/or examples read or otherwise learned of violence and/or alternatives to violence. (Where more details, you may wish to use a case analysis sheet for certain items.)

Item No.	Date	Facts and source	Your analysis of what happened, why and what, if anything, might otherwise have been done

NOTE:
Back of sheet and additional pages to be added as needed. (From time to time, please mail a copy of this report to Peace GROWS, Inc., 513 West Exchange Street, Akron, OH 44302. It will help our upcoming teaching.)

©1986, 1990, 1992, 1993, 1994, 1995 PEACE GROWS, Inc., 513 W. Exchange St., Akron, OH 44302 (216)864-5442.

ALTERNATIVES TO VIOLENCE

SUMMARY OF CONCEPTS
As related to the subjects listed on worksheet #20

1. *What are some things I have learned I can do?*
   Examples will reflect skills, strategies and principles of conflict resolution and nonviolence.

2. *About what would I like to learn?*
   Answers will vary.

3. *How can we celebrate growth?*
   Answers will vary.

> **Major point to remember:**
> - Nonviolence is rewarding! It is fun! It works!

©1986, 1990, 1992, 1993, 1994, 1995 PEACE GROWS, Inc., 513 W. Exchange St., Akron, OH 44302 (216)864-5442.

Session 20
REFLECTION AND CELEBRATION
Additional reading

DeAngelis, Barbara. *Real Moments.* NY: Delacorte Press, 1994.

Fluegelman, Andrew. *More New Games: And Playful Ideas From The New Games Foundation.* Garden City, NY: Doubleday, 1981.

Keen, Sam. *Hymns To An Unknown God: Awakening The Spirit In Everyday Life.* NY: Bantam Books, 1994.

LeFevre, Dale N. *New Games For The Whole Family.* NY: Perigee Books, 1988.

Luks, Allan and Peggy Payne. *The Healing Power Of Doing Good.* NY: Fawcett Columbine, 1991.

Sobel, Jeffrey. *Everyone Wins: Non-Competitive Games For Young Children.* NY: Walker, 1983.

ALTERNATIVES TO VIOLENCE

PARTICIPANT CONCERNS SHEET

Please fill out this sheet as an assignment before our second gathering. Its purpose is to guide our course/workshop toward your relevant needs. If space proves too small, you may add blank pages and refer to them.

Please answer the following questions in one or two words, or if that is not possible, no more than one or two sentences:

(1) Why did you sign up for this program? _____
_____
_____
_____

(2) What do you hope or want to learn from it? _____
_____
_____
_____

(3) Please describe a violent/conflict tension or injustice problem in your situation which has been especially difficult to handle. Specific details will help in the analysis. If you have found a solution that satisfies you, please describe it. (The case may come from your personal/neighborhood/job/religious institution or whatever or wherever some human problem exists which you have observed, heard about, or better yet, experienced.)
_____
_____
_____
_____

©1986, 1990, 1992, 1993, 1994, 1995 PEACE GROWS, Inc., 513 W. Exchange St., Akron, OH 44302 (216)864-5442.

(4) Please list what you feel are the basic causes of this and other similar problems:
_____
_____
_____

(5) What skills do you feel you might need to strengthen or further develop your ability to handle these situations?
_____
_____
_____

(6) Please list the kinds of violence/conflict that disturb you the most: _____
_____
_____
_____

Hopefully we will be directing some of our learning toward relevant problem solving for you and/or your institution. We all will share not only our problems but also our ideas for solutions. Thank you!

PEACE GROWS, *Alternatives to Violence* **Project, 513 West Exchange Street, Akron, OH 44302.**

Name (optional) _____

Course location _____ Facilitator _____

APPLICATION PAPER GUIDELINES

Real learning requires doing it.

The application paper's objective is to try out something you have learned in the course and then report what happened and analyze the results.

Content is important. Length and format are not.

You are expected to select any particular learning from the course that suits you and apply it wherever it seems appropriate, or could be tried, on your job, somewhere in your daily life, in your family, in some conflict you are experiencing.

Your write-up should:

(1) Explain the background of the situation, if appropriate.

(2) Narrate what you tried and how you tried it.

(3) Tell what happened then.

(4) Reveal whether you felt it was successful or not.

(5) Make clear why you think you obtained the results you did. If it failed, then propose what you think might have been done differently to change the results.

Should you have any questions not answered here, ask them of your class facilitator.

Please follow the scheduled due dates for turning in your application papers.
   Thank you.

ALTERNATIVES TO VIOLENCE

REFLECTION PAPER GUIDELINES

The purpose of the reflection paper, to be turned in at, or before, the last class, is to cause you to think about and articulate what this class has meant to you.

Here are some of the things this paper might cover:

(1) What were my feelings about the course? What particularly pleased me? What disappointed me?

(2) What did I learn in the course which I had not realized before? What surprised me in the course? On what would I like to have spent more time?

(3) How has the course helped me? Where have I applied it and with what results?

(4) What applications do I plan to make in the future? How did the course aid me to grow in understanding? What would I like to have understood better?

(5) Whatever other reflections you have of any sort pertaining to the course should be added.

(6) What, if anything, do I plan to do in the future to prevent violence and promote nonviolence?

If you have been able to maintain a journal, this task will be much easier. Probably, you, mainly, will need to enter some of the major highlights from that journal.

Further questions always will be answered willingly by the facilitator.

Again, this reflection paper is due on or before the last class session.

GLOSSARY OF TERMS

Active listening. Making a conscious effort to hear, understand, and respond to what is said.

Active nonviolence (Direct action). Denotes a wide range of methods of confronting conflict which do not use any violent force: examples include strikes, sit-ins, boycotts, rallies, street theatre, personal witness, letter campaigns, leafletting, etc.

Affirmation. The assertion of the positive value of a person or idea.

American. Is used to denote any one of the following: a Native American (an "Indian"); a citizen of any part of North, Central, or South American continents; (and/or) a United States citizen.

Anarchism. "A doctrine advocating the abolition of government as the indispensable condition for full liberty." (*The Random House Dictionary*)

Antisemitism. Systemmic and/or individual discrimination, prejudice, or persecution against Jews.

Arbitration. Binding settlement of a dispute by an impartial third party (an ARBITRATOR), for example by a judge or jury.

Assertive. Stating positively but without aggression.

Boycott. To join together in refraining from dealing with or buying from.

Brainstorm. To freely share suggestions, inspirations, or ideas without discussion or evaluation.

Capitalism. An economic system based upon private ownership for profit of the means of production and their products.

Civil disobedience. Nonviolent refusal to obey a law (intended to influence government policy).

Civilian-based defense (Nonviolent national defense). Nonviolent protection (as, of a homeland) by non-military personnel, usually an entire able population.

Classism. Systemmic and/or individual prejudice against or oppression of people on the basis of their lesser wealth, education, or social status.

Collective. Non-hierarchical group organization or process.

Communism. The theory and economic system of collective ownership of the means of production by a local community with all members sharing in the work and the products.

Compromise. The process of mutual concession to resolve differences (conflict).

Conflict. Opposition of actions or ideas; a problem or disagreement.

Confront. To face or meet (as, a problem); to deal with.

Conscientious objector. A person who is unwilling to participate in war and/or the military for reasons of personal belief about violence.

Consensus. General agreement; willingness of all members of a group to go along with a particular solution or action.

Cooperative (Co-op) An association formed to help its members buy, sell, or live jointly to better mutual advantage; a communally owned and run operation.

Dehumanization. The deprivation of human qualities, rights, or understanding.

Democracy. Government by elected representatives of the people; a country with democratic government where all citizens have equal rights and opportunities.

Diffuse. To scatter, dilute, or confuse a problem so as to make confrontation less likely and resolution impossible or postponed.

Dilemma strategy. A nonviolent action strategy of creating a situation wherein the party in power has to choose between alternatives it might not consider advantageous. For example, if the government chooses its party line, it will appear unfair, and if it chooses to recognize/give in to the demonstrators, it will feel it is losing power. Setting up a dilemma for the party in power means it will be more likely to change/negotiate with its opponent.

Disarmament. Reduction in the size and/or equipment (weapons) of the armed forces.

Draft. To select persons for mandatory service in the armed forces.

Equitable. Fair and just, distributed on the basis of need.

Escalation. An increase in the magnitude or intensity; a build up making resolution more difficult.

GLOSSARY OF TERMS (continued)

Facilitator. A person who helps a meeting or negotiation to run smoothly and effectively; one who disencumbers group process (FACILITATES) to make way for mutually satisfying conflict resolution and action.

Fascism. Totalitarian and unresponsive governmental system.

Feminism. 1: The doctrine advocating equal social, economic, and political rights for women. 2: The assertion of the importance of processes, work, and ideas traditionally considered "feminine." 3: Opposition to patriarchy and patriarchal forms of behavior.

Genocide. The systematic and planned killing of a racial, political, or cultural group of people.

Global responsibility. The feeling of obligation to be concerned with the welfare of the earth and its inhabitants, including outside national boundaries.

Heterosexism. Systemmatic and/or individual persecution, discrimination or prejudice against homosexuals, and sometimes suspected homosexuals and bisexuals.

Holocaust. 1: Any widespread destruction, especially by fire. 2: The Holocaust refers to the genocidal incarceration and murder of Jews and others by the German Nazi state, 1933-1945.

Human rights (Civil rights). Just claims for equitable legal, economic, and social power in a society or country.

Imaging. A technique of picturing and depicting verbally our dreams or ideas.

Imperialism. The policy or practice of extending or trying to extend the dominion of a government, ideology, or nation over a widening territory.

Institutional violence. The deprivation of any person or group of their basic human rights or needs, imposed or condoned by an institution or society.

Mediation. Helping to settle differences by having someone (a MEDIATOR) go between opposing parties, negotiating with each and suggesting non-binding resolutions.

Military-industrial complex. The private corporation and governmental institutions which control and equip the U.S. military: mainly the Pentagon, the Department of Defense, the Department of Energy (nuclear weapons and research), and the private contractors which operate military production plants for a profit.

Negotiation. Discussion "with a view to reaching agreement" (*Webster's New World Dictionary*); talking about a conflict where both parties give and take to reach a resolution.

New international economic order (NIEO). A United Nations study and campaign for redistribution of world resources: poor nations would be paid more for the raw material and labor they provide to wealthy nations, international loans would be reexamined so as to be less harsh on developing nations.

Noncooperation. A kind of active nonviolence entailing a (usually collective) refusal to help or work together with an institution or group in power.

Nongovernmental organization (NGO). A group working to resolve international problems which is not directed, paid, or sponsored by any government.

Nonresistance. A conscious, usually preplanned response to violence entailing not opposing or protecting oneself. Commonly used by activists demonstrating against institutional violence as a response to physical retaliation by police or bystanders.

Nonviolence. Confrontation of violence with intent not to injure and/or rectify injury or injustice.

Nuclear freeze proposal. A proposal for an immediate moratorium on further production, development, or deployment of any nuclear weapons. It has been proposed unilaterally (U.S. only), bilaterally (U.S. and U.S.S.R.), and multilaterally (all nuclear weapons producers).

Ombudsman/Ombudswoman. A public official responsible for fact-finding to aid conflict resolution: s/he investigates complaints from private citizens and/or consumers, especially those involving abuses of power by government officials.

GLOSSARY OF TERMS (continued)

Oppression. "Exists when any entity (society, institution, group or individual), intentionally or unintentionally, inequitably distributes resources, maintains inflexible or unresponsive structures, refuses to share power, and/or pursues an unclarified mission while ignoring diversity for its own supposed benefit, and rationalizes its action by blaming or ignoring the victim." (—Jean Alvarez) *Synonym:* Institutional violence.

Pacifism. A belief that disputes should be settled by nonviolent means.

Peace. Freedom from violence and war and the causes thereof.

Peace churches. The three Christian churches, Society of Friends (Quaker), Brethren, and Mennonite, which hold pacifism at the core of their religious philosophies.

Peacekeeper (once called Peace marshall). A person at a demonstration or convocation responsible for helping to resolve problems peacefully and preventing violence.

Peace research. Investigation and study into the causes of and alternatives to war and other violence and into how to encourage peace and nonviolence.

Pluralism. The doctrine or belief that there is more than one kind of "correct" or "good" person or way of life.

Prejudice. Preconceived or biased, usually unfavorable, ideas about a person, group, or place.

Racism. The systemmic and/or individual persecution, discrimination, or prejudice against a person or group on the basis of race, specifically of persons with dark skins by people/groups with white or other-colored skins.

Rape. "The crime of having sexual intercourse with a woman forcibly and without her consent." (*Webster's New World Dictionary*); the act of a man forcing any sexual contact upon another man, woman, or child.

Role playing. A learning technique in which two or more people act out characterizations of other people or other communication styles.

Satyagraha. The Indian word for Truth-Force, or nonviolent action, coined by Mahatma Mohandas Gandhi.

Security. "A feeling of being free from fear, danger, etc." (*Webster's New World Dictionary*)

Sexism. Systemmatic and/or individual discrimination or prejudice against women; the devaluation of people, objects, and ideas considered "feminine."

Simple living. Reducing one's detrimental effect upon the world and its finite resources by, for example, growing own food, buying direct from producers, recycling, etc.

Socialism. The theory and political-economic system of society/government ownerships of the means of production and distribution, in which all members are required to work and are paid equally.

Street theatre (guerilla theatre). A nonviolent action strategy in which a person or persons performs a skit and/or wears a costume(s) to dramatize and explain a problem or viewpoint to the public. Takes place in public places or on the street.

Strike. Nonviolent refusal to continue to work until a problem is resolved. Types of strikes include the following:

Hunger strike. To refuse to eat until a problem is resolved.

One-hour (one day) strike. To stop work for a pre-determined length of time as a protest or warning.

Sit-down strike. To occupy a workplace or other institutions while refusing to work or support it.

Walk-out. To leave in the middle of a meeting or workday to protest what goes on there.

Wildcat strike. A strike which is illegal and/or not sanctioned by a recognized union.

Work slowdown. To slow or impede, rather than stop, work.

Tax resistance. Refusal to pay taxes as a form of nonviolent civil disobedience. *War tax resistance*, then is the refusal to pay the percentage of one's taxes which would go to fund military operations (past, present, and future). This is illegal. See also **World Peace Tax Fund.**

Town meeting (also called public meeting, open meeting). A community gathering to learn about and discuss an issue of concern.

Transarmament. The period and process of conversion from a national security system based on military force to a nonviolent, civilian-based defense system.

©1986, 1990, 1992, 1993, 1994, 1995 PEACE GROWS, Inc., 513 W. Exchange St., Akron, OH 44302 (216)864-5442.

GLOSSARY OF TERMS (continued)

Transnational corporation (multinational). A business which operates in more than one country (for example, mining or growing raw materials in one country, and refining and selling them in another, or shipping parts to another country to be assembled by a less-paid labor force than the home country's).

Vigil. A nonviolent watch or silent demonstration to protest, honor or express concern, and sometimes to encourage others to do likewise.

Violence. Force used to injure or take advantage of someone; hurt imposed. Types of violence include physical, verbal, psychological, and institutional (including oppression).

World federalism. The belief in or practice of world government.

World peace tax fund bill. If passed, this bill would make possible legal conscientious objection to war taxes: taxes of a conscientious objector which would have paid for war would instead go into a federally administered World Peace Tax Fund, working to end the causes of war.

ALTERNATIVES TO VIOLENCE

ORGANIZATIONAL INDEX

- AEROSPACE ENGINEERS/WORKERS FOR SOCIAL RESPONSIBILITY, P.O. Box 21471, Los Angeles, CA 90021 (213)641-8929

- AFSC NUCLEAR WEAPONS FACILITIES PROJECT, 1660 Lafayette Street, Denver, CO 80218 (303)832-4508

- AMERICAN ASSOCIATION OF UNIVERSITY WOMEN, 2401 Virginia Avenue NW, Washington, DC 20037 (202)785-7800

- AMERICAN COMMITTEE ON EAST-WEST ACCORD, 109 11th Street SE, Washington, DC 20003 (202)546-1700

- AMERICAN CONSERVATIVE UNION, 38 Ivy Street SE, Washington DC 20003 (202)546-6555

- AMERICAN FEDERATION OF STATE, COUNTY AND MUNICIPAL EMPLOYEES, 1625 L Street NW, Washington, DC 20036 (202)452-4800

- AMERICAN FRIENDS SERVICE COMMITTEE (AFSC), 1501 Cherry Street, Philadelphia, PA 19102 (215)241-7177

- AMERICAN SECURITY COUNCIL, P.O. Box 8, Boston, VA 22713 (703)547-1776

- AMERICANS FOR DEMOCRATIC ACTION, 1411 K Street NW, Suite 850, Washington, DC 20006 (202)638-6447

- ANOTHER MOTHER FOR PEACE, 407 North Maple Drive, Beverly Hills, CA 90210 (213)274-9665

- ARCHITECTS FOR SOCIAL RESPONSIBILITY, 225 Lafayette Street, New York, NY 10012 (212)334-8104

- ARMS CONTROL AND DISARMAMENT AGENCY (ACDA), 320 Twenty-First Street NW, Washington, DC 20451 (202)632-0392

- ARMS CONTROL ASSOCIATION, 11 Dupont Circle NW, Washington, DC 20036 (202)797-6450

- ARMS RACE EDUCATION PROJECT, P.O. Box 76600, Washington, DC 20013 (301)270-1141

- ARTISTS FOR SURVIVAL, 65 Inman Street, Cambridge, MA 02139

- ATHLETES UNITED FOR PEACE, P.O. Box 1776, Lawrence, KS 66044 (913)843-6435

- BIMILLENNIUM FOUNDATION, 2100 Pennsylvania Avenue NW, Washington, DC 20037 (202)466-5716

- BLACKS AGAINST NUKES, 3728 New Hampshire Avenue NW, Suite 202, Washington, DC 20037 (202)882-7155

- BRANDT COMMISSION, P.O. Box 2619, North Canton, OH 44720 (216)494-6924

- BROOKINGS INSTITUTION, 1775 Massachusetts Avenue NW, Washington, DC 20036 (202)797-6000

- BULLFROG FILMS, INC., Oley, PA 19547 (215)779-8226

- BUSINESS EXECUTIVES FOR NATIONAL SECURITY, 21 Dupont Circle NW, Suite 401, Washington, DC 20036 (202)429-0600

- CABLE NEWS NETWORK (CNN), 2133 Wisconsin Avenue NW, Washington, DC 20007 (202)342-7900

- CALVERT SOCIAL INVESTMENT FUND, 1700 Pennsylvania Avenue NW, Washington, DC 20006 (800)368-2748

- CAMPAIGN AGAINST MX, 711 G Street SE, Washington, DC 20003 (202)546-2660

- CATHOLIC PEACE FELLOWSHIP, 339 Lafayette Street, New York, NY 10012 (212)673-8990

- CENTER FOR DEFENSE INFORMATION, 600 Maryland Avenue SW, Suite 303, West Washington, DC 20024 (202)484-9490

- CENTER FOR INTERNATIONAL POLICY, 120 Maryland Avenue NE, Washington, DC 20002 (202)544-4666

- CENTER FOR NATIONAL SECURITY STUDIES, 122 Maryland Avenue NE, Washington, DC 20002 (202)544-5380

- CENTER FOR PEACE STUDIES, Georgetown University, Washington, DC 20057 (202)625-4240

- CENTER FOR THE STUDY OF RESPONSIVE LAW, P.O. Box 19367, Washington, DC 20036 (202)387-8030

- CENTER ON THE CONSEQUENCES OF NUCLEAR WAR, 3244 Prospect Street NW, Washington, DC 20007 (202)337-4706

- CHILDREN'S CAMPAIGN FOR NUCLEAR DISARMAMENT, 14 Everit Street, New Haven, CT 06511 (203)787-5262

©1986, 1990, 1992, 1993, 1994, 1995 PEACE GROWS, Inc., 513 W. Exchange St., Akron, OH 44302 (216)864-5442.

ORGANIZATIONAL INDEX (continued)

- CHURCHES' CENTER FOR THEOLOGY/PUBLIC POLICY, 4500 Massachusetts Avenue NW, Washington, DC 20016 (202)363-3088

- CINEMA GUILD, 1697 Broadway, Suite 802, New York, NY 10019 (212)246-5522

- CITIZEN INVOLVEMENT TRAINING PROJECT, 225 Fureolo Hall, University of Massachusetts, Amherst, MA 01003 (413)545-2038

- CITIZENS AGAINST NUCLEAR WAR, 1201 Sixteenth Street NW, Washington, DC 20036 (202)822-7483

- CITIZENS EXCHANGE COUNCIL, 18 East Forty-First Street, New York, NY 10017 (212)889-7960

- CITIZENS POLICY CENTER, 1515 Webster Street, #401, Oakland, CA 04609 (415)839-9037

- CLERGY AND LAITY CONCERNED (CALC), 198 Broadway, Room 308, New York, NY 10038 (212)964-6730

- COALITION FOR A NEW FOREIGN AND MILITARY POLICY, 120 Maryland Avenue NE, Washington, DC 20002 (202)546-8400

- COALITION FOR PEACE THROUGH STRENGTH see AMERICAN SECURITY COUNCIL

- COMMISSION FOR ADVANCEMENT OF PUBLIC INTEREST ORGANIZATIONS, 1875 Connecticut Avenue NW, Suite 1010, Washington, DC 20009 (202)462-0505

- COMMITTEE AGAINST NUCLEAR WAR, 401 C Street NE, Suite 103, Washington, DC 20002 (202)547-5480

- COMMITTEE FOR NATIONAL SECURITY, 1742 N Street NW, Fourth floor, Washington, DC 20036 (202)833-3140

- COMMON CAUSE, 2030 M Street NW, Washington, DC 20036 (202)833-1200

- COMMUNICATORS FOR NUCLEAR DISARMAMENT, 354 Congress Street, Boston, MA 02110 (617)423-7886

- COMPUTER PROFESSIONALS FOR SOCIAL RESPONSIBILITY, P.O. Box 717, Palo Alto, CA 94301 (415)322-3778

- CONCORD FILMS COUNCIL, LTD., 201 Felixstone Road, Ipswich, Suffolk, IP3-9BJ, England

- CONGRESSIONAL CLEARINGHOUSE ON THE FUTURE, House Annex #2, Room 555, Washington, DC 20515 (212)226-3434

- CONSERVATIVE CAUCUS, 501 Church Street NE, Room 317, Vienna, VA 22180 (703)893-1550

- CORINTH FILMS, 410 Est Sixty-Second Street, New York, NY 10021 (212)421-4770

- COUNCIL FOR A LIVABLE WORLD, 100 Maryland Avenue NE, Washington, DC 20002 (202)543-4100

- COUNCIL ON ECONOMIC PRIORITIES, 30 Irving Place, New York, NY 10003 (212)420-1133

- CREATIVE INITIATIVE, 222 High Street, Palo Alto, CA 94301 (415)328-7756

- CRUISE AND PERSHING PROJECT, 119 Constitution Avenue NE, Washington, DC 20002 (202)543-2482

- DEFENSE AUDIO-VISUAL AGENCY, Building 168, NDW, Anacostia, Washington, DC 20374 (202)433-2166

- DEFENSE NUCLEAR AGENCY, 6801 Telegraph Road, Alexandria, VA 22310 (202)325-7120

- DEPARTMENT OF DEFENSE, Office of Assistant Secretary of Defense, Public Affairs, Room 1E776, The Pentagon, Washington, DC 20301 (202)695-6108

- DIRECT CINEMA, LTD., P.O. Box 69589, Los Angeles, CA 90069 (213)656-4700

- EDUCATIONAL FILM AND VIDEO PROJECT, 1725-B Seabright Avenue, Santa Cruz, CA 95062 (408)427-2627

- EDUCATORS FOR SOCIAL RESPONSIBILITY, 23 Garden Street, Cambridge, MA 02138 (617)492-1764

- EMPLOYMENT RESEARCH ASSOCIATES, 474 Hollister Building, Lansing, MA 48933 (517)485-7655

- FEDERATION OF AMERICAN SCIENTISTS, 307 Massachusetts Avenue NE, Washington, DC 20002 (202)546-3300

- FELLOWSHIP OF RECONCILIATION, P.O. Box 271, Nyack, NY 10960 (914)358-4601

- FILM FUND, 80 East Eleventh Street, New York, NY 10003 (212)475-3720

- FORUM INSTITUTE, 1225 Fifteenth Street NW, Washington, DC 20005 (202)462-4243

ORGANIZATIONAL INDEX (continued)

- FORWARD MOVEMENT PUBLICATIONS, 412 Sycamore Street, Cincinnati, OH 45202 (513)721-6659

- FREEZE VOTER, 2000 K Street NW, Suite 451, Washington, DC 20006 (212)822-0661

- FRIENDS COMMITTEE ON NATIONAL LEGISLATION, 245 Second Street NE, Washington, DC 20002 (202)547-6000

- FRIENDS OF THE EARTH, 1045 Sansome Street, San Francisco, CA 94111 (415)433-7373

- FUND FOR CONSTITUTIONAL GOVERNMENT, 122 Maryland Avenue NE, Washington, DC 20002 (202)546-3732

- FUND FOR PEACE, 345 East Forty-Sixth Street, Suite 207, New York, NY 10017 (212)661-5900

- GAUDETE PEACE AND JUSTICE CENTER, 634 Spruce Street, Madison, WI 53715

- GENERAL ELECTRIC STOCKHOLDERS ALLIANCE, P.O. Box 966, Columbia, MD 21044 (301)730-0178

- GLOBAL PERSPECTIVES IN EDUCATION, 218 East Eighteenth Street, New York, NY 10003 (212)475-0850

- GOVERNMENT PRINTING OFFICE, Superintendent of Documents, Washington, DC 20402 (202)783-3238

- GREEN MOUNTAIN POST FILMS, P.O. Box 229, Turners Falls, MA 01376 (413)863-4754

- GREENPEACE, 2007 R Street NW, Suite 300, Washington, DC 20009 (202)462-1177

- GROUND ZERO, 806 Fifteenth Street NW, Washington, DC 20005 (202)638-7402

- GROUND ZERO CENTER FOR NONVIOLENT ACTION, 806 15th Street NW, Suite 421, Washington, DC 20002 (202)638-7402

- GROUND ZERO PAIRING PROJECT, 7135 SW Thirty-Sixth Street, Portland, OR 97219 (503)245-3519

- HARVARD NUCLEAR NEGOTIATION PROJECT, 500 Pound Hall, Cambridge, MA 02138 (617)495-1684

- HEALTH AND ENERGY INSTITUTE, 236 Massachusetts Avenue NE, Suite 506, Washington, DC 20009 (202)543-1070

- HERITAGE FOUNDATION, 214 Massachusetts Avenue NE, Washington, DC 20002 (202)546-4400

- HIGH FRONTIERS FOUNDATION, 1010 Vermont Avenue NW, Suite 1000, Washington, DC 20005 (202)737-1979

- HIGH TECHNOLOGY PROFESSIONALS FOR PEACE, 639 Massachusetts Avenue, Room 316, Cambridge, MA 02139 (617)497-0605

- HIROSHIMA NAGASAKI MEMORIAL COLLECTION, Wilmington College, Pyle Center, P.O. 1183, Wilmington, OH 45177 (513)382-5338

- ICARUS FILMS, 200 Park Avenue South, New York, NY 10003 (212)674-3375

- IMPACT, 100 Maryland Avenue NE, Suite 502, Washington, DC 20002 (202)544-8636

- INDEPENDENT SECTOR, 1828 L Street NW, Washington, DC 20036 (202)223-8100

- IN THE PUBLIC INTEREST, 2000 P Street NW, Suite 315, Washington, DC 20036 (202)887-6737

- INSTITUTE FOR DEFENSE AND DISARMAMENT STUDIES, 2001 Beacon Street, Brookline, MA 02146 (617)734-4216

- INSTITUTE FOR POLICY STUDIES, 1901 Q Street NW, Washington, DC 20009 (202)234-9382

- INSTITUTE FOR SECURITY AND COOPERATION IN SPACE, 1776 Massachusetts Avenue NW, Washington, DC 20036 (202)547-3336

- INSTITUTE FOR SOVIET-AMERICAN RELATIONS, 2738 McKinley Street NW, Washington, DC 20015 (202)244-4725

- INSTITUTE FOR SPACE AND SECURITY STUDIES, 7720 Mary Cassatt Drive, Potomac, MD 20854

- INSTITUTE FOR THE STUDY OF WORLD POLITICS, 345 East Forty-Sixth Street, New York, NY 10017 (212)661-5900

- INTERFAITH CENTER ON CORPORATE RESPONSIBILITY, 475 Riverside Drive, Room 566, New York, NY 10027 (212)870-2936

- INTERFAITH CENTER TO REVERSE THE ARMS RACE, 132 North Euclid Avenue, Pasadena, CA 91101 (213)449-9430

- INTERHELP, 330 Ellis Street, Room 505, San Francisco, CA 94102 (415)673-5433

ORGANIZATIONAL INDEX (continued)

- INTERNATIONAL ASSOCIATION OF MACHINISTS & AEROSPACE WORKERS, 1300 Connecticut Avenue NW, Washington, DC 20036 (202)857-5200

- INTERNATIONAL INSTITUTE FOR STRATEGIC STUDIES, 23 Tavistock Street, London, WC2E 7NG, England

- INTERNATIONAL PHYSICIANS FOR PREVENTION OF NUCLEAR WAR, 225 Longwood Avenue, Boston, MA 02115 (617)738-9404

- INTERSECTION ASSOCIATES, 56 Chestnut Street, Cambridge, MA 02139 (617)492-5200

- JAPANESE AMERICAN PROFESSIONALS AGAINST NUCLEAR OMNICIDE, Denison University, Granville, OH 43023 (614)587-2327

- JOBS WITH PEACE CAMPAIGN, 76 Summer Street, Third floor, Boston, MA 02110 (617)338-5783

- JOINT STRATEGY AND ACTION COMMITTEE, 475 Riverside Drive, Room 560, New York, NY 10115 (212)870-3105

- JONAH HOUSE, 1933 Park Avenue, Baltimore, MD 21217 (301)669-6265

- JOURNAL FILMS INC., 903 Pitner Avenue, Evanston, IL 60202 (800)323-5448

- LABOR RESEARCH ASSOCIATION, 80 East 11th Street, New York, NY 10003 (212)473-1042

- LAWYER'S ALLIANCE FOR NUCLEAR ARMS CONTROl, 43 Charles Street, Suite 3, Boston, MA 02114 (617)227-0118

- LEADERSHIP INSTITUTE, 8001 Braddock Road, #550, Springfield, VA 22151 (703)321-8580

- LEAGUE OF WOMEN VOTERS, 1730 M Street NW, Washington, DC 20036 (202)429-1965

- LEGACY, 1275 Goldfinch Trail, Stow, OH 44224 (216)688-1253

- MEDIA ACCESS PROJECT, 1609 Connecticut Avenue, NW, Washington, DC 20009 (202)232-4300

- MEDIA NETWORK, 208 West 13th Street, New York, NY 10011 (212)620-0877

- MICHIGAN MEDIA RESOURCE CENTER, 400 4th Street, Ann Arbor, MI 48103 (313)764-5360

- MICROSECOND, 1636 Ashland Avenue, Santa Monica, CA 90405 (213)452-1609

- MID-PENINSULA CONVERSION PROJECT, 2 C View Street, Mountain View, CA 94041 (415)968-8798

- MIT PRESS, 28 Carleton Street, Cambridge, MA 02142 (617)253-2884

- MOBILIZATION FOR SURVIVAL, 853 Broadway, Suite 2109, New York, NY 10003 (212)533-0008

- NATIONAL ACTION RESEARCH ON THE MILITARY-INDUSTRIAL COMPLEX (NARMIC/AFSC), 1501 Cherry Street, Philadelphia, PA 19102 (215)241-7175

- NATIONAL ASSOCIATION OF ATOMIC VETERANS, 236 Massachusetts Avenue, NE, Suite 306, Washington, DC 20002 (202)543-7711

- NATIONAL ASSOCIATION OF BROADCASTERS, 1771 N Street NW, Washington, DC 20036 (800)368-5644

- NATIONAL CAMPAIGN TO SAVE THE ABM TREATY, 1346 Connecticut Avenue NW, Suite 1117, Washington, DC 20036 (202)463-4213

- NATIONAL CAMPAIGN TO STOP THE MX, see CAMPAIGN AGAINST MX

- NATIONAL COMMITTEE OF SOCIAL WORKERS FOR PEACE & DISARMAMENT, 7981 Eastern Avenue, Silver Spring, MD 20910 (301)565-0333

- NATIONAL CONSERVATIVE POLITICAL ACTION COMMITTEE, 1001 Prince Street, Alexandria, VA 22311 (703)684-1800

- NATIONAL COUNCIL FOR THE SOCIAL STUDIES, 3501 Newark Street NW, Washington, DC 20016 (202)966-7840

- NATIONAL COUNCIL OF CHURCHES, 110 Maryland Avenue NE, Washington, DC 20002 (202)544-2350

- NATIONAL EDUCATION ASSOCIATION, 1201 Sixteenth Street NW, Washington, DC 20036 (202)833-4000

- NATIONAL EUROMISSILE CLEARING HOUSE, P.O. Box 43243, Washington, DC 20010 (202)328-0897

- NATIONAL PEACE ACADEMY CAMPAIGN, 110 Maryland Avenue NE, Suite 409, Washington, DC 20002 (202)546-9500

ALTERNATIVES TO VIOLENCE

ORGANIZATIONAL INDEX (continued)

- NATIONAL TECHNICAL INFORMATION SERVICES, 5285 Port Royal Road, Springfield, VA 22161 (202)487-4650

- NETWORK, 806 Rhode Island Avenue NE, Washington, DC 20036 (202)526-4070

- NEW CENTURIES POLICIES, P.O. Box 2715, Boston, MA 02208 (617)354-5811

- NEW MANHATTAN PROJECT, 15 Rutherford Place, New York, NY 10003 (212)598-0972

- NEW YORKER FILMS, 16 West 61st Street, New York, NY 10023 (212)247-6110

- NUCLEAR ARSENAL PROJECT, 2216 Race Street, Denver, CO 80205 (303)377-7998

- NUCLEAR FREE AMERICA, 2521 Guilford Avenue, Baltimore, MD 21218 (301)235-3575

- NUCLEAR FREE ZONE REGISTRY, P.O. Box 172, Riverside, CA 92502 (714)674-6576

- NUCLEAR INFORMATION AND RESOURCE SERVICE, 1346 Connecticut Avenue, NW, 4th floor, Washington, DC 20036 (202)296-7552

- NUCLEAR TIMES, Room 542, 298 Fifth Avenue, New York, NY 10001 (212)563-5940

- NUCLEAR WAR GRAPHICS PROJECT, 100 Nevada Street, Northfield, MN 55057 (507)645-7736

- NUCLEAR WEAPONS FREEZE CAMPAIGN, 3195 South Grand Boulevard, St. Louis, MO 63118 (314)771-6211

- NUKEWATCH, 315 West Gorham Street, Madison, WI 53703 (608)256-4146

- NURSES ALLIANCE FOR PREVENTION OF NUCLEAR WAR, P.O. Box 319, Chestnut Hill, MA 02167 (617)232-5167

- OFFICE OF TECHNOLOGY ASSESSMENT, U.S. Congress, Washington, DC 20510 (202)224-8996

- PACKARD MANSE MEDIA PROJECT, Box 450, Stoughton, MA 02072 (617)344-9634

- PARENTS/TEACHERS FOR SOCIAL RESPONSIBILITY, P.O. Box 517, Moretown, VT 05660 (802)229-0137

- PASTORAL COUNSELORS FOR SOCIAL RESPONSIBILITY, 2439 McGregor Boulevard, Ft. Myers, FL 33901 (813)332-2273

- PAX CHRISTI, USA, 6337 West Cornelia Street, Chicago, IL 60634 (312)736-2113

- PAX WORLD FUND, 224 State Street, Portsmouth, NH 03801 (603)431-8022

- PEACE CHILD FOUNDATION, P.O. Box 33168, Washington, DC 20033 (202)628-6262

- PEACE LINKS-WOMEN AGAINST NUCLEAR WAR, 723 1/2 Eighth Street SE, Washington, DC 20003 (202)544-0805

- PEACE MEDIA PROJECT, 1801 18th Street, Washington, DC 20009 (202)328-9001

- PEACE NOW EDUCATION FUND, 331 East 38th Street, New York, NY 10016 (212)944-2403

- PEACEFUL USES OF OUTER SPACE, Room 3361-A, United Nations, New York, NY 10017

- PERFORMING ARTISTS FOR NUCLEAR DISARMAMENT, 225 Lafayette Street, New York, NY 10042 (212)431-7921

- PHYSICIANS FOR SOCIAL RESPONSIBILITY, 639 Massachusetts Avenue, Cambridge, MA 02139 (617)491-2754

- PRESBYTERIAN CHURCH (USA), 475 Riverside Drive, Room 1244M, New York, NY 10027 (212)870-2137

- PROFESSIONALS COALITION, 1345 Connecticut Avenue, Suite 1117, Washington, DC 20036 (202)887-6764

- PROJECT ON MILITARY PROCUREMENT, 201 Massachusetts Avenue NE, Suite 402, Washington, DC 20017 (202)636-3037

- PSYCHOLOGISTS FOR SOCIAL RESPONSIBILITY, 1841 Columbia Road NW, Suite 216, Washington, DC 20009 (202)797-7907

- PUBLIC CONCERNS FOUNDATION, Washington Spectator, P.O. Box 442, Merrifield, VA 22116 (703)691-1271

- PUBLIC INTEREST VIDEO NETWORK, 1736 Columbia Road NW, Washington, DC 20009 (202)797-8997

- PUBLIC MEDIA CENTER, 25 Scotland Street, San Francisco, CA 94133 (415)434-4403

- PUBLIC MEDIA INC., 119 West 57th Street, Suite 1511, New York, NY 10019 (212)247-9050

- PYRAMID FILMS, P.O. Box 1048, Santa Monica, CA 90406 (213)828-7577

©1986, 1990, 1992, 1993, 1994, 1995 PEACE GROWS, Inc., 513 W. Exchange St., Akron, OH 44302 (216)864-5442.

ORGANIZATIONAL INDEX (continued)

- RAINBOW SIGN: JEWISH PROJECT TO PREVENT NUCLEAR HOLOCAUST, 7041 McCallum Street, Philadelphia, PA 19119 (215)247-1081

- RELIGIOUS TASK FORCE MINORITY COALITION WORKING GROUP, 85 South Oxford Street, Brooklyn, NY 11217 (212)858-6882

- RESOURCE CENTER FOR NONVIOLENCE, P.O. Box 2324, Santa Cruz, CA 95063 (408)423-1626

- RIVERSIDE CHURCH DISARMAMENT PROGRAM, 490 Riverside Drive, New York, 10027 (212)870-6700

- SANE, 711 G Street SE, Washington, DC 20003 (202)546-7100

- SANE-RADIO PROGRAM, 5808 Greene Street, Philadelphia, PA 19144 (215)848-4100

- SEARCH FOR COMMON GROUND, 1346 Connecticut Avenue, NW, Suite 1126, Washington, DC 20002 (202)835-0777

- SHALOM CENTER, Church Road and Greenwood Avenue, Wyncote, PA 19095 (215)576-0800

- SISTER CITIES INTERNATIONAL, 1625 Eye Street NW, Washington, DC 20006 (202)293-5504

- SOCIAL GRAPHICS, 1120 Riverside Avenue, Baltimore, MD 21230 (301)837-3857

- SOJOURNERS, P.O. Box 29272, Washington, DC 20017 (202)636-3637

- SOUTHERN CHRISTIAN LEADERSHIP CONFERENCE, 334 Auburn Avenue, Atlanta, GA 30312 (404)522-1420

- STANLEY FOUNDATION, 420 East Third Street, Muscatine, IA 52761 (319)264-1500

- STATE DEPARTMENT, OFFICE OF PUBLIC PROGRAMS, Room 5831, Washington, DC 20520 (202)632-5927

- STOCKHOLDERS ALLIANCE AGAINST NUCLEAR WEAPONS, 119 Crooked Lane, Apt. B3, King of Prussia, PA 19406 (215)279-2214

- STOCKHOLM INTERNATIONAL PEACE RESEARCH INSTITUTE (SIPRI), Bergshamra, S-171 73 Solna, Sweden

- STUDENT/TEACHER ORGANIZATION TO PREVENT NUCLEAR WAR, Box 232, Northfield, MA 01360 (413)498-5311

- TRADE UNION COMMITTEE FOR THE TRANSFER AMENDMENT & ECONOMIC CONVERSION, see LABOR RESEARCH ASSOC.

- TRANSNATIONAL INSTITUTE, 20 Paulus Pottserstraat, Amsterdam, 1007, Holland

- TRAPROCK PEACE CENTER, Woolman Hill, Keets Road, Deerfield, MA 01342 (413)773-7427

- U.S. CATHOLIC CONFERENCE/PASTORAL LETTER, 1312 Massachusetts Avenue, NW, Washington, DC 20005 (202)659-6600

- U.S. CHAMBER OF COMMERCE, 1615 H Street NW, Washington, DC 20036 (202)659-6000

- U.S. PACIFIC NETWORK, 1346 Connecticut Avenue NW, #533, Washington, DC 20036 (202)296-8152

- U.S. CATHOLIC CONFERENCE, 1312 Massachusetts Avenue NW, Washington, DC 20005, (202)659-6785

- UNICEF, 866 United Nations Plaza, New York, NY 10017 (212)754-1234

- UNION OF AMERICAN HEBREW CONGREGATIONS, 2027 Massachusetts Avenue NW, Washington, DC 20005 (202)387-2800

- UNION OF CONCERNED SCIENTISTS, 26 Church Street, Cambridge MA 02238 (617)547-5552

- UNITED AUTO, AEROSPACE, & AGRICULTURAL IMPLEMENT WORKERS, 8000 East Jefferson Avenue, Detroit, MI 48214 (313)926-5000

- UNITED CAMPUSES TO PREVENT NUCLEAR WAR, 1346 Connecticut Avenue NW, #1019, Washington, DC 20036 (202)223-6206

- UNITED DOCUMENTARIES, (Women Make Movies Film Library), P.O. Box 315, Franklin Lakes, NJ 07417 (201)891-9240

- UNITED METHODIST SEMINARS ON NATIONAL AFFAIRS, 100 Maryland Avenue NE, Washington, DC 20002 (202)488-5644

- UNITED NATIONS, Public Inquiry Unit, New York, NY 10017 (212)754-6927

- UNITED NATIONS ASSOCIATION-USA, 300 East 42nd Street, New York, NY 10017 (212)697-3232

ORGANIZATIONAL INDEX (continued)

- US-USSR TRADE & ECONOMIC COUNCIL, INC., 805 3rd Avenue, New York, NY 10022 (212)644-4550

- VISION OF AMERICA AT PEACE, P.O. Box 9820, Berkeley, CA 94709 (415)496-0233

- WAR CONTROL PLANNERS, P.O. Box 19127, Washington, DC 20036 (202)785-0708

- WAR RESISTERS LEAGUE, 339 Lafayette Street, New York, NY 10012 (212)228-0450

- WILMINGTON COLLEGE PEACE RESOURCE CENTER, Pyle Center, Box 1183, Wilmington, OH 45477 (513)382-5338

- WITNESS FOR PEACE, P.O. Box 29241, Washington, DC 20017 (202)636-3642

- WOMEN AGAINST MILITARY MADNESS, 3255 Hennepin Avenue S, Minneapolis, MN 55408 (612)827-5364

- WOMEN STRIKE FOR PEACE, 145 South 13th Street, Philadelphia, PA 29107 (215)923-0681

- WOMEN'S ACTION FOR NUCLEAR DISARMAMENT, P.O. Box 153, New Town Branch, Boston, MA 02258 (617)643-6740

- WOMEN'S INTERNATIONAL LEAGUE FOR PEACE AND FREEDOM, 1213 Race Street, Philadelphia, PA 19107 (215)563-7110

- WORKING ASSETS MONEY FUND, 230 California Street, San Francisco, CA 94111 (800)543-8800

- WORLD CONSTITUTION AND PARLIAMENT ASSOCIATION, 1480 Hoyt Street, Suite 31, Lakewood, CO 80215

- WORLD FEDERALIST ASSOCIATION, P.O. Box 15250, Washington, DC 20003 (202)296-0941

- WORLD FUTURE SOCIETY, 4916 St. Elmo Avenue, Bethesda, MD 20814 (301)656-8274

- WORLD PEACEMAKERS, 2025 Massachusetts Avenue NW, Washington, DC 20036 (202)265-7582

- WORLD POLICY INSTITUTE, 777 United Nations Plaza, New York, NY 10017 (212)490-0010

- WORLD PRIORITIES, Box 1003, Leesburg, VA 22075 (617)253-5646

- WORLD SERVICE AUTHORITY, 1012 14th Street NW, Suite 1101, Washington, DC 20045 (202)638-2662

- WORLD WITHOUT WAR PUBLICATIONS, 420 South Wabash, Chicago, IL 60605 (312)663-4250

- Y.W.C.A., 135 West 50th Street, New York, NY 10020 (212)621-5189

©1986, 1990, 1992, 1993, 1994, 1995 PEACE GROWS, Inc., 513 W. Exchange St., Akron, OH 44302 (216)864-5442.

ALTERNATIVES TO VIOLENCE   For use with all cases

NONVIOLENT POWER
Case analysis sheet

1. What are the facts of the conflict?

2. Why use nonviolence?
   (Refer to reading on Use of Nonviolence, *Workbook,* Page 10.)

3. What human need(s) are being denied or are perceived to be denied?

4. What is the nonviolent solution or suggested solution?

5. What nonviolent tactic(s) were used or proposed?
   (Refer to reading on Differences Between Violence and Nonviolence, Principles and Techniques, *Workbook* Pages 15 - 16.)

6. Why did or would the tactics work?

YOUR NAME_____

©1986, 1990, 1992, 1993, 1994, 1995 PEACE GROWS, Inc., 513 W. Exchange St., Akron, OH 44302 (216)864-5442.

ALTERNATIVES TO VIOLENCE For use with all cases

NONVIOLENT POWER
Case analysis sheet

1. What are the facts of the conflict?

2. Why use nonviolence?
   (Refer to reading on Use of Nonviolence, *Workbook,* Page 10.)

3. What human need(s) are being denied or are perceived to be denied?

4. What is the nonviolent solution or suggested solution?

5. What nonviolent tactic(s) were used or proposed?
   (Refer to reading on Differences Between Violence and Nonviolence, Principles and Techniques, *Workbook* Pages 15 - 16.)

6. Why did or would the tactics work?

YOUR NAME_____

©1986, 1990, 1992, 1993, 1994, 1995 PEACE GROWS, Inc., 513 W. Exchange St., Akron, OH 44302 (216)864

ALTERNATIVES TO VIOLENCE

NONVIOLENT POWER
Case analysis sheet

1. What are the facts of the conflict?

2. Why use nonviolence?
   (Refer to reading on Use of Nonviolence, *Workbook,* Page 10.)

3. What human need(s) are being denied or are perceived to be denied?

4. What is the nonviolent solution or suggested solution?

5. What nonviolent tactic(s) were used or proposed?
   (Refer to reading on Differences Between Violence and Nonviolence, Principles and Techniques, *Workbook* Pages 15 - 16.)

6. Why did or would the tactics work?

YOUR NAME_____

©1986, 1990, 1992, 1993, 1994, 1995 PEACE GROWS, Inc., 513 W. Exchange St., Akron, OH 44302 (216)864-5442.

ALTERNATIVES TO VIOLENCE — For use with all cases — 260

NONVIOLENT POWER
Case analysis sheet

1. What are the facts of the conflict?

2. Why use nonviolence?
   (Refer to reading on Use of Nonviolence, *Workbook,* Page 10.)

3. What human need(s) are being denied or are perceived to be denied?

4. What is the nonviolent solution or suggested solution?

5. What nonviolent tactic(s) were used or proposed?
   (Refer to reading on Differences Between Violence and Nonviolence, Principles and Techniques, *Workbook* Pages 15 - 16.)

6. Why did or would the tactics work?

YOUR NAME_____ _____

©1986, 1990, 1992, 1993, 1994, 1995 PEACE GROWS, Inc., 513 W. Exchange St., Akron, OH 44302 (216)864-

ALTERNATIVES TO VIOLENCE   For use with all cases

NONVIOLENT POWER
Case analysis sheet

1. What are the facts of the conflict?

2. Why use nonviolence?
   (Refer to reading on Use of Nonviolence, *Workbook,* Page 10.)

3. What human need(s) are being denied or are perceived to be denied?

4. What is the nonviolent solution or suggested solution?

5. What nonviolent tactic(s) were used or proposed?
   (Refer to reading on Differences Between Violence and Nonviolence, Principles and Techniques, *Workbook* Pages 15 - 16.)

6. Why did or would the tactics work?

YOUR NAME_____

©1986, 1990, 1992, 1993, 1994, 1995 PEACE GROWS, Inc., 513 W. Exchange St., Akron, OH 44302 (216)864-5442.

ALTERNATIVES TO VIOLENCE

NONVIOLENT POWER
Case analysis sheet

1. What are the facts of the conflict?

2. Why use nonviolence?
   (Refer to reading on Use of Nonviolence, *Workbook,* Page 10.)

3. What human need(s) are being denied or are perceived to be denied?

4. What is the nonviolent solution or suggested solution?

5. What nonviolent tactic(s) were used or proposed?
   (Refer to reading on Differences Between Violence and Nonviolence, Principles and Techniques, *Workbook* Pages 15 - 16.)

6. Why did or would the tactics work?

YOUR NAME_____

©1986, 1990, 1992, 1993, 1994, 1995 PEACE GROWS, Inc., 513 W. Exchange St., Akron, OH 44302 (216)864-

ALTERNATIVES TO VIOLENCE

NONVIOLENT POWER
Case analysis sheet

1. What are the facts of the conflict?

2. Why use nonviolence?
   (Refer to reading on Use of Nonviolence, *Workbook,* Page 10.)

3. What human need(s) are being denied or are perceived to be denied?

4. What is the nonviolent solution or suggested solution?

5. What nonviolent tactic(s) were used or proposed?
   (Refer to reading on Differences Between Violence and Nonviolence, Principles and Techniques, *Workbook* Pages 15 - 16.)

6. Why did or would the tactics work?

YOUR NAME_____

©1986, 1990, 1992, 1993, 1994, 1995 PEACE GROWS, Inc., 513 W. Exchange St., Akron, OH 44302 (216)864-5442.

ALTERNATIVES TO VIOLENCE   For use with all cases   264

NONVIOLENT POWER
Case analysis sheet

1. What are the facts of the conflict?

2. Why use nonviolence?
   (Refer to reading on Use of Nonviolence, *Workbook,* Page 10.)

3. What human need(s) are being denied or are perceived to be denied?

4. What is the nonviolent solution or suggested solution?

5. What nonviolent tactic(s) were used or proposed?
   (Refer to reading on Differences Between Violence and Nonviolence, Principles and Techniques, *Workbook* Pages 15 - 16.)

6. Why did or would the tactics work?

YOUR NAME_____

©1986, 1990, 1992, 1993, 1994, 1995 PEACE GROWS, Inc., 513 W. Exchange St., Akron, OH 44302 (216)864-

ALTERNATIVES TO VIOLENCE   For use with all cases

NONVIOLENT POWER
Case analysis sheet

1. What are the facts of the conflict?

2. Why use nonviolence?
   (Refer to reading on Use of Nonviolence, *Workbook,* Page 10.)

3. What human need(s) are being denied or are perceived to be denied?

4. What is the nonviolent solution or suggested solution?

5. What nonviolent tactic(s) were used or proposed?
   (Refer to reading on Differences Between Violence and Nonviolence, Principles and Techniques, *Workbook* Pages 15 - 16.)

6. Why did or would the tactics work?

YOUR NAME_____

©1986, 1990, 1992, 1993, 1994, 1995 PEACE GROWS, Inc., 513 W. Exchange St., Akron, OH 44302 (216)864-5442.

ALTERNATIVES TO VIOLENCE   For use with all cases

NONVIOLENT POWER
Case analysis sheet

1. What are the facts of the conflict?

2. Why use nonviolence?
   (Refer to reading on Use of Nonviolence, *Workbook,* Page 10.)

3. What human need(s) are being denied or are perceived to be denied?

4. What is the nonviolent solution or suggested solution?

5. What nonviolent tactic(s) were used or proposed?
   (Refer to reading on Differences Between Violence and Nonviolence, Principles and Techniques, *Workbook* Pages 15 - 16.)

6. Why did or would the tactics work?

YOUR NAME_____

©1986, 1990, 1992, 1993, 1994, 1995 PEACE GROWS, Inc., 513 W. Exchange St., Akron, OH 44302 (216)864-5

ALTERNATIVES TO VIOLENCE

NONVIOLENT POWER
Case analysis sheet

1. What are the facts of the conflict?

2. Why use nonviolence?
   (Refer to reading on Use of Nonviolence, *Workbook,* Page 10.)

3. What human need(s) are being denied or are perceived to be denied?

4. What is the nonviolent solution or suggested solution?

5. What nonviolent tactic(s) were used or proposed?
   (Refer to reading on Differences Between Violence and Nonviolence, Principles and Techniques, *Workbook* Pages 15 - 16.)

6. Why did or would the tactics work?

YOUR NAME_____

ALTERNATIVES TO VIOLENCE — For use with all cases

NONVIOLENT POWER
Case analysis sheet

1. What are the facts of the conflict?

2. Why use nonviolence?
   (Refer to reading on Use of Nonviolence, *Workbook,* Page 10.)

3. What human need(s) are being denied or are perceived to be denied?

4. What is the nonviolent solution or suggested solution?

5. What nonviolent tactic(s) were used or proposed?
   (Refer to reading on Differences Between Violence and Nonviolence, Principles and Techniques, *Workbook* Pages 15 - 16.)

6. Why did or would the tactics work?

YOUR NAME_____

©1986, 1990, 1992, 1993, 1994, 1995 PEACE GROWS, Inc., 513 W. Exchange St., Akron, OH 44302 (216)864-

ALTERNATIVES TO VIOLENCE

NONVIOLENT POWER
Case analysis sheet

1. What are the facts of the conflict?

2. Why use nonviolence?
   (Refer to reading on Use of Nonviolence, *Workbook,* Page 10.)

3. What human need(s) are being denied or are perceived to be denied?

4. What is the nonviolent solution or suggested solution?

5. What nonviolent tactic(s) were used or proposed?
   (Refer to reading on Differences Between Violence and Nonviolence, Principles and Techniques, *Workbook* Pages 15 - 16.)

6. Why did or would the tactics work?

YOUR NAME_____

ALTERNATIVES TO VIOLENCE

NONVIOLENT POWER
Case analysis sheet

1. What are the facts of the conflict?

2. Why use nonviolence?
   (Refer to reading on Use of Nonviolence, *Workbook,* Page 10.)

3. What human need(s) are being denied or are perceived to be denied?

4. What is the nonviolent solution or suggested solution?

5. What nonviolent tactic(s) were used or proposed?
   (Refer to reading on Differences Between Violence and Nonviolence, Principles and Techniques, *Workbook* Pages 15 - 16.)

6. Why did or would the tactics work?

YOUR NAME_____

©1986, 1990, 1992, 1993, 1994, 1995 PEACE GROWS, Inc., 513 W. Exchange St., Akron, OH 44302 (216)864

ALTERNATIVES TO VIOLENCE   For use with all cases

NONVIOLENT POWER
Case analysis sheet

1. What are the facts of the conflict?

2. Why use nonviolence?
   (Refer to reading on Use of Nonviolence, *Workbook,* Page 10.)

3. What human need(s) are being denied or are perceived to be denied?

4. What is the nonviolent solution or suggested solution?

5. What nonviolent tactic(s) were used or proposed?
   (Refer to reading on Differences Between Violence and Nonviolence, Principles and Techniques, *Workbook* Pages 15 - 16.)

6. Why did or would the tactics work?

YOUR NAME_____

©1986, 1990, 1992, 1993, 1994, 1995 PEACE GROWS, Inc., 513 W. Exchange St., Akron, OH 44302 (216)864-5442.

ALTERNATIVES TO VIOLENCE

NONVIOLENT POWER
Case analysis sheet

1. What are the facts of the conflict?

2. Why use nonviolence?
   (Refer to reading on Use of Nonviolence, *Workbook*, Page 10.)

3. What human need(s) are being denied or are perceived to be denied?

4. What is the nonviolent solution or suggested solution?

5. What nonviolent tactic(s) were used or proposed?
   (Refer to reading on Differences Between Violence and Nonviolence, Principles and Techniques, *Workbook* Pages 15 - 16.)

6. Why did or would the tactics work?

YOUR NAME_____

©1986, 1990, 1992, 1993, 1994, 1995 PEACE GROWS, Inc., 513 W. Exchange St., Akron, OH 44302 (216)864-

ALTERNATIVES TO VIOLENCE

NONVIOLENT POWER
Case analysis sheet

1. What are the facts of the conflict?

2. Why use nonviolence?
   (Refer to reading on Use of Nonviolence, *Workbook,* Page 10.)

3. What human need(s) are being denied or are perceived to be denied?

4. What is the nonviolent solution or suggested solution?

5. What nonviolent tactic(s) were used or proposed?
   (Refer to reading on Differences Between Violence and Nonviolence, Principles and Techniques, *Workbook* Pages 15 - 16.)

6. Why did or would the tactics work?

YOUR NAME_____

©1986, 1990, 1992, 1993, 1994, 1995 PEACE GROWS, Inc., 513 W. Exchange St., Akron, OH 44302 (216)864-5442.

ALTERNATIVES TO VIOLENCE

NONVIOLENT POWER
Case analysis sheet

1. What are the facts of the conflict?

2. Why use nonviolence?
   (Refer to reading on Use of Nonviolence, *Workbook,* Page 10.)

3. What human need(s) are being denied or are perceived to be denied?

4. What is the nonviolent solution or suggested solution?

5. What nonviolent tactic(s) were used or proposed?
   (Refer to reading on Differences Between Violence and Nonviolence, Principles and Techniques, *Workbook* Pages 15 - 16.)

6. Why did or would the tactics work?

YOUR NAME_____

©1986, 1990, 1992, 1993, 1994, 1995 PEACE GROWS, Inc., 513 W. Exchange St., Akron, OH 44302 (216)864

ALTERNATIVES TO VIOLENCE **For use with all cases**

NONVIOLENT POWER
Case analysis sheet

1. What are the facts of the conflict?

2. Why use nonviolence?
   (Refer to reading on Use of Nonviolence, *Workbook,* Page 10.)

3. What human need(s) are being denied or are perceived to be denied?

4. What is the nonviolent solution or suggested solution?

5. What nonviolent tactic(s) were used or proposed?
   (Refer to reading on Differences Between Violence and Nonviolence, Principles and Techniques, *Workbook* Pages 15 - 16.)

6. Why did or would the tactics work?

YOUR NAME_____

©1986, 1990, 1992, 1993, 1994, 1995 PEACE GROWS, Inc., 513 W. Exchange St., Akron, OH 44302 (216)864-5442.

ALTERNATIVES TO VIOLENCE — For use with all cases

NONVIOLENT POWER
Case analysis sheet

1. What are the facts of the conflict?

2. Why use nonviolence?
   (Refer to reading on Use of Nonviolence, *Workbook,* Page 10.)

3. What human need(s) are being denied or are perceived to be denied?

4. What is the nonviolent solution or suggested solution?

5. What nonviolent tactic(s) were used or proposed?
   (Refer to reading on Differences Between Violence and Nonviolence, Principles and Techniques, *Workbook* Pages 15 - 16.)

6. Why did or would the tactics work?

YOUR NAME_____

©1986, 1990, 1992, 1993, 1994, 1995 PEACE GROWS, Inc., 513 W. Exchange St., Akron, OH 44302 (216)86-

CASE HISTORIES

OF
PEACEFUL
CONFLICT
RESOLUTION

from the

ALTERNATIVES TO VIOLENCE Course and *Workbook*

produced by

PEACE GROWS — Grass Roots Outreach Works

PREFACE

The *ALTERNATIVES TO VIOLENCE* curriculum uses a case analysis approach—learning from successful applications. The folowing cases are examples from history, from current newspaper and magazine articles, and from experiences of students while taking the *ALTERNATIVES TO VIOLENCE* course.

The case numbers correspond to the session numbers in the *ALTERNATIVES TO VIOLENCE WORKBOOK*. For instance, Case 5-A means this is an application of the principles, strategies and/or techniques presented in Session 5.

In the course, offered in schools, colleges and churches, we role play and analyze the cases to help us not only think about but also feel alternative responses to conflict. If these skills worked for others, they might work for you, also. These cases can give you insight into working on your own "alternatives."

LIST OF CASES

CASE 1-A: QUICK CHANGE ARTIST
CASE 1-B: GREETINGS!
CASE 1-C: BUDDHIST ABBOT'S COURAGE
CASE 2-A: RIVER OF DEATH IN BRAZIL
CASE 2-B: ME FIRST!
CASE 2-C: PUT ON A HAPPY FACE
CASE 2-D: DE-ESCALATING CONFLICT
CASE 3-A: ROSA'S QUIET COURAGE
CASE 3-B: UP TO THEIR SHOULDERS IN FLOODWATERS
CASE 3-C: GETTING INVOLVED
CASE 3-D: STUDENT PARTICIPATION
CASE 4-A: BEDROOM INTRUDER
CASE 4-B: GANDHI'S FAMOUS "SALT MARCH"
CASE 4-C: STEERING A TATTLER
CASE 4-D: SYNTHIA'S LEARNING
CASE 4-E: NEW KINDERGARTEN REBEL
CASE 4-F: WITH CALM WORDS,
CASE 5-A: QUAKER JUSTICE FORGES PEACE
CASE 5-B: LINGUISTIC MIRACLES
CASE 5-C: QUAKER DOCTOR'S ANSWER
CASE 5-D: DISCUSSION IMPROVES
CASE 5-E: ANOTHER TEACHER'S EXPERIENCE
CASE 5-F: FAMILY CIRCLE
CASE 5-G: CHALLENGE OF REALLY LISTENING
CASE 5-H: TAKE YOUR TURN
CASE 6-A: AN ABERRANT STUDENT
CASE 6-B: HANDLING ANGER
CASE 6-C: NEW APPROACH
CASE 6-D: SMILE
CASE 7-A: TROUBLE IN THE SUBWAY
CASE 7-B: HANDLING TEACHER ANGER
CASE 7-C: THOSE ANGRY PHONE CALLS
CASE 7-D: FIRST GRADERS TALK TO THEMSELVES
CASE 7-E: NAME CALLING
CASE 7-F: STEP BY STEP
CASE 8-A: MEDIATION SUCCEEDS
CASE 8-B: A TOUGH CHALLENGE FOR MEDIATION
CASE 8-C: MEDIATION QUICKIE
CASE 8-D: DISPUTE BECAME BLOODY
CASE 9-A: HOW DO YOU RESPOND TO BEING KNIFED?
CASE 9-B: CELL BLOCK RAPE THREATENED
CASE 9-C: MUGGER DIVERTED FROM VIOLENCE
CASE 9-D: HOLDUP
CASE 9-E: CRAZY LIKE TWO FOXES
CASE 9-F: ALLEY ATTACK
CASE 9-G: HE SCREAMED ANYWAY
CASE 10-A: JOHN WHO?
CASE 10-B: IT TAKES STIFF COURAGE
CASE 10-C: MERCY VOYAGES OF THE PHOENIX
CASE 10-D: SOFT ANSWER WORKS
CASE 10-E: FOLLOWING A HIGHER LAW
CASE 11-A: A TORMENTING MAJORITY
CASE 11-B: STOLEN EAR MUFFS
CASE 11-C: SPONTANEOUS STUDENT REACTIONS
CASE 11-D: NONVIOLENT INTERVENTION
CASE 11-E: RESTROOM MANNERS
CASE 11-F: A CONFLICT SITUATION:
CASE 12-A: ZEROING IN ON A PROBLEM
CASE 12-B: A WAVE OF IDEAS
CASE 12-C: THOSE DARN KIDS
CASE 13-A: BATTLE OF NERVES
CASE 13-B: GRAPES OF WRATH
CASE 13-C: CONTEMPORARY INQUISITION
CASE 13-D: UNION BASHING
CASE 13-E: WOMEN SUFFRAGISTS ASK:
CASE 13-F: SHOOTING OUR OWN CITIZENS IN KENT
CASE 14-A: WHEN INVASION OCCURS
CASE 14-B: STEMMING THE TIDE
CASE 14-C: A QUICK KISS
CASE 14-D: OVERCOMING SOCIETAL VIOLENCE
CASE 15-A: THOSE WHO LIVE BY THE SWORD
CASE 15-B: CANOES BLOCK ARMS TO PAKISTAN
CASE 15-C: MILESTONE TOWARD PEACE
CASE 15-D: NATIVE AMERICANS ON A WARPATH
CASE 15-E: KING CHRISTIAN PROVES
CASE 15-F: NONVIOLENT HEROISM
CASE 16-A: CITIZENS OF THE PLANET
CASE 16-B: EFFECTIVE TECHNIQUE
CASE 17-A: NONVIOLENT COMMITMENT
CASE 17-B: STRAIGHT TALK
CASE 18-A: WIDOW COMBS VS. CAPERTON COAL
CASE 18-B: A BETTER FUTURE
CASE 18-C: IDEAS TO TRY

BIBLIOGRAPHY
for historical cases

Crane, Mary. "Rape Avoidance And Resistance: A Nonviolent Approach." *WIN Magazine,* Apr. 26, 1979.

Crowell, Suzanne. *Appalachian People's History Book.* Louisville: Southern Conference Educational Fund, 1971.

Gregg, Richard B. *The Power Of Nonviolence.* New York: Schocken Books, 1959 (1st ed. 1939).

Hunter, Allan A. *Courage In Both Hands.* New York: Ballantine Books, 1962.

Lynd, Alice. *We Won't Go: Personal Accounts Of War Objectors.* Boston: Beacon Press, 1968.

Matthiesson, Peter. *Sal Si Puedes: Cesar Chavez And The New American Revolution.*

Morris, Mark. "Nonviolent Self Defense." *WIN Magazine,* 1974.

Samuel, Dorothy T. *Safe Passage On City Streets.* Nashville: Abingdon Press, 1975.

Sharp, Gene. *The Politics of Nonviolent Action.* Boston: Extending Horizons Books (Porter Sargent Publishers, 11 Beacon Street, Boston, MA 02108), 1973.

Sibley, Mulford Q. *The Quiet Battle: Writings On The Theory And Practice Of Nonviolent Resistance.* Boston: Beacon Press, 1963.

War Resisters League. *Nonviolent Struggle Around the World.* (1978 Peace Calendar from WRL: 339 Lafayette Street, New York, NY 10012).

Woolman, John. *The Journal of John Woolman.* Secaucus, NJ: Citadel Press, 1961.

QUICK CHANGE ARTIST

turns muggers into helpers.

An older woman was walking down a city street carrying her heavy shopping bags. Two young men came up behind her and overtook her on both sides. She knew what they were up to but she was far from any residence or person she knew.

Before they got close enough to touch her or to say anything, she turned and grinned at each of them, thrust her packages into their arms, and told them how relieved she felt now that they had come along.

"I was rather nervous on this street," she said, "and these bags are so heavy. Would you help me?" The men took the bags instinctively, and off the three of them walked together, the woman thanking the two men all the while for being such good and helpful people.

See *Safe Passage on City Streets* (Samuel), p. 89.

GREETINGS!
(and forget what you were thinking).

One night at about midnight, I was walking to my house in Alliance down the main street. As I walked past a group of kids who were busy harassing passers-by, I looked over and said hello.

At first, this just prompted some nasty comments about my appearance. I just ignored them and walked on, but soon I became aware that two of them were following me on foot. I continued to ignore them and they continued to get closer. Soon, when they were right up behind me, I spun around and greeted them, "Good morning, how are you?". They looked at each other, confused, turned around and left.

**from David Schall, September, 1986.
Reported personal experience of a college junior.**

BUDDHIST ABBOT'S COURAGE
converts a warrior king to nonviolence.

In India, about 261 B.C., a Buddhist abbot confronted King Asoka, a famous warrior, who had pursued an enemy into his monastery. The King commanded, "Stand aside or I'll cut you down!" The abbot replied fearlessly, "You have the power but if you do you will find that the law which is now speaking through this body will stand always in front of you, accusing you." In spite of further harassment, the abbot continued to refuse until King Asoka decided to withdraw.

Subsequent thought about the situation and about the abbot's courage followed, during which Asoka himself was won over to the idea of nonviolence. In about 259 B.C. he established the world's first nonviolent empire. For thirty years uninterrupted peace was maintained. Trees were planted far and wide. Wells were dug; hospitals built. Medicines were distributed, and the aged and infirm taken care of. Women achieved a more equitable position in society. Swords gave way to education. Missionaries went to other countries, not to impose but to share the way of life of the new empire.

When India became a free nation again in 1947, her flag contained only Asoka's symbol: a wheel and the Sanskrit motto, "Truth Conquers."

See *Courage in Both Hands* (Hunter), pp. 100-101.

RIVER OF DEATH IN BRAZIL

Persistent effort over 37 years brings peace.

For centuries, the white colonists' Indian program in Brazil was one of extermination only. "Shoot the Indians on sight" was the general policy. The Chavantes Indians, living close to the center of South America, made a specialty of answering white people's atrocities with their own atrocities. Over 300 years ago, the river in their territory was renamed the River of Death after it supposedly ran red with the blood of a party of white adventurers who thought they could invade Chavantes country militarily. White rubber prospectors, celebrating on a Saturday night, would grab an Indian, pour kerosene over him or her, light it and fire shots at the fleeing flames as the victim ran for the river in the dark.

Onto this scene came Candide Rondon, an officer in the Brazilian army excited by the creative possibilities of a new approach. Rondon was eventually successful in instating a totally new policy: "Die if you must, but never kill an Indian." By 1910 he had persuaded the Brazilian government to establish the Indian Protection Service. It was a long struggle.

Once, six of his representatives went into the jungle to make friendly contact with the Chavantes but were misunderstood and massacred. Even though guns for animal protection were with them they were found in their boxes **unopened**. Apparently, these men really believed that it was better to be murdered by the Indians than to kill an Indian.

Gradually, the message began to get through to the Chavantes that the white people were no longer there to harm them. In 1945, Francisco Meireles and ten helpers planted peace offerings near Chavantes dwellings. Eventually some disappeared, replaced by broken arrows. Interpreting this as a gesture of friendship, Meireles and his friends shouted greetings. The Indians came out, more and more at once. As the Brazilians' presents gave out, hostility again developed and they had to flee a rain of arrows which killed one white man and one horse. But Meireles remained persistent.

Finally in 1947, he heard of large numbers of Chavantes gathering on the opposite river bank. Without hesitating he went over to meet them. No sooner had he stepped ashore than Apoena himself, the formerly ruthless chief, rushed forward, threw his arms around Meireles, and wept. As Candide Rondon wired Meireles, "This is a victory of patience, suffering and love."

See *Courage in Both Hands* (Hunter), pp. 89-92.

ALTERNATIVES TO VIOLENCE

ME FIRST!

Better a compromise.

When I asked row two of my first grade class to line up for a morning restroom break Monday, two six-year-old boys walked quickly to the line, each hoping to stand behind Andy, the line leader. Each believed he deserved that "honored" position and was very willing to let the other know through verbal barbs.

I had observed the incident and was, of course, hoping the boys would be able to solve their problems. However, after approximately ten seconds, I realized that they were unable to do so and that the children near them were becoming agitated.

I then calmly walked over to the two rascals, and in a soft voice said, "Why don't you stand side by side as friends often do?"

Immediately, one of the two, with a smile spreading quickly over his face, looked at the other and said in an amusing voice, "Oh, yeah!" Both boys then stood side by side, right behind the line leader.

Submitted by a teacher from Akron, Ohio, while taking the *ALTERNATIVES TO VIOLENCE* course.

PUT ON A HAPPY FACE

Learning also occurs in school's corridor.

Gina, Lisa and Erin, three hearing-impaired students had a disagreement with Jill, a student who could hear. The three hearing-impaired students told their teacher about the problem. Gina and Lisa had made faces at Jill and Jill made a face back. Soon they were making faces at each other every time they met in the hall.

By the time the teacher heard about it, the conflict had escalated. The students were now bumping shoulders while passing in the hall. Although Erin is hearing-impaired, her speech is very good. Erin called Jill some names and also told her to stop her bumping into the girls. At this point, Jill's friends started making faces and bumping shoulders with the girls in the school hall.

The teacher spent two health classes brainstorming ideas to de-escalate the conflict and help solve the problem. Finally, Gina, Lisa and Erin decided to try smiling instead of making faces and bumping shoulders. They decided to try this technique for one week. The three students wrote an agreement and had it witnessed by another classmate. They wrote: "For the next week, every time we see Jill, we will smile. We will not make faces or call her names."

By the end of the week, Gina and Lisa were walking with Jill and Jill's friends without any more unfriendly gestures. Erin, however, had continued to make faces but kept some distance from Jill in the hall. Sometime later she decided to approach Jill to talk about the problem.

Submitted by a teacher from Mayfield Heights, Ohio, while taking the ALTERNATIVES TO VIOLENCE course.

ALTERNATIVES TO VIOLENCE CASE 2-D

DE-ESCALATING CONFLICT

with good humor.

My new mother-in-law was coming for dinner Sunday for the first time. Probably because of nervousness, I had been arguing with my husband about going to Click's for a new sweeper belt. (important stuff!)

To make a long story short, my husband did a "natural" de-escalator of conflict. This blessed man has never taken a course on this. The minute his mom came through the door he took her over to a picture I recently gave him. In a warm, sincere voice he said, "Look what my wife bought me, Mom." The inscription on the picture says, "Happiness is being married to your best friend." His humor and good nature immediately melted my angry feelings.

Submitted by a participant from the Interparish School of Religion, Akron, Ohio, while taking the *ALTERNATIVES TO VIOLENCE* course.

©1986, 1990, 1992, 1993, 1994, 1995 PEACE GROWS, Inc., 513 W. Exchange St., Akron, OH 44302 (216)864

ROSA'S QUIET COURAGE
Her refusal to be intimidated started the Civil Rights Movement.

On December 1, 1955, Rosa Parks, a Black seamstress, boarded a bus in Montgomery, Alabama, on her way home from work. Tired, she sat in the first row of seats behind the full white section. When more white people boarded, as was the custom, Ms. Parks was asked to move farther back to give seats to the whites. The Black section was full by this time, so she would have had to stand. Three other Black people, sitting in the same row, did move back, but she quietly and with dignity refused.

The driver called the police, and Rosa Parks was arrested for violating the city's segregation ordinance. Probably because she was so highly respected in the Black community, her arrest triggered the long-smoldering resentment of the Black community into action. At the suggestion of the (Black) Women's Political Council, a mass meeting of Black citizens decided to boycott all buses on Monday, December 5th, and to meet that night to determine further action.

The boycott was a complete success. Not more than a tiny handful of Montgomery's 50,000 Black citizens rode a bus that day. They realized, though, that one day's effort, would mean little. At Monday's mass meeting, the community decided unanimously to continue the boycott until:

(1) courteous treatment of Blacks by bus operators was guaranteed,

(2) seating on a first-come, first-served basis, whites beginning in the front and Blacks in the back, and

(3) Black bus operators to be employed on predominantly Black routes. To direct the bus boycott, they formed the Montgomery Improvement Association and chose as its president a young, well-educated minister, Martin Luther King, Jr.

With many trials and tribulations, the bus boycott continued for over one year. The whole world knew what was going on, not only regarding the unjust seating, but regarding the bombings, harassment arrests, the unjust legal treatment. Opinion was so in sympathy that when the U.S. Supreme Court itself acted, the boycott finally ended.

When Dr. Martin Luther King, Jr. boarded the first bus, the driver smiled cordially and said, "You're Dr. King, aren't you? We're glad to have you this morning."

Violence against Black people in Montgomery and elsewhere did not end with the end of the bus boycott, but the widespread belief that Blacks approved of their inferior status under segregation was shattered, and the Civil Rights movement began.

See *The Power of Nonviolence* (Gregg), pp. 36-41, and *Nonviolence* (Miller), pp. 298-305.

ALTERNATIVES TO VIOLENCE

UP TO THEIR SHOULDERS IN FLOODWATERS

Months long vigil overcomes caste barrier.

For centuries a caste system was maintained in India. Brahmans had refused the (lower-caste) 'untouchables' the use of a particular road through the village of Vykom, in southern India, for generations.

Some followers of Mohandas Gandhi decided it was only just that the road should be open to all human beings. They started the struggle by taking several 'untouchable' friends with them along the road into the Brahman quarter. Beatings and arrests resulted.

Volunteers all over India heard about the action and poured in to replace them. The state forbade more arrests but ordered the police to prevent any of the reformers from using the road. The police set up a barricade across the road. The reformers simply stood before this barrier in an attitude of prayer. They organized themselves into six-hour, round-the-clock shifts, and a hut was built nearby.

The duties were undertaken on a religious basis. Never did the demonstrators use any violence, though the vigil went on for months. They rainy season came: the road was flooded. The volunteers continued to stand, sometimes with water up to their shoulders, while the police continued their barricade in small boats. Due to the hardships, the length of shifts shortened, with more and more volunteers taking part in the action. The position of the authorities seemed more and more unreasonable both to the public and to the government itself.

Finally the Brahmans' hearts were melted. The Vykom road was opened to all comers. Reverberations were felt throughout India in removing other restrictions and strengthening the cause of tax reform.

See *The Power of Nonviolence* (Gregg), pp. 19-20; and *Courage in Both Hands* (Hunter), pp. 77-78.

GETTING INVOLVED

solves pupil problems.

One day a third-grader was constantly throwing spit balls during the entire period she was in my room. Why? I asked myself—only for attention—she loved to hear the other children complain to me. I could ignore it, but they couldn't.

I sent the child with another responsible child on an errand to another classroom—the farthest one from my room. While they were out, I explained to the class that the student needed special attention and help from all of us.

I would review classroom rules with her—letting her decide which one she had broken. Then I told the class the next time one of them "received" one of her spit balls to just quietly return it to her and ask if she had forgotten the rule or if they could sit with her and help her participate or do her class work. She was shocked at their calm manner over the spit balls and did accept their help.

Submitted by a teacher from Akron, Ohio, while taking the *ALTERNATIVES TO VIOLENCE* course.

ALTERNATIVES TO VIOLENCE   CASE 3-D

STUDENT PARTICIPATION
produces a cooperative atmosphere.

A Columbus, Ohio, inner city high school which had been predominantly black was integrated under a black principal. Much conflict, trouble and violence was anticipated.

However, through student participation and easy direct access for every student to the administration, it became an outstanding high school with a good spirit and a friendly, cooperative, non-violent atmosphere. The school had a large enough auditorium to bring the whole student body together. Their problems were discussed and ways of handling them determined. The rules of conduct were established there together. They constituted a contract voluntarily joined into by the students and the administration. Having understood the problems, why they were problems and having helped workout the solutions made the student body supportive of, not antagonistic to, the regulations.

Rather than eating his lunch in a secluded faculty lounge or somewhere outside the school, the principal every noon possible took his tray through the regular student cafeteria line and sat right down at a table in the middle of the cafeteria to eat with the students. Thus, he came to know them personally by name on a one-to-one basis. They were coming up during the whole lunch hour to talk with him. He knew them well enough to ask questions, showing real interest in the things they were doing. With that kind of relationship, the chance of any causing him problems was slim.

Reported from a personal experience of an *ALTERNATIVES TO VIOLENCE* teacher.

BEDROOM INTRUDER

Jane Addams' calm understaning succeeds.

Jane Addams was the famous founder of Hull House, a service center and shelter in Chicago's inner city. Converted from an old mansion, Hull House no doubt seemed an oasis of wealth in an otherwise very poor area. Though Ms. Adams lived in Hull House, there was really nothing of monetary value in it.

One night a man broke in—not an uncommon occurrence there. Jane Addams was awakened as he made his way into her own bedroom, looking for money or jewelry. Instead of being terrified, she greeted him very naturally.

"What do you want?" she asked.

"I want money."

"Well, what is the trouble?" she asked, just as she did all needy visitors to Hull House.

"I need money. I'm out of work."

"I have no money," Jane Addams answered honestly and without defensiveness, "But if you will come around in the morning, I'll try to find a job for you."

Because of the natural way she spoke, he seemed not to doubt her word. The burglar left, unthreatened, and did indeed return in the morning. He even identified himself when the same calm Ms. Addams met him at the door, unassisted by police or weapons. She was, in fact, able to find him a job.

See *Safe Passage on City Streets* (Samuel), pp. 19-20.

ALTERNATIVES TO VIOLENCE

GANDHI'S FAMOUS "SALT MARCH"

tested the sinews of nonviolent protest.

The "Salt March" was one of the most famous non-violent actions initiated by Gandhi. In defiance of British police, volunteers walked to the ocean to get their own salt, rather than buying it from the British colonists.

Here are excerpts from the New York *Telegram's* report of May 22, 1930, on the demonstration: The scene "was astonishing and baffling to the Western mind accustomed to see violence met by violence, to expect a blow to be returned and a fight result. During the morning I saw hundreds of blows inflicted by the police, but saw not a single blow returned by the volunteers. So far as I could observe the volunteers implicitly obeyed Gandhi's creed of nonviolence. In no case did I see a volunteer even raise an arm to deflect the blows. There were no outcries from the beaten Swarajists, only groans after they had submitted to their beating . . . . . Much of the time the stolid native Surat police seemed reluctant to strike . . . I saw many instances of the volunteers pleading with the police to join them . . . At other times . . . the beating would be done earnestly . . . Sometimes the scenes were so painful that I had to turn away momentarily."

See *The Power of Nonviolence* (Gregg), pp. 24-26.

STEERING A TATTLER
toward a positive outlook.

One of my six-year-old students often tattles to any adult or child who will listen. Throughout the past month, I have had this boy first relate something positive about the student he was about to "tell on," and this procedure has greatly reduced his number of tattling incidents.

After reading the section on "tattling" in your handout, I decided to try the suggested solution with Adam. Well, it didn't take long for me to "put it to the test!" When Adam ran up to me on the playground the very next day, I quickly but calmly said to him, "I want you only to tell on good behavior or if there is danger to a child's life or to a thing."

He seemed shocked by my words, but he said, "Yeah, but it's important!" I repeated the above statement, and Adam slowly turned and walked back to the swings.

Submitted by a teacher from Akron, Ohio, while taking the *ALTERNATIVES TO VIOLENCE* course.

SYNTHIA'S LEARNING
required facing herself.

Six-year-old Synthia was resisting doing math all week. By Thursday she had built herself up to absolute refusal and tears.

I talked and worked with her for 10 minutes. Even had my arm around her and hugged her but it got worse. She started really wailing.

Frustrated, I took her over to the door and told her to stand there and finish crying facing the door, and to tell me when she was ready to come back and be part of the class. It went on about 15 minutes. She stood and cried, then laid down, then sat up, was finished and finally came over to me and said she was ready to sit at her seat again.

It was amazing that the whole class was able to ignore her and not get upset. She has not cried since and after conferencing with Mom she is now doing her math.

Submitted by a teacher from Akron, Ohio, while taking the *ALTERNATIVES TO VIOLENCE* course.

NEW KINDERGARTEN REBEL
yields to gentle firmness.

I have a girl who has been in my class only two weeks, but she is one of those students that teachers truly dread. A real nightmare. She has demonstrated violent behavior **daily** since she came to us—kicking, screaming, throwing tantrums, and insubordination.

Yesterday we had an "indoor" recess, where my kindergartners had to be in the classroom with sixth grade monitors for about 25 minutes. Each child was to be coloring a picture on paper provided for them. This particular girl, along with another feisty girl in my class, decided to color the yellow chairs instead!

They were taken to the office, and I met up with them there. I took them back to the room, where I gave them the proper materials to clean the chairs. I expected my newer student to really throw a fit! So I gave the materials to the other young lady and let her clean first.

When it came to my new student, she knew what to do. To my surprise she got right to work. When she became frustrated and started crying, I told her to rinse the chair off and dry it—and told her she'd done a good job, and that I **knew** it was hard work. No tantrums! I was really surprised!

Submitted by an Akron City teacher while taking the *ALTERNATIVES TO VIOLENCE* course.

WITH CALM WORDS,
students learn quickly.

Two students from another class were in a fist fight in the boys' restroom. Upon entering, I saw punches being delivered from both young men. When they saw me, they both stopped immediately. I didn't say a word. I just motioned for them to follow me.

I walked them back to their classroom teacher where we decided to deal with this problem in 15 minutes. Both teachers were very calm. We asked each young man to tell his story.

Then I proceeded to ask each student if they could have handled this problem in a different way. They both answered yes and made several recommendations on different ways to act.

Since the incident had to be written up, the principal intervened and both students were suspended for breaking a building rule.

Both young men now come to me with serious problems and ask for help rather than deciding on solutions immediately by themselves. We have built up an informal support system.

Submitted by a teacher from Akron, Ohio, while taking the *ALTERNATIVES TO VIOLENCE* course.

QUAKER JUSTICE FORGES PEACE

Why wasn't William Penn scalped?

The early American colonists took land from the Native Americans by force and taught the Native Americans the art of scalping. The colonists could not speak the language of the Indians; communication was difficult.

By contrast, when William Penn was given his Pennsylvania grant he began at once to learn the Native American language. At his initial meeting with them, he spoke peaceably and in their tongue.

Instead of taking their land by force, he paid for it fairly, clearly defining the boundaries. He asked that the Native Americans report any future injustices on the part of Pennsylvania colonists.

As Voltaire said, this was the only treaty never written down and the only one never broken. As a result of these just relationships, a real friendship was forged.

When Quakers were gone from home, sometimes for days at a time, who took care of their children? The Native Americans were their babysitters—sometimes members of the same tribes were scalping other colonists. The Quaker latchstrings were always open for Native Americans to come and go day and night with complete mutual trust.

As Pope Paul said, "If you want peace, then work for justice."

See *The Quiet Battle* (Sibley), pp. 210-217.

LINGUISTIC MIRACLES

How Frank Laubach bridged wide chasms.

Frank Laubach, founder of the "Each One Teach One" campaign which is credited with bringing literacy to millions of human beings, felt he was 'getting nowhere' with the Philippine Moros. He didn't know what to do about this savage people.

Then he realized that he might have been hiding from himself (but not from the Moros) a sense of racial, cultural and religious superiority. Immediately he passed around the word that he wanted to study the Moros' sacred book, the Koran, under their leadership. A crowd of Mohammedan teachers swarmed around his tent by the next morning.

With help, Laubach was soon mastering the language of the Moros, which had never been printed. Eventually, he stumbled on the discovery that only three words contained all the consonants necessary to speak the language. Each, "mother," "hand," and "work," had four syllables. From this point, it was simple to construct reading charts.

Laubach has now successfully carried this technique to many other languages. As he left the Philippines, the Mohammedan leader prayed that his American friend would have the blessing of Allah as he went around the world "introducing to less fortunate nations the method we (Moros) helped him make into the easiest lessons in the world for teaching people to read."

See *Courage in Both Hands* (Hunter), pp. 85-89.

QUAKER DOCTOR'S ANSWER
de-fangs the Viet Cong.

Marge Nelson was a Quaker doctor working at the prosthesis center in Quang Ngai, Vietnam, operated by the American Friends Service Committee. At that time, most of the surrounding area was controlled by the Viet Cong. The fact that she had taken the time to learn Vietnamese before this incident was, of course, helpful.

She was asked to identify herself. Captured armed forces personnel are only supposed to give their name, rank and serial number. Presumably, captured pacifist civilians are not expected to say much, either. However, when Marge was asked she replied in a different way.

"My name is Marge Nelson—and what is yours?" The ice was broken. About six weeks later she was released unharmed.

See International Division, AFSC, 1501 Cherry Street, Philadelphia, PA 19102.

DISCUSSION IMPROVES
using listening practise.

In my Basic English 9 class I tried the activity using erasers as the object giving students the right to speak. The assigned subject was to identify what problems the class was having. (Behavior is a continuous, on-going problem and I wanted to find out if students saw it the same way I did.)

After I explained the rules, I put the students into groups of four. As with all activities in this class, it took a while to get started.

However, the students settled in and did a good job identifying the problems. The hardest part for these kids was listening well enough to repeat what the previous speaker had said. Initially, there was some frustration at taking turns, but the prop (the eraser) really seemed to help.

In a follow-up discussion of solutions to the problem that had been identified, the whole group did not do very well in taking turns speaking and I wish now that I had continued the use of the eraser with the whole group of sixteen.

I see value in having students repeat the responses of other students and am using that technique in class on a regular basis.

Submitted by a teacher from Gahana/Jefferson, Ohio, while taking the *ALTERNATIVES TO VIOLENCE* course.

ANOTHER TEACHER'S EXPERIENCE
with the listening technique.

Freshman students in my English class were divided into groups of four. Each group was given an orange piece of paper and the rules for the activity were explained:

1. Only the person holding the orange paper is allowed to speak.
2. The speaker should tell what he feels is the theme of the short story read as homework the previous night.
3. After speaking, the speaker should pass the orange paper to the person on his right.
4. That person should then paraphrase what he believes the previous speaker said and then give his own impression of the short story's theme.

Students were not good listeners at first but soon realized that they had to listen in order to repeat the previous speaker's ideas.

In discussion after the activity, the students expressed difficulty in containing themselves. They wanted to comment and interject as the speaker explained his ideas—especially if they disagreed with those ideas. No student admitted any feelings of satisfaction at being the center of attention in the speaker role. As a matter of fact, most said they felt uncomfortable being in the limelight. However, some students expressed pleasure at the power they sensed in having control of the orange paper and the right to speak.

Submitted by a teacher from Gahana/Jefferson, Ohio, while taking the *ALTERNATIVES TO VIOLENCE* course.

FAMILY CIRCLE
benefits from listening exercise.

I tried the listening technique demonstrated in class last week with my family. We used a beanbag as a prop and sat in a circle in the livingroom. The question I posed to the group was, "How can we work together as a family?"

I took the first turn. My suggestion was to have a message center or bulletin board.

My six-year-old son David was next to hold the beanbag. He repeated my suggestion and he added that he thought we should all help each other doing chores around the house.

The beanbag next went to Christen, my four-year-old who was too shy to talk at first but with a little coaxing, we got her to say she wanted a bulletin board.

My husband, John, had the next turn. He is usually a complainer so he had a bit of trouble not complaining and trying to come up with a positive suggestion, but finally said, "Teamwork."

Brian, age eight, was next. He restated his dad's idea and added that he thought that we should stop fighting so much and then we could work together better.

Lastly, I took the beanbag and repeated Brian's suggestion.

The technique worked fairly well. Christen was too young perhaps to understand how to participate, but with time I think she would become more confident and talk in her turn. This experience was also good in that one person was not allowed to dominate the conversation and there was only one topic being discussed at one time, instead of two or more.

In many family conflicts, going off on more than one topic can hinder anything from being done.

Submitted by a parent from the Interparish School of Religion, Akron, Ohio, while taking the *ALTERNATIVES TO VIOLENCE* course.

CHALLENGE OF REALLY LISTENING
leads to better problem solving.

Because I teach math at the middle school level, I had some difficulty deciding on a meaningful listening activity. The skill seemed to lend itself easily to the area of English or social studies, and I thought of several applications in these academic areas. After some thought, I finally decided to apply active listening in the area of problem-solving. It seemed logical to use this phase of math because all of our conflict resolutions depend on creative problem-solving techniques. So I planned my lesson with this goal in mind.

At the beginning of my pre-algebra class, I discussed the difference between hearing and listening. Once the students distinguished between the two, I listed, with their input, various active listening techniques. Next, I had the students name the steps in solving a work problem. I listed the following steps on the board: 1) What is the question or what is the problem that I am being asked to solve? 2) What information or data do I have? 3) What are some ways that I can use to solve this problem (strategies)?

1. Nannette, Jay and Brad have a total of 80 pieces of bubble gum. The total number of pieces that Nannette and Brad have equals the number of pieces that Jay has. Jay has four times as many as Brad.
How many pieces of gum does each child have?
Nannette?
Brad?
Jay?

At this time, I divided the class into five groups with five in each group. (I had five rows, so I chose groups by rows of students). I explained the activity, and I used math symbols for the speakers to hold. As a warmup exercise, I asked the students to express their feelings about homework.

It was immediately evident that one student was uncomfortable with this activity. He was isolated and given the assignment to complete independently. It was also apparent that one of the groups was overloaded with "talkers" and lacking in "listeners." However, I continued without changing the players for the sake of curiosity.

Following the warmup activity, we discussed impressions and feelings. Much to my surprise, most students enjoyed being the speaker and seemed quite comfortable getting the attention.

At this point, I distributed four problems for each group to solve. They would receive ten points for each correct solution. I suggested that each individual read the problem carefully and think about problem-solving steps one and two. Then each student was to share a strategy for solving the problem, as other students practiced active listening skills.

The students were excellent in employing the listening skills, but the passing of the item from one person to the next became cumbersome. After the first problem was solved in each group, I allowed them to continue without using the symbol when speaking.
(continued next page)

2. Ralph read a book with more than 100 pages and less than 200 pages. The total of the three digits is 10. The second digit is twice the last digit. How many pages did Ralph's book have?

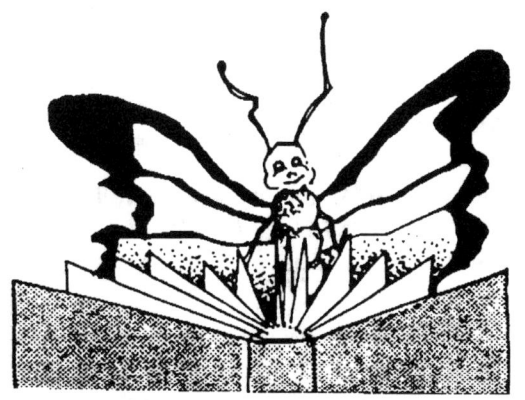

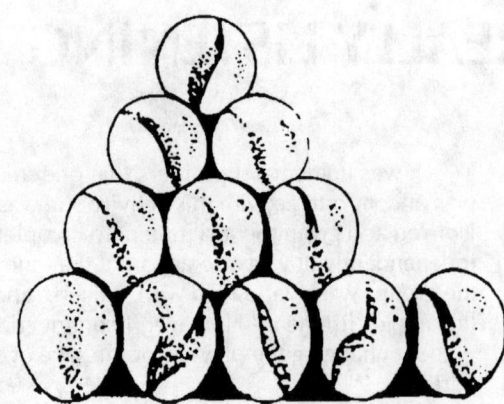

3. Three children collect marbles. Martha has twice as many as Wally. The three children have a total of 1,454 marbles. If Joe had one more marble, he would have 210 marbles. How many marbles does each child have?
Martha?
Wally?
Joe?

4. Ruth has three red hens, six speckled hens, one white hen and seven black hens. How many of the hens can say they are the same color as another hen?

As expected, the results proved to be quite interesting. Four of the five groups did remarkably well. Two groups were able to solve three problems. These four groups were extremely cooperative and successfully used the active listening techniques.

The last group did not fare as well. This very same group had difficulty during the warmup exercise, so it was not surprising to discover that they could only solve one problem, and that solution came at the very end of the activity. This group required constant reminders about speaking one at a time. They also spent much time bickering about their strategies. It was clear that their cooperative learning skills were deficient. The other groups were pleased with their results. The last group was not surprised that they did poorly. They recognized their problem. Unfortunately, they did nothing to correct it. As a result, they performed below par.

As the students left class, nearly everyone expressed a desire to do this activity again. They also told my other pre-algebra class about the activity. More importantly, they were able to recognize the importance of listening to each other's ideas and working together to solve problems. As a result, I plan to use this technique frequently in my classes.

Submitted by an Akron City teacher while taking the ALTERNATIVES TO VIOLENCE course.

TAKE YOUR TURN

Alternatives to Violence Course technique proves itself.

I used the listening technique in my first grade classroom during circle group presentation for Drug Awareness Week. We used it all three days when the class sat in a circle for discussion.

Naturally, as we started talking, everyone had comments or stories to share about drugs and everyone wanted to talk. I allowed one statement from each child and they passed the eraser around for their turn to talk. It seemed much easier for them to wait their turn—knowing their turn was coming around (they could visually see it).

They also had the option of passing and not saying anything. Even those students got to touch the eraser as it went around—so they were really participating too.

It really helped when I was talking because when someone started talking out of turn I just held up the eraser to show that it was my turn. It really helped the discipline without having to say anything. An added benefit was that it seemed to make it easier for some students to speak when they were focusing on the eraser.

Submitted by a teacher from Akron, Ohio, while taking the *ALTERNATIVES TO VIOLENCE* course.

AN ABERRANT STUDENT
can be nudged to improve.

Recently I had a problem with a student's behavior and attitude. I planned in advance what I wanted to say and how I would say it. I decided to use "I" statements and to concentrate on speaking calmly and slowly.

When the student came in, I was able to speak with him alone for about twenty minutes. He hung up his jacket before I started to talk but, when I started to speak, he stayed by the closet door, leaving it open.

I started out telling how I felt about what was going on and was very careful to use "I" statements. As usual he became very angry and once went in to get his jacket to leave. I continued to talk to him calmly and did not mention his move to leave.

After we talked for about ten minutes, he finally, on his own, moved to his seat and continued to talk. When we were out of time in the classroom, we moved to the hall and wrapped up the conversation. While long-range problems were not solved, his behavior and attitude were greatly improved and have stayed good for several days.

During the discussion, the student became upset, as he usually does, but did not storm out as he is likely to do. I really think the "I" statements, planning ahead and the calm, controlled atmosphere greatly influenced the outcome of the discussion.

Submitted by an Akron City teacher while taking the *ALTERNATIVES TO VIOLENCE* course.

HANDLING ANGER

Fifth graders learn a spectrum of techniques.

I teach 28 fifth grade students. Using role playing, journal writing and discussion, I tried the hassle line exercise for handling anger.

We used a situation where 14 students owned a new bike that the other 14 had run over and wrecked. They were given 45 seconds to "go at" each other.
Then I randomly asked; "How do you feel?"
Responses: Upset, Angry, Mad, . . .

We used the same "story" and I instructed students to only use "I" statements—"I think," "I need," "I want," "I wish," . . . etc.
Again, they went "at it" for 45 seconds. When asked how they felt about the second situation.
Responses: I couldn't argue, I couldn't fight, It didn't work, (meaning I couldn't fight) etc.

Then we discussed, with whom do you have conflicts:
Responses were (1) siblings (2) parents and (3) friends/peers.

I then told them to "talk" to their journals about a conflict. Use the "I" statements only. List at least four.

Students became so quiet. All were wrapped up in this. At R.R. break, there were five or six students who **rushed** to share their "conflict" and "I" statements with me. I encouraged them to try these statements at home to try to resolve the troublesome conflict.

Submitted by an Akron City teacher while taking the *ALTERNATIVES TO VIOLENCE* course.

NEW APPROACH

offers something to gain.

Every weekend my family faces what every other family faces . . . **an argument over a dirty house**. Try as I may I always lose it. It seems there are so many activities and overwhelming chores.

This week instead of threatening, insisting that I need a clean house, and putting all three of my children in their place because they did not handle their responsibilities, I tried something different. At our family meeting, I told them how I felt—overloaded and angry because of all the "stuff" I had to do to keep things in order. We discussed how they felt about my anger, about their feelings and what possible solutions we could implement.

We came up with two solutions: 1) an infraction list and 2) attitude enhancement list. After discussing the problem and implementing the solution, the week was fun. And because everyone did his or her part, the weekend workload was cut in half.

Submitted by a parent from the Interparish School of Religion, Akron, Ohio, while attending the *ALTERNATIVES TO VIOLENCE* course.

SMILE (AND BEHAVE)

You're on candid camera.

A teacher in an Akron, Ohio, high school was having trouble with students scuffling and acting up in various ways in class. He found an interesting, nonviolent way to stop it. In his desk drawer, he kept a camera complete with flashbulb. Whenever such an incident started, he pulled out his camera, aimed it and pressed the button! All trouble stopped immediately and good order was maintained through the students themselves.

Submitted by a teacher while taking the *ALTERNATIVES TO VIOLENCE* course.

TROUBLE IN THE SUBWAY
Friendly persistence averts threatening clash.

LS: Last December at about 11:30 p.m., I boarded the subway at 14th Street on my way back from a meeting in Washington. About a dozen passengers got on the empty car with me, an old one with seats running its full length so that all the passengers could see each other.

I found myself sitting opposite two black men. "A" was on the plump side; "B," thin, wiry and intense. I noticed A looking upset as he got up in anger and moved away from B, who was smoking.

B: (disdainfully, glancing over at A): What's the matter, don't you like my smoke?

A: No, you blew it right in my face.

(By now, most people in the car were aware of the conflict.)

A: Well, if you don't like it, you know what you can do!

A: I'm not saying anything. I just want to move away.

B: (with hostility): You better keep your mouth shut!

A: (sheepishly, and with obvious fear): I'm saying nothing.

B: (looking around triumphantly, as if daring anyone to challenge him): You better not!

LS: Dead silence enveloped the car. Some people inched away from the scene of the conflict. There was a clear consensus that it was something to stay out of. Three or four minutes passed.

LS (standing and walked over to B, speaking quietly and considerately): My friend, I'm really very sensitive to smoke. It's hard on my lungs. You wouldn't mind putting out your cigarette for the sake of my health, would you? (with a smile.)

B: You're over on that side and I'm over here. My smoke doesn't go over there.

LS (returning to seat): It's not as bad over here, but some does come over, and it does bother me. I'm quite sensitive, you know. (Everyone in the car was listening carefully now, but trying not to look at B.)

B: I **know** it doesn't go over there.

LS (earnestly): You know, smokers can't really notice it so much; they're used to it. It's different with those of us who are sensitive. I know you don't like to make it difficult for people.

B (less hostile): You ask me in a nice way. You're not a "schmuck" (with a nod toward A to indicate that he is one.)

LS: As he went on smoking in silence, I smiled at him, but tried to show by my expression that I wasn't joining in the denunciation of A. At this point, another black man nodded approvingly in my direction, taking care to do so when B wasn't looking.
(continued on next page)

B: I have to apologize. (At his words, fear in the car seemed to melt away.)

LS: I appreciate that. I know how you feel. But you know, it really doesn't help.

LS: B repeated his apology three times, each time after a short period of reflection in which he carefully scrutinized my face. I showed appreciation, but continued to indicate—by means of imploring looks—that apologies were not enough, that the smoke really bothered me. After another minute or so, B took a last puff, put his cigarette on the floor and crushed it with his shoe. He looked at me with a faint smile.

B: You talk like a gentleman. (By now, the other passengers looked incredulous, as if they had just witnessed a miracle.)

LS: Well, I try, but I'm not always able to. But I really appreciate your putting out your cigarette. You're a gentleman, too.

B: I apologize. You were right. I'm not a schmuck, but when someone else acts like a schmuck, you have to act that way, too.

LS: Not really. Sometimes you can change the situation by acting nice.

B: (with a knowing look): You're right there, too. (He smiled, obviously wanting to be my friend. I smiled back.) He's my brother (nodding toward A and clearly indicating that he meant soul brother.)

LS: Yes, we're all brothers.

LS: B nodded in enthusiastic agreement as the train, which had stopped for passengers, started off. As the noise grew, we looked across at each other to communicate that it was useless to try to shout over the din. B continued to smile and look pleased. At Union Square, the train filled up with passengers who stood between us, blocking our view. When I got up to leave, at Third Avenue, I walked over to B. "Have a good evening, friend," I said. He looked up, pleased.

On the stairs leading up to the street, a young woman hurried up from behind to tell me that she could hardly believe what she had just seen happen. Because of what I had done, the passengers lost their fear and were filled with good feeling, she said. How was I able to be so friendly to someone who seemed so threatening? I walked with her to the corner, telling her that I worked with Quakers in nonviolence training and conflict resolution.

"It doesn't always work," I said, "but it usually does. All people have good inside them, and it's a challenge to try and draw it out." She agreed and indicated deep satisfaction with my explanation. She warmly returned my greeting as we went our separate ways.

Lee Stern is administrative secretary of the Quaker Peace and Social Action Program, which serves a tri-state area from an office in New York City. A longtime FOR member, he was a member of the national staff for many years. "Turning Things Around on the Subway" by L. Stern from *Fellowship Magazine* 10/80, pp. 17-18.

HANDLING TEACHER ANGER

Administrator applies Alternatives to Violence principles.

I recently had an irate faculty member come bursting into my office with a long list of complaints about his teaching assignment. He was emotionally upset and unable to control his temper. I consciously utilized some of the techniques presented in class in an attempt to de-escalate his anger.

I first got him to sit down and began to restate what I heard him complaining about. I employed "I" statements as a means to deflate the level of emotion. I lowered the volume of my voice in sharp contrast to his initial shouts and loud comments. I indicated a personal interest in helping him to resolve some of the constraints which were complicating his teaching situation. I was specific about a time line we would follow to begin addressing his many concerns. I acknowledged the teacher's tremendous contributions to the school district, and his commitment to children. I reminded him of other problems that we had resolved together and indicated my confidence in our ability to solve these issues together, too.

The teacher eventually began to relax and his anger eventually began to dissipate. We agreed to jointly develop a plan of action to resolve the difficulties the following afternoon.

Submitted by an administrator while taking the *ALTERNATIVES TO VIOLENCE* course in the Shaker Heights School District.

ALTERNATIVES TO VIOLENCE CASE 7-C

THOSE ANGRY PHONE CALLS
Handling techniques work for business.

The following is an office memorandum for handling angry phone callers.

1. Focus on the problem. When someone is angry, it is easy to take what they say personally. Instead, focus on the caller's problem, even if the problem might appear to be the result of your actions. Listen to the caller. Help the caller to focus on the problem by summarizing what is said and asking if that is correct. For example:

The irate customer says: "I don't understand you people. I told you to check my credit when I placed the order. Now I'm on C.O.D. and nobody told me. My credit's good! What's the matter, don't you trust anybody?"

You could reply: "Let me see if I understand the problem. You asked for terms when you placed the order; you were given terms of C.O.D. and no one told you."

2. Once the problem is clarified to both parties' satisfaction, then it is our job to resolve the problem. In the above example, one response might have been:

You: "I've reviewed your account and we can give you Net 30 terms. I'm sorry that no one told you earlier."

3. It helps to say you're sorry or express concern that their needs were not met, or not met in a timely manner. However . . .

4. Use your own words and **only say what's true**. If you don't feel sorry, don't say so. People can tell if you aren't sincere and usually that just makes them more angry. Something along the lines of, "I wish we had been able to take care of this earlier" might help calm things down.

5. If, once the problem is clarified, you are not the person who can resolve the problem, transfer the call to the person who can. Tell the caller what you are doing and why. If possible, tell the person to whom you are transferring the call what the call is about. If you are the person to whom the call is being transferred, be aware this person has been transferred once and be wary of transferring again.

6. If you have any questions about how best to resolve a problem, ask the Office Manager or a co-worker familiar with the area.

7. If at any time a caller is verbally abusive or threatening, involve the Office Manager **immediately.**

8. If we stay calm, clarify the problem and do our very best to resolve the problem, the amount of time we spend on angry callers should be minimal and much easier on all concerned.

Submitted by the office manager who completed the *ALTERNATIVES TO VIOLENCE* course.

©1986, 1990, 1992, 1993, 1994, 1995 PEACE GROWS, Inc., 513 W. Exchange St., Akron, OH 44302 (216)8

FIRST GRADERS TALK TO THEMSELVES
as alternative to name calling.

In my first grade health lesson I used the Talking to Yourself technique as an alternative response to name calling. We sat in our circle group. I listed the steps on chart paper to read together.

We defined name calling and I asked for a show of hands of those who had ever heard anyone call someone else a name. I then let them share all the examples they could think of. (None were too bad; dummy, idiot, fool, brat, "cuss word"). This kept it very impersonal. They couldn't tell who said what.

I explained the talking to yourself steps. Then I modeled the process on myself. We then discussed why someone would lash out at someone else and how we would feel as the victim. We also discussed how it could escalate if both persons kept doing something back—in a fight and a bloody nose. Again, I let them all have a chance to share how they would feel if they were the victim.

I then let a very secure and able student practice the technique in front of the group. I needed to remind her of each step, but she did really well.

We then practiced as a group how we would talk to ourselves. I led them through it but they all participated and "owned it." They were wiggly but I know they got something from it. I think next time I might use characters on a flannelboard or puppets. We will practice again in a few days. I built them up that if they got a chance to use this in the next few days—they could come and share it with me and maybe with the class. This was very timely as we had had several instances of name calling this last week.

Submitted by an Akron City teacher while taking the *ALTERNATIVES TO VIOLENCE* course.

NAME CALLING

"Fatty" learns alternative response.

A student came to me after class to show me a story that another student had written in language arts class. The story had been carefully written and word processed on the computer as an assignment to be handed in for a grade. The story was about a "fat" boy and his adventures in the sea. It was very descriptive and quite crude. The name of the character in the story was the same as the student who came to me after class. This student is quite obese, and I know he had taken offense at this story, which was an obvious put down. However, he joked about it, and said, "This is so funny."

Here was the opportunity for me to use **alternative response to name-calling technique**. I tried it and I think the young, obese student felt much better after we talked.

I first asked him how the story made him feel. He admitted that it made him feel hurt and angry.

"Why do you think this other student used your name in the story and then showed it to you?" I asked. He said that all the kids tease him about his weight.

I asked him if he thought he was overweight. He said, "yes," but that he was on a diet. I said I thought that was great and told him that he was a good person. He said, "Yes, I guess I am."

I suggested that he go and tell the student who wrote the story that it had made him feel hurt. I don't know yet if he did or what the response was. But, hopefully the obese student will know how to handle such put downs in the future.

Submitted by a teacher from the Talawanda Middle School, Oxford, Ohio, while taking the ALTERNATIVES TO VIOLENCE course.

ALTERNATIVES TO VIOLENCE   CASE 7-F

STEP BY STEP

away from name calling.

My students and I discussed the questions below as part of a Social Studies unit entitled "Me." I asked these questions of 21 first-graders. The results are as follows:

Have you ever called someone a name?	18 yes	3 no
If you answered no, think about it and try again:	21 yes	0 no

Why did you call someone a name?
I was mad. My brother hit me. Sherry wouldn't play with me. I just wanted to.
He calls me names, so I call him names, too.

How did it make you feel?
Glad. Happy! At first I was glad; then we fighted. Sad. She shouldn't have called me a name 'cause it was her fault.

What else could you have done?
Played with someone else. Not get into a fight, just talk. I could have told my mom.
We should play a game we both like. Go home.

Have you ever been called a name?   Yes! (21 students)

Why were you called it?
I was fighting with Adam. I didn't share my bike with her. She was mad at me.
My friend didn't like me 'cause I couldn't play at his house.

How did it make you feel?
Sad. Angry! Sad because it wasn't my fault. She called me something I wasn't and I cried.
I didn't pay attention to her but I was mad.

What did you do?
I just went home. I called her a name back. I told my mom and dad. I hit her.
I didn't play with her for two days. My friends and me wouldn't play with her.

Teacher comment: I expected most of the above comments because of the students' ages (6 and 7) and their environment. This week we will be discussing alternatives to name calling.

Submitted by an Akron City teacher while taking the *ALTERNATIVES TO VIOLENCE* course.

MEDIATION SUCCEEDS
in settling a personal feud.

Background:
Karen received a note from Sue that was filled with threats, accusations and profanity. A teary-eyed, shaking Karen shared the note with me after class.

I struggled that night with thoughts of what to do. It seemed a perfect opportunity to attempt a mediation conference.

With the approval of Sue and Karen and the help of a fellow teacher who acted as a recording secretary, we sat down together in hopes of settling differences.

Mediation:
Using the six-step mediation procedure, the girls revealed emotional wounds, misunderstandings, and peer pressures that undermined what had once been a friendship. With these factors as a backdrop, negative interactions escalated between them to a point where groups were involved and neither was in control. Both girls expressed hope for a renewed friendship in time, but in the interim generated a four-part contract that would ameliorate their present situation.

Karen and Sue signed an agreement that contained these provisions or guidelines:
1) We won't write notes to each other.
2) Karen will not listen to others' opinions of Sue, but will form her own.
3) Sue will not listen to others' opinions of Karen, but will form her own.
4) We agree to ask our friends to stop taunting, name-calling and threatening. These intimidating actions which had been directed at each of us had escalated to an uncomfortable level.

I'm writing up this case about one month after the mediation took place and to this date there has been no evidence of conflict between Sue and Karen. Both girls have expressed that their differences have been settled.

I was delighted with the outcome of this mediation and with the meaningfulness and depth of the communication between the girls.

Submitted by a teacher from the Talawanda Middle School, Oxford, Ohio, while taking the ALTERNATIVES TO VIOLENCE course.

A TOUGH CHALLENGE FOR MEDIATION

How did it work for Ron and grandma?

Last Thursday, Mrs. S. and I held my first mediation conference with a freshman student (Ron, age 15—not his real name) and his guardian (his 81-year-old grandmother). We went to the home in West Akron and after introductions had been made, we were told that the grandmother had a stroke earlier this year.

Grandmother had called me earlier in the week indicating that Ron had not been home for three days. He had left the house on Saturday night and had not returned by Tuesday. She had called the police and the detention home. They weren't much help. I indicated to her that I would talk to Ron in my office as he was coming to school.

Grandmother was concerned about him staying out past 10 p.m. on weekends, losing his key, picking up his clothes and leaving other people's belongings alone. She was threatening to send Ron back to California (to Dad) if he ever stayed out past curfew again. Ron said he would run away before going back to California.

After talking to Ron, I called Grandmother and she okayed the mediation session for Thursday after school. We used a peer mediation work-sheet that Mrs. S. had been using at school.

The grandmother kept indicating that she would not change any of her "house rules." I was afraid that someone 81-years-old, and having suffered a stroke, might be too inflexible and rigid for the mediation to work. But after hearing what Ron said he would do to change, Grandmother did make some minor concessions.

Both participants signed the agreement and I promised that I would continue working with Ron at school, to improve his grades (another of Grandmother's concerns). Both mediators would follow up with Grandmother after about a week.

The mediation process worked much better than I expected for this case. I'm encouraged to try it again as soon as I get a chance.

Submitted by an Akron City teacher while taking the ALTERNATIVES TO VIOLENCE course.

MEDIATION QUICKIE

led by a capable teacher.

In my eighth grade social studies class, I discovered that two students had cheated on a homework assignment. Their answers were identical. I talked to the two girls after class and told them that since their answers were identical, that they would have to share the grade. An 85% divided by two is an "F" for each student.

They were not too happy about this and started blaming and accusing each other. They were good friends and I didn't want to see their friendship hurt, yet they had to learn that cheating is not acceptable. Had they come to me before doing the assignment and asked to work together in completing it, I would have agreed to it. But, they tried to pass it off as individual work.

The conflict began to escalate so I thought a mini-mediation was in order. I helped them identify the problem without placing blame. I asked each to tell how they were feeling. Then I asked each to tell her side of the story while the other listened without interrupting. I asked the girls to identify the problem and to come up with a couple of suggestions about how to solve it.

The problem seemed to be that one girl felt obliged to give her friend her work to copy in order to keep her friendship. The other assured her that she was her friend, no matter what, and she would not ask to copy work again.

I repeated to them the resolution that they seemed to have reached. The girls smiled at each other and said, "Let's go to lunch before all the tables are full." That was it!

I tried to let the girls do all the talking and reach a resolution on their own. The whole process took no more than five minutes. It was five minutes well spent!

Submitted by a teacher from the Talawanda Middle School, Oxford, Ohio, while taking the *ALTERNATIVES TO VIOLENCE* course.

DISPUTE BECAME BLOODY
How did mediation help?

The need for a mediation conference developed suddenly as a bloodied John pinned Ken to an unforgiving cement floor. As the disappointed crowd of boys dispersed, I escorted both Ken and John to my closet-like room at one of the dorms at an outdoor education center.

In a brief interview held separately with each boy, I discovered they had a history of misunderstandings and escalating tension. Conflicts had arisen around little things in the fall that cumulatively would erupt into war in the winter. Words had been exchanged, negative body language acted out, and a crowd's enthusiasm sparked, then lit the fuse of a knock-down-drag-out fight.

Both boys admitted that violence was not the way to settle things and apologized for their behavior. They were disappointed with themselves for losing control, especially since each boy had targeted his propensity for fighting as a flaw, not an asset. Having completed the interviews. I felt the time was ripe for settling differences together.

We sat down and recapped the fight. Long-standing negative feelings were probed and diffused as by-products of misperception. Each boy listened attentively to the other as they faced off in an exchange of hurt feelings. They admitted that a friendship between them was unlikely, but that peaceful getting along with each other was necessary.

Though it was an informal mediation conference, the outcome was impressive. The battle was over and so was the war.

Submitted by a teacher from the Talawanda Middle School, Oxford, Ohio, while taking the *ALTERNATIVES TO VIOLENCE* course.

HOW DO YOU RESPOND TO BEING KNIFED?

Forgiveness is one alternative.

Harold Schultz, an associate of Candide Rondon in Brazil, once did not have enough presents to go around in a negotiation with the Chavantes Indians. An Indian man, taking this as a personal insult, ran a knife into Schultz's shoulder up to the hilt!

He escaped and came back a year later, his arm still in a sling, but with plenty of presents. He sought out the Indian who had nearly killed him and ceremoniously presented him with a beautiful new knife! The tribe was so moved by this forgiving act that they took in Schultz as a member.

See *Courage in Both Hands* (Hunter), pp. 90-91.

CELL BLOCK RAPE THREATENED
hardened criminal responds to nonviolence.

Mark Morris had received a five-day jail sentence in San Francisco County Prison No. 2 for participating in a demonstration organized by the Committee for Nonviolent Action. To Mark, both the jail's facilities and its oversight were severely inadequate.

Crowded conditions caused doubling up, during the day, in what were intended to be one-man cells. Guards rarely were seen. At night half the inmates, including Mark, were bedded down in the hallway floor on filthy mattresses.

The prison, more than most, was run by inmates. Bobby, a young black 'trusty,' clearly the most powerful prisoner on the tier, arranged with the guards to have Mark transferred to his cell. Bobby was cruel, arrogant, manipulative and terrorized nearly everybody.

Females are not the only victims of rape. From the very first Bobby verbally made sexual advances and threats to Mark. However, there was no opportunity for them to become physical until the night before Mark was to be released.

That evening when the prisoners were locked up in the cells, Bobby stayed out in the hallway, having persuaded another prisoner to take his cell. While the mattresses were being pulled out, he showed Mark a home-made stiletto he had filed down from a kitchen knife into 'a really mean-looking blade,' as Mark described it. "At the same time," Mark said, "Bobby told me he was going to fuck me." Bobby saved a mattress for Mark at the far end of the hall.

Mark decided to keep talking loudly, but it did no good. Everyone else dropped off to sleep anyway. Meanwhile, Bobby held the stiletto against Mark's throat. But, Mark kept on talking. Bobby kept on ordering Mark to remove his clothes.

Mark said he would not and kept talking on and on. Finally, Bobby said he was going to undress Mark and tore at his pants forcefully enough to rip off the buttons. Mark's shirt also got torn.

Right after that, a guard with a flashlight came through on a routine count of the prisoners. Bobby was terrified. He was sure Mark would turn him in. Being found out of his cell, he would be thrown in 'the hole' and lose his good time. If the knife were found, Bobby would be in even more trouble.

Bobby started to threaten Mark to keep him quiet. Before any words really could get out, Mark softly whispered to Bobby not to worry, he did not want to get Bobby into trouble. Mark said he considered Bobby his friend! As the guard went by both stayed deathly still.

Things at that point turned around; Bobby made no more advances. For a long time the two talked with Mark's hand resting gently on Bobby's chest. Bobby told Mark about his loneliness and his sexual frustrations. Finally, Bobby even cried a little. He said it was the first time he had cried since he was a child.

They also talked about Carl, a very young and inexperienced demonstrator, also arrested with Mark. Bobby had been threatening Carl, too, so much so that Carol, on the same night, was lying on his mattress both crying and trembling from fear.

The next morning Bobby found a piece of contraband string for Mark to use in holding up his pants. Also, Bobby promised Mark that he would not touch Carl, who had to serve for a few more days.

Why did Bobby respond so well to this nonviolent approach? Mark listed eight specific nonviolence techniques:

1. Be clear about your objectives.
2. Don't be frightened (or, if you are, don't show it).
3. Don't be frightening.
4. Don't be afraid of stating the obvious.
5. Don't behave like a victim.
6. Seek to befriend your opponent's better nature.
7. In response to physical violence, play it by ear, keeping the confrontation on a verbal-emotional-intellectual level, resisting as firmly as you can without escalating the violence.
8. Keep talking. Keep listening. It humanizes both parties. The rapist or attacker tends to think of the intended victim only as a 'thing,' not as a human being. It is hard to attack someone perceived as a real human person.

From an article by Mark Morris in the former *WIN Magazine* issue of January 24, 1974.

MUGGER DIVERTED FROM VIOLENCE
by continuous, calm talking.

In 1972, two young women were walking home on a dark, empty Philadelphia street. Suddenly a tall young man confronted them. Holding a knife at the throat of the woman nearest him, he demanded money. "I have to have money," he pleaded. Clearly he was a junkie desperate for a fix. "If I don't get money, someone is going to get hurt," he threatened.

Although they said they had none, he still threatened. The women offered as many alternatives as they could think of.

"Look," said the smaller woman, "I'll stay here with you. Let Mary go back to my apartment and get you the money."

"No way," he replied, "She'll call the cops."

"No, she won't. Really she won't. And I'll be here. She wouldn't call the cops while I was still here." But the assailant wouldn't give in. So, there in the empty street, she suggested that all three of them go to the apartment. He gave many reasons for not; it was clear he was frightened, too.

"Look, trust us. Come on," she said, looking him straight in the eye. Crazed and irrational as he was, the junkie began to understand that there was no better way out. He finally agreed.

Still threatening with the knife, the man walked with them up the street and into the apartment build- ing, while the women talked to him quietly and normally, not showing their fear. The woman whose apartment it was went in and returned with a ten dollar bill, all she had.

"Is that all you have?" he shouted. Her heart sank. "But I only need five dollars. I don't have any change. I'm sorry." He stood there uncertainly.

"Take it, take it. That's all right." Finally, he ran down the stairs and out of the building.

See *Safe Passage on City Streets* (Samuel), pp. 13-18.

HOLDUP

Trading butter for a gun.

A traveller coming out of a bus station was accosted by a hold-up man threatening him with a gun and muttering something about demanding money.

Ignoring the gun and the muttering, the traveller said, calmly, "It's cold. Why don't you take my jacket?" The assailant fumbled, and the traveller continued his expression of concern, "I was just going for something to eat. Why don't you join me?"

Later, he even offered the hold-up man some money, but the relationship by now was so well established that the money was refused.

See *Safe Passage on City Streets* (Samuel), pp. 89-90.

CRAZY LIKE TWO FOXES

Muggers' quarries use wits.

Joe and his friend Peter were waiting for a bus in a bus shelter in a deserted section of Cleveland. They had about $200 with them. Two other men also were in the shelter.

Suddenly they turned on Joe and Peter. With something under their coats, like guns, they shouted, "Give us your money!"

Joe looked at the sky behind the attackers and yelled, "Wow, look! Here they come!" Peter joined in. Both talked and acted rather crazy.

The robbers didn't know what to think. Confused, they ran away.

Someone who took the *ALTERNATIVES TO VIOLENCE* course (1980).

ALLEY ATTACK

nonviolence defends intended rape victim.

A man grabbed a woman in an alley, obviously to rape her. He said he was sorry. He did not want to hurt her, but he just had to do it. He was very messy and in really poor condition.

For a long time the woman talked to him saying, mostly, reinforcing things. She told him he did not have to rape; that rape is evil; that he could be attractive, if he would clean himself up.

She told him about her two children. She said he was "not really a bad person and didn't really want to do that to her."

Then, he thanked her for caring enough to talk to him as she had. He told her that no one had ever done that before and that he was lonely. He said she had saved him from doing something bad and told her to leave. They went their separate ways.

**From "Dealing Nonviolently with Rape"
by Ray Chandler as reported by Mary Crane
in an article in the former WIN Magazine
of April 26, 1979 entitled "Rape Avoidance
and Resistance: A Nonviolent Approach."**

HE SCREAMED ANYWAY
which turned out quite luckily.

Six years ago I experienced the most violent situation of my life. As I was ready to enter the back door of my house, after getting out of my car, a man came up to me and said that someone wanted to see me in front of my house.

I was taken aback when I saw the man, but I just talked to him calmly, questioning why someone needed to see me. As our conversation continued, I realized it was all a ruse to try to get me to leave the door and go to the front of the house.

I just continued to resist verbally when I suddenly saw a second man enter my house. It was then that I realized that this was a very serious and frightening situation.

The first man suddenly had his hand near his pocket, told me he had a gun and that I should not scream. After seeing the second man enter my house and knowing that if I entered the house, I would be at their mercy, I gambled and chose to scream, hoping my neighbors would hear me.

At that moment, I heard a gunshot but did not see that a gun was pointing at me. After the shot resounded, the man inside my house ran out and down the driveway and the man holding me also ran away.

From these actions, I realized that the gun must just have gone off accidentally and consequently scared the two "would-be robbers" and saved me!

I certainly did not feel calm but looking back at the incident with the thoughts gained from our workshop, I realized I saved myself because I did not act like a victim. I tried to talk calmly and reasonably to a person who may, in some ways, have been frightened himself of whatever he was doing.

Perhaps I surprised him by my actions and he no longer felt in control of the situation. I feel thankful that I did remain fairly calm but I was not consciously aware of "doing the right thing!!"

Submitted by a teacher from the Shaker Heights School District, Cleveland, Ohio, while taking the *ALTERNATIVES TO VIOLENCE* course.

JOHN WHO?

He paved the way to freedom for slaves.

Most Americans would probably contend that the Civil War and Abraham Lincoln ended slavery. Most probably never heard of John Woolman. Yet John Woolman, who lived in the 18th century, probably did more to end slavery than Abraham Lincoln. How?

He dedicated his life and his energy to overcoming the injustice of slavery. His first act was to refuse to write a will for a man in New Jersey who wanted to bequeath his slaves. He travelled extensively through the colonies talking and acting against slavery. He wouldn't wear the traditional blue Quaker hat and overcoat because the indigo was raised using slave labor.

As a result of Woolman's efforts and the efforts of those who followed him, the political climate was such that seventy years later Abraham Lincoln could end chattel slavery in the United States.

See *The Journal of John Woolman.*

IT TAKES STIFF COURAGE
to stand tall under police beatings.

The Chicago *Daily News* of June 21, 1930, told of the non-violent demonstration near Bombay, India, during the Indian struggle for independence from British colonization.

First, the ambulance unit arrived and lined up with stretchers. Then came the processions of white-robed volunteers, toward whom the police marched. The police began beating with lathis those who did not flee. No volunteer resisted or defended himself; only leaving the field when carried off on a stretcher. Then the police began beating up fifty Sikhs (religious leaders) who had arrived.

The news report goes, " . . . I stood within five feet of a Sikh leader as he took the lathi blows . . . he stood straight. His turban was knocked off. The long black hair was bared with the round top knot. He closed his eyes as the blows fell until at last he swayed and fell to the ground. No other Sikhs had tried to shield him, but now, shouting their defiance, they wiped away the blood streaming from his mouth . . . the Sikh gave me a smile and stood for more. And then the police threw up their hands. 'You can't go on hitting a blighter when he stands up to you like that.'"

See *The Power of Nonviolence* (Gregg), pp. 26-28.

ALTERNATIVES TO VIOLENCE

MERCY VOYAGES OF THE PHOENIX
versus U.S. duplicity.

In 1967, the 50-foot sailboat *Phoenix* sailed to Haiphong, in the Democratic Republic of Vietnam, sponsored by a Quaker Action Group of Philadelphia. She carried ten thousand dollars worth of medical supplies, consigned to the Red Cross, to be used for the relief of civilian casualties of U.S. bombing there. The United States government was placed in an embarrassing position. It had two choices, neither of which fit its chosen policy: the boat could be allowed to go ahead, which would strengthen the anti-war movement, or it could be stopped, which would show clearly to the watching world the inhumaneness of its Vietnam policy. The decision was finally made at the White House. The *Phoenix* was allowed to proceed to Vietnam, where it received a warm welcome.

On a second trip, *Phoenix* attempted a similar mission to what was then South Vietnam. This time the South Vietnamese government, with U.S. help, repelled repeated attempts at delivering the medical supplies. The *Phoenix* finally sailed to Cambodia instead.

See *Nonviolent Struggle Around the World* (War Resisters League 1978 calendar), and "Voyage of the Phoenix" (film by Canadian Broadcasting Co.).

ALTERNATIVES TO VIOLENCE CASE 10-D

SOFT ANSWER WORKS
Without guns, Maori Chief uses his wits.

The native Maori Indians of New Zealand were in the stone age when the English colonists first landed. They were cannibals. They did not have modern weapons, so it was easy for the English to take over more and more of the Maori land by force.

One chief, however, had considerable wisdom. When he learned that English armed forces were about to attack his village, he called the tribe together and pointed out that the English were invading with guns. The Maoris could try to defend themselves with their spears and stones, but he had another idea.

He asked the men and boys to gather in the village center without weapons, the women to make cakes and other food, and the children to dress in their brightest garments and to gather flowers and make wreaths. The latter he sent to meet the invaders with songs, dances and games!

The invading soldiers, of course, were dumb-founded, and all they could do was follow the celebrating procession back to the village. There the chief stepped forward and greeted his would-be attackers with great dignity and friendliness. All the English soldiers could do was accept the hospitality and refreshments. Then they withdrew, leaving the Maoris in full possession of their land. This was said to be the last British expedition against the Maoris.

See *Courage in Both Hands* (Hunter), pp. 122-123; and *Nonviolent Struggle Around the World* (War Resisters League 1978 calendar).

FOLLOWING A HIGHER LAW

Thoreau's civil disobedience.

Henry David Thoreau felt the Mexican War was unjust and did not want either the Mexicans or the Americans to suffer from it. The only effective protest he could see was to refuse to pay the tax being used to finance it. He knew tax resistance would lead to his arrest, and it did.

Thoreau's **Civil Disobedience** inspired Gandhi many years later. Not obeying an unjust law, or obeying a divine law which is in conflict with a secular law, is part of the non-violent technique of civil disobedience. One must realize the consequences, however, and be willing to suffer them in order to inspire and educate others.

See "Which Way the Wind" (AFSC film) and *Civil Disobedience* (Thoreau).

A TORMENTING MAJORITY

What can a minority of one do?

Carlotta was the first and only Black student in a white high school classroom after integration began in the South. Fearful and hesitant, she was placed up front, making her an easy target for juicy spitballs. Some of these even had a bit of metal inside which made them hurt.

When they hit her cheeks and forehead she had managed to control her temper as her non-violent training sessions had taught. She was afraid, however, that the white kids would think she had no feelings like theirs because she didn't react to their attacks.

When the class would laugh uproariously as she wiped her face, she wanted to crawl out of the room and never return. So Carlotta came up with another approach.

The next time she was hit with a spitball, she stooped to the floor, picked it up, and personally delivered it back to the obviously guilty person. With all her possible charm she laid it down in front of him, smiling, and in a very friendly fashion said, "This is yours, isn't it?" Then she turned and, with dignity, returned to her seat. The class howled with laughter, but at her embarrassed tormentor, not at her.

See *Courage in Both Hands* (Hunter), p. 25.

ALTERNATIVES TO VIOLENCE

STOLEN EAR MUFFS
lead to more than their return.

Terra lost her earmuffs yesterday. Since Terra is in first grade, you often need to prompt a child to get through the tears to find out why they're upset.

I asked my inquiring questions and found that Terra was missing her **new** earmuffs. Terra had remained in the room to wash the boards while I dismissed the class and one of her fellow students had picked them up. I knew that Terra was upset because they were new, but I wanted her to realize that she did have a course of action she could take.

We went to the phone and called Chris (the new owner of the earmuffs) and told him to bring them tomorrow.

In the morning Terra arrived at school early and we came up with a list of words that described how she was feeling. When Chris arrived, Terra went over the list of feeling words.

Chris wasn't permitted to just say "I'm sorry." We asked him to tell us using three feeling words what it was like to receive Terra's phone call and to know that I then got on the phone and spoke to his mom. I labeled this CONSEQUENCE. (We wrote this all on chart paper).

I asked Chris to tell us what he would do the next time he desired something that wasn't his. I think he better understood the word consequence; they both learned how to dialogue feelings and to come to a resolution.

(This case was suggested by the worksheet: Responding to Aggressive Behavior.)

Submitted by an Akron City teacher while taking the *ALTERNATIVES TO VIOLENCE* course.

SPONTANEOUS STUDENT REACTIONS
reveal depth of violence conditioning.

My freshmen are very aggressive young people. They are active and emotional. I decided to give them the "Responding to Aggressive Behavior" sheet and I was shocked by their responses.

I knew they were aggressive, but I didn't realize how violent they were. And I mean **very** violent. Also, I was shocked that **all** of them chose fighting as their course of action in at least one of the five situations. They knew that the short-term and/or the long-range effects could be suspension from school or getting into trouble, but they still chose the violence.

The two situations that elicited the most violent responses were:

Angela just pushed you hard in the hall, and Francine is calling you names.

Here are some responses to the Angela situation:

1. Tell her to stop pushing and beat her up.
2. Push her back.
3. I would beat the heck out of her after asking her why.
4. Push her harder.
5. Smack her like a mack.
6. I will hit her and throw her down the stairs etc.
7. Beat her up.
8. Get my sister to kick her butte.

Here are some responses to the Francine situation:

1. Talk about her so bad in front of her friends, humiliate her, and make her cry.
2. I'll smack her and say her mama.
3. Call her names back and fight.
4. Tell her to say it to my face, and if she does, hit her.
6. Kick it on her so bad she'd cry.
7. Give her a finger.

The students did this exercise in a serious manner. They were working individually and were not sharing their answers or trying to show off.

I just don't think that they consider any non-violent alternatives. I intend to discuss these situations with them and maybe as a class they can come up with some more peaceful solutions. I also intend to share some of the cases from the *ALTERNATIVES TO VIOLENCE* notebook with them and discuss why these particular solutions worked.

Submitted by an Akron City teacher while taking the *ALTERNATIVES TO VIOLENCE* course.

NONVIOLENT INTERVENTION

spurs students to solve their own problems.

Within my classroom we had had problems of constant bickering, inappropriate touching and leaving the bathroom a mess. These small problems usually lead to someone finally going off and ending up in time out. The problems had been escalating over the last two weeks. Instead of taking privileges away, we held a meeting, stated the problems and brainstormed ways to solve the problems or resolve the conflicts.

The students came up with many good ideas. The consequences they set were much tougher than I would have set. We typed up the problems with the agreed upon consequences, each student signed it and received a copy. As a result, the problems have lessened (though not disappeared) and when students receive a consequence, there is much less complaining and more overall support by the rest of the class.

Submitted by a teacher from Akron, Ohio, while taking the *ALTERNATIVES TO VIOLENCE* course.

RESTROOM MANNERS
Role playing helps kindergarteners.

At the Kindergarten level, there constantly seem to be problems using the restroom. The problems are not usually major, but enough of a problem to be a constant source of frustration.

Recently, during a restroom break, there were a lot of noise and loud talking coming from the boys' restroom. I approached the entrance and called all of the boys out. As they filed out, Bobby and Nicholas were in tears and each of the other boys had an explanation about the noise. Of course, all were giving their explanations at the same time.

I made sure that Bobby and Nicholas were not hurt. Then, I had the boys line up quietly and told them we would discuss it in the room when Bobby and Nicholas had a chance to collect themselves and everyone else had a chance to settle down.

The problem was that while Bobby was using the restroom, Nicholas decided to "peek" in the curtain. (Bobby is a shy child and was embarrassed.)

Anthony came to Bobby's rescue and pushed Nicholas away from the curtain and Nicholas, in turn, fell and hurt his leg. This became the forum for some role playing lessons.

We practiced walking in a line into and out of the restroom. We discussed and role played manners in the restroom, and following rules like being quiet, giving others privacy, washing hands, and coming out immediately—not staying there to play.

The incident also led to discussions about feelings. We role played showing different feelings when faced with different situations. This is an excellent way for children like Bobby, who are shy, to express themselves. They learn that everyone has feelings and that there are different ways to express feelings.

All of our restroom problems have not been eliminated. However, our attempts at role playing respectful behavior have helped.

Submitted by an Akron, Ohio, city teacher while taking the *ALTERNATIVES TO VIOLENCE* course.

ALTERNATIVES TO VIOLENCE CASE 11-F

A CONFLICT SITUATION:
not getting to sit with friend in lunch room . . .

I developed the following plan for my third graders:

The Conflict Situation: Not getting to sit with a friend in the lunch room.
(happens sometimes to most students)

Drama: *Narrator:* It is time to put our books away and clean up for lunch. Putting books away and washing hands. Talking about what it means to be good friends. Have students line up as if they were getting ready to go to the lunch room. Have everyone listen as different students talk about lunch room rules.

Discussion: Divide the class into 5 small groups and plan some ways they can solve the problem of getting to sit with their friend. Brainstorm ideas they could use in order to get to sit with their best friend.

Drama: Re-enter the drama in the lunch room. (Now I am in the role as the lunch room monitor.) Enact events that occur in the lunch room. Stop the drama as conflict escalates.

Discussion: This is the time to put in force some of their brainstormed ideas of getting to sit by their friend. If necessary, call on the principal to give his input. Review lunch room rules. Choose a class leader. This person may take the place of the teacher. Discuss what works and what doesn't work in getting everyone seated in the lunch room.

Drama: Try the different solutions to getting to the lunch room with a friend for a week. Have class vote on the best way.

Submitted by a teacher from Akron, Ohio, city schools while taking the *ALTERNATIVES TO VIOLENCE* course.

ALTERNATIVES TO VIOLENCE   CASE 12-A

ZEROING IN ON A PROBLEM
Eighth graders practise consensus skills.

As often as possible I try to implement group problem-solving activities in my eighth grade social studies classroom. One objective is to help students develop skills in achieving consensus. An example of such an activity is as follows:

Students are divided up into small groups of four. They are provided with a problem to solve. One such problem is the story of a farm family moving to the city of Boston in the early 20th century. The family encounters a variety of problems and difficulties related to and caused by the rapid growth of the city.

The group, after reading the story, must decide what the **four** most important problems are, such as overcrowded housing, lack of a police force, frequent fires, unemployment, etc.

The group must then prioritize the problems and come up with **three** possible solutions to each problem. It sounds like an easy task, but the students soon realize that differences in opinions get in the way of solving the problem.

They are then asked to begin again, but first must lay ground rules, such as: a) everyone has the right to an opinion, b) everyone must have equal opportunity to speak, c) there will be no name calling, d) differences of opinion are settled by a vote.

This activity has several positive effects. The most important one is that students who tend to dominate discussion learn to listen to other students who are normally passive. Students develop a sense of group unity. And finally, many creative ideas flow as the group becomes involved in discussion.

The consensus skill is one that must be developed in the classroom if students are to be expected to participate in an active and positive way in the larger society.

Submitted by a teacher from the Shaker Heights School District, Cleveland, Ohio, while taking the *ALTERNATIVES TO VIOLENCE* course.

ALTERNATIVES TO VIOLENCE CASE 12-B 346

A WAVE OF IDEAS

can flow from young children.

Kindergarten children are usually anxious to share ideas and help each other. They always seem to have something to say. I thought the **brainstorming** technique might be fun and enlightening to try with my class. As a part of Drug Awareness Week, we brainstormed a drug-related idea.

I explained the brainstorming process to the children. We discussed the rules in simple language as follows:

1. Say something you think of (about the subject).
2. Listen, but don't say anything about what someone else says. Everyone has the right to say whatever he/she wants.
3. Say whatever comes to your mind, even if you think it might sound silly.
4. Say the first thing you think of.

Problem to be addressed:

What Would You Do If Some Big Kids Gave You Pills (Drugs) And Wanted You To Take Them?

We were seated on our carpet area and I recorded the children's ideas on a chart. The following is a list of ideas the children were able to come up with:

Say, No way, Jose!	Don't smoke and drive
Walk away	Just say, "NO!"
Don't smoke	Run
Dont' take drugs	Tell my teacher
Don't drink and drive	Smash them
Tell my brother	Don't ever eat pills
Run and hide	Tell my parents
Call the police	Call 9-1-1

After our ideas were all recorded, I reread them from the chart to the children.

Submitted by a teacher from Akron, Ohio, city schools while taking the ALTERNATIVES TO VIOLENCE course.

©1986, 1990, 1992, 1993, 1994, 1995 PEACE GROWS, Inc., 513 W. Exchange St., Akron, OH 44302 (216)864

ALTERNATIVES TO VIOLENCE — CASE 12-C

THOSE DARN KIDS

respond to creative teaching.

Last week, while passing in the hall, many students from my third grade class were rude to a first-grader who had been bitten in the face by a dog. Her face was badly bruised and my students made unkind remarks to her.

I thought brainstorming about other responses when faced with an uncomfortable situation might help students not to repeat their behavior. The following is a flow chart of their suggestions; those ideas marked * were acted upon.

Problem: **Being Rude To Someone Younger. What Are Other Responses?**

Are you OK or can I help you?
Apologize for rude remarks or expressions.
Write a note saying you are sorry.
*Next time you see them try to be extra nice.
If you can't say something nice, don't say it at all.
Keep your feelings to yourself.
*If you must have "gross feelings," try and keep them to yourself and not show them.
Make a chart of these things so we don't do them again.
*Put yourself in their shoes—see how you would feel.
Write an apology note.
*Send get better cards or do a nice deed for her.
Treat people like you want them to treat you.

Submitted by a teacher from Akron, Ohio, city schools while taking the *ALTERNATIVES TO VIOLENCE* course.

ALTERNATIVES TO VIOLENCE

BATTLE OF NERVES

What stopped the swing of a meat cleaver?

In 1961 Leon Green, an eighteen year-old Black university freshman, participated in a sit-in protesting segregation at an Atlanta lunch counter. He sat still and held the menu in both hands.

The enraged manager grabbed a meat cleaver and yelled, "Get your hands off that counter or I'll cut off one of them." He ripped the menu from Leon's hands and raised the knife.

Leon firmly held what was left of the menu and looked straight ahead. They both had a hard time during the next few seconds of silence. Then the manager turned and walked back to the kitchen to think it over.

See *The Quiet Battle* (Sibley), pp. 291-299 and *Courage in Both Hands* (Hunter), pp. 84-85.

GRAPES OF WRATH
fail to turn farm workers from their cause.

The United Farm Workers, led by Mr. Cesar Chavez, have reported on many infractions and abuses of their civil rights during the famous agricultural strike begun in September, 1965.

A stationary line of picketing strikers stand along the edge of a public road. In front of them across the way are two strike breakers loading grapes into cartons. A grower comes up and shouts to the picketers to go back to work in the fields. Grabbing up a bunch of grapes from a box, he starts eating them as he walks down the picket line, leering and shaking his fist.

A sheriff and a deputy arrive. Through a bullhorn he shouts at the picketers, "All right, get along here—get moving! Go back to the fields." The deputy strides along the silent line of picketers pushing people back with his fist on their shoulders or chests. Several of the demonstrators are women; one is pregnant. There is murmuring and jostling behind the front line of picketers. One woman falls down. Angry at the wall of faces, the deputy kicks one man in the stomach.

Someone calls to the picketers, "Sing!" and gradually the voices join and sing as the demonstrators turn and continue down the road in slow procession.

See *Sal Si Puedes* (Mattheisson) *The Politics of Nonviolent Action* (Sharp), pp. 263-264.

CONTEMPORARY INQUISITION

Racism in our system of justice.

Black Panthers in New Haven, Connecticut, had begun to help inner city residents through concrete programs such as: (1) free health programs, (2) free children's breakfast programs, (3) day care programs, and (4) free clothing for women and children in need. Then fourteen of the Black Panthers were arrested and charged with conspiracy, murder and kidnapping in connection with the death of Alex Rackley, a former Panther, in May of 1969. After they had been held in jail for six months without even a trial, a support action was planned.

The Black Panthers claimed that the charge was trumped up, that the police wanted them off the streets, out of their communities, and away from the people they wanted to serve. Similar arrests, harassment, and police killings had been happening to Black Panthers all over the country.

Five of the fourteen held were women. Rose Smith, Loretta Luce, and Francis Carter were pregnant at the time of their arrest. The women were all denied the right to physical exercise, good food, fresh air, and proper maternity clothes. Lights flooding their cells and the sound of sirens outside day and night prevented them from sleeping. They were kept in solitary confinement and denied the right to choose lawyers to represent them.

Frances Carter, in such poor condition that she was in labor thirty hours before a Caesarian section was performed, gave birth under armed guard. Rose Smith and Loretta Luce were both due in December. Indicative of her treatment, Ms. Smith gained only one pound during the entire six months of her pregnancy spent in jail. All of the babies were to be taken, against their mothers' wills, to be raised by the state.

On Saturday, November 22, 1969, Women's Liberation, the Black Panther Party, and the Welfare Rights Organization staged a protest march. Thousands of Black and white people marched through the streets of New Haven, ending at an inspiring rally at the Courthouse. The marchers demanded the freeing of the pregnant women on their own recognizance and of the rest on reasonable bail.

UNION BASHING
A present threat to workers' rights.

After the crash of 1929, miners were desperate in eastern Kentucky. Without a union and with wages at rock bottom they lived precariously. The United Mine Workers did not have the power to organize, but a new union, the National Miners Union, came to Harlan and Bell Counties to do so.

In February of 1931 they called a strike. Thousands went out. The union set up soup kitchens and collected and distributed clothes. The Red Cross would not help because the strike was not a "natural disaster."

The mine operators hired 325 armed guards, many of whom were made sheriff's deputies. The miners called them "gun thugs." In April a guard shot and wounded William Burnett, who shot back and killed the guard. On the morning of May 5th the deputies set out to run off some men picketing a mine. At a railroad crossing, they were met by a carload of miners. Miners were in the hills on both sides of the tracks. The Battle of Evarts began. It is said a thousand shots were fired. At least four people were killed, among them deputy sheriff Jim Daniels.

Governor Flem Sampson sent in hundreds of National Guardsmen to stop the union organizing. Thirty-four miners and one guard were arrested. Their trial was moved from Harlan to Winchester because the prosecutor felt he would have trouble getting convictions in Harlan. Some miners were sent to the state prison. The NMU drive failed. The miners nearly starved and couldn't hold out during the strike.

The Harlan County Coal Operators Association not only controlled the sheriff and his deputies. In a senate hearing, Senator La Follette asked George Ward, secretary of the Association, if it took any part in the politics of Harlan County. Ward replied, "No sir, it does not."

La Follette: "Who is the Chairman of the Republican Committee of Harlan County?

Ward: "I am."

La Follette: "Who is the Chairman of the Democratic Committee of Harlan County?"

Ward: "Mr. S. S. Dickenson."

La Follette: "What position, if any, does Mr. Dickinson hold with the Harlan County Coal Operators Association?"

Ward: "President."

See *Appalachian People's History Book* (Crowell), pp. 65 + 78.

WOMEN SUFFRAGISTS ASK:

Make the world safe for whom?

The first time the White House was ever picketed was in 1917 by Women's Suffragists. They began picketing Woodrow Wilson during the patriotic fervor of World War I: President Wilson was spurring people on with the slogan, "Make the World Safe For Democracy," when half the adult citizens of the United States were denied their voting rights on the basis of sex.

At first, no one interfered officially, but when picketers were still there after six months, more and more women were arrested. Jail sentences were progressively lengthened.

But public sympathy began to grow. People who objected to Women's Suffrage objected even more strongly to the cruel way the Suffragists were treated.

Wilson's stands for 'democracy' but against women's right to vote presented such a dilemma to him that he was finally forced to include Women's suffrage as one of his war aims.

As Alice Paul, one of the militant leaders, explained the **dilemma strategy**, "If a creditor stands before a man's house all day long, demanding payment of his bill, the man must either remove the creditor or pay the bill."

See *The Politics of Nonviolent Action* (Sharp), pp. 133, 141+ 735.

ALTERNATIVES TO VIOLENCE — CASE 13-F

SHOOTING OUR OWN CITIZENS IN KENT

How reliance on weapons leads to crazy behavior.

In the spring of 1970, the Vietnam War and anti-war activity were at their peak. Early in May, President Nixon surprised the world by escalating the war through an invasion of Cambodia. In Kent, the night the word got out, frayed tempers exploded on the Water Street bar row, the scene of many past fights. This time the police were ordered to close down the bars and the action moved out and grew in the streets.

Saturday night was pretty much the same as the previous night, but crowds moved from downtown toward the campus where the ROTC building was burned down. It is not clear who was responsible for the arson. Over one hundred students and townspeople were arrested. The situation was tense but not nearly riot-level. Then Governor Rhodes called out the National Guard, who happened to be in nearby Ravenna dealing with a trucking strike disturbance. The Guard members were extremely tired already from too many days and nights on call without sleep in Ravenna. In spite of the situation, classes went on Monday morning. A rally was called, to be held on the Commons, a traditional forum spot, to discuss the Cambodian action. The rally was publicized through normal channels, including an announcement on the commercial radio station in Kent. Perhaps a thousand people gathered, many out of curiosity, some just on their way between classes.

Meanwhile, the governor had apparently issued an order against public assembly. He had lashed out at students, following the earlier lead of President Nixon and Vice President Agnew. The National Guard came to the Commons that Monday noon from the far end, approaching people and asking them to leave. The crowd broke up, going both ways around Taylor Hall on top of the hill above the Commons. The National Guard split up and followed them, as the crowd began to disperse. The Guard contingent on the west side of the building marched up Blanket Hill and down the other side, across a playing field at the bottom and right into a wire fence. Then they turned around and marched back up the hill. At the top, they turned and were ordered to fire at the crowd. Many did fire, later in court claiming self defense. In court, Adjutant General Del Corso stated sixteen times before a grand jury that what happened here was "indiscriminate firing."

Bill Schroeder, 19, was shot dead 380 feet away from the nearest Guardsman (a football field is 300 feet long). Sandy Scheuer, 19, was 390 feet away when killed; Allison Krause, 19, over 345 feet away, and Jeff Miller, 20, the closest, were 265 feet away when killed. Dean Kahler was 300 feet when he fell to the ground shot; he was shot a second time as he fell. Although he was not killed, the second bullet left him paralyzed for life. Bobby Stamps, 500 feet away, was shot and injured while handing a pretzel to a friend. None of the victims were armed. Five years later, the officer who had said he found a weapon on Jeffrey Miller's body admitted he had lied.

See KSU Center for Peaceful Change.

WHEN INVASION OCCURS
The case for nonviolent resistance.

Strikes by civil servants and closings of bazaars and shops by business people in Kabul and other Afghanistan cities are counteractions to the presence of the USSR.

Afghanistan, after all, is separated from India only by Kashmir, which is under India's control. And it was in India under Mohandas K. Gandhi that many strategies were used effectively in the 1920s against Britain.

The techniques of non-violent resistance, while by no means historically restricted to the Indian subcontinent, fit well into the Afghanistan situation, although not entirely in textbook fashion.

They are strategies particularly suitable when an oppressor is militarily too strong to be dealt with by physical weapons. Depending upon how much military assistance is available to the Moslem Insurgents and how effective they are in using it, the non-violent resistance may be either a preliminary softening-up device or may develop into a regular policy as it did in India and in Denmark against the Nazis.

If reports that the government of President Babrak Karmal is falling are correct, the failure of his regime may be the first victory of the protesting strikers. And if resistance to the Soviets continues in civil protests, we may see a repetition of several other strategies used elsewhere.

In India, Mahatma Gandhi and other leaders less widely known in the United States led the rank and file opposition to the British colonial rulers.

Gandhi planned the campaigns. He first warned the people against hatred of the British or anyone else. Then he asked them to refuse to pay taxes, to defend themselves without violence if attacked, to go to jail gladly for their disobedience, to have nothing to do with lawlessness, such as cutting telegraph wires and destroying buildings, and to publish underground papers.

Skeptics about the efficacy of such strategies say the British rulers were not oppressors like the Soviets. They were more humane. But their humanity was challenged at many points, most dramatically at Dharsana during the famous instance of the salt flats march. Gandhi had already been imprisoned, but one of his sons and others led the advance. The unarmed satyagrahis, as the believers in non-violent resistance were called, marched on as their battering continued. Two were killed and 320 wounded by 435 Indian police commanded by British officers. Armed with long clubs tipped with steel, the police swung them on the line of marchers, kicking the men and women once they were down.

After hours of that brutality not enough of the Indian police could carry on in the face of the satyagrahis' courage and the assault ended.

But such "decent" oppressors were not even in Denmark in 1940, when Germany occupied that country. The ruthless Nazi military machine was not resisted with force; there was neither time nor ability to do so.

King Christian refused to comply with Nazi demands. The people defied the invaders by helping Jews to escape or sheltering them in their homes. For two and a half years Danes refused to work in either Germany or Norway (which also was overrun).

In Denmark they worked badly for the Germans, took part in slowdowns, refused to go into theaters if German military entered, would not trade or do business with them, and secretly printed illegal newspapers, some of which now are major dailies in Copenhagen. Although under house arrest, King Christian each day rode, erect on his horse, through Copenhagen to encourage his people.

The campaign was effective until the Danes were persuaded by the Allies to resort to violence.

Whether the Moslem Insurgents plan to attack the Soviet presence with both violent and non-violent tactics simultaneously is not yet clear. The strength of their military defense has surprised the Russians. Non-cooperation has slowed the occupation and could make matters still more difficult for the USSR.

by Rojand E. Wolseley. Wolseley, a resident of Syracuse, is the author or co-author of four books about India, where he worked for more than a year. From the Cleveland *Plain Dealer*, March 7, 1980.

ALTERNATIVES TO VIOLENCE   CASE 14-B

STEMMING THE TIDE
Czech's vigorous, nonmilitant resistance to invaders.

When half a million Soviet and Warsaw Pact troops invaded Czechoslovakia in August, 1968, they expected to take over the country easily—within a matter of a few days. Instead, they encountered massive non-violent resistance by the people of Czechoslovakia. Even though spontaneous and untrained, the resistance movement was able to prevent Soviet military takeover for a full eight months. The Soviets were forced to negotiate with the very Czech government officials they had planned to replace.

Immediately upon hearing of the invasion, Czechoslovakians began their resistance. The Czech news agency would not issue the Soviet press release saying that the invasion had been requested by members of their government. A clandestine radio network was set up instead, issuing counter statements.

The National Assembly and other government bodies were able to meet and make it clear they opposed the invasion.

Workers all over Czechoslovakia held one hour general strikes. Rail workers slowed the transport of military-related equipment from the USSR. The underground radio continued to broadcast, playing a vital role in preventing rumors, responding to emergencies (like finding people to harvest the potatoes and hops), and reporting important information as it became available.

Compare eight months of civilian resistance, which resulted in a compromise with the Soviets, to the estimate that the Czech army would have been able to hold out for four days. The compromise reached, called the Moscow Protocol, while far from perfect, set the stage for the increasing independence of European communist countries, and for a massive Eastern European human rights movement still progressing today.

See Gene Sharp T*he Politics of Nonviolent Action*, the Fellowship of the Reconciliation's flier, "Disregarded History," and the WRL 1978 Peace Calendar.

ALTERNATIVES TO VIOLENCE   CASE 14-C

A QUICK KISS
intercepts a clenched fist.

Once, in Damascus years ago, when I was strolling along the street called Straight—wondering whether it is truly the most ancient street in the world that has served continuously as a marketplace—I watched as a man who was riding slowly through the crowd on a bicycle with a basket of oranges precariously balanced on the handlebars was bumped by a porter so bent by a heavy burden that he had not seen him. The burden was dropped, the oranges scattered and a bitter altercation broke out between the two men, surrounded by a circle of onlookers.

After an angry exchange of shouted insults, as the bicyclist moved toward the porter with a clenched fist, a tattered little man slipped from the crowd, took the raised fist in his hands and kissed it. A murmur of approval ran through the watchers, the antagonists relaxed, then the people began picking up the oranges and the little man drifted away. I have remembered that as a caring act, an act of devotion there on the street called Straight by a man who might have been a Syrian Muslim, a Syrian Jew or a Syrian Christian.

We thank Waring Smith for sending this to us. In a letter from Kenneth W. Morgan, professor of religion emeritus at Colgate University to the *New York Times*, January 30, 1991.

OVERCOMING SOCIETAL VIOLENCE

Students begin to see better alternatives.

I introduced the activity by recalling previous discussions on how to handle a problem situation (conflict). I was delighted to find out that the students' responses were not nearly as violent as the first assignment.

One of the students even wrote "forgive him" in response to the question of name calling. Many chose to ignore a situation, talk it out or explain their feelings/position on an issue (copying homework). I frequently hear the students say, "No put downs!" in response to name calling in the classroom. I am pleased to see that some of our discussions have made an impact.

I found that my students were very violent in relationship to being invaded by another planet. It appeared that they were less violent in handling day-to-day conflict, but extremely protective of national defense.

The greatest benefit of introducing non-violent concepts into the classroom has been seeing the students stop and think about their actions before acting violently. They have begun to recognize violent actions as including put downs and name calling. So many of my students are so used to violence, it has become "normal." Some of them are beginning to realize that things don't have to be that way.

Submitted by an Akron City teacher while taking the *ALTERNATIVES TO VIOLENCE* course.

THOSE WHO LIVED BY THE SWORD
can, like these Austrians, be foiled.

In the mid-nineteenth century, the Austri-ns were trying to subordinate the Hungarians to their power, contrary to the original treaty of the union, which called for equal participation. The Hungarians were feeling helpless, being too weak to fight.

Fenenc Deak, a Catholic landowner, urged action, saying, "The nation that submits to injustice and oppression without protest is doomed." His plan was to refuse, non-violently, all recognition and support of the Austrian government.

He started to organize a plan for independent Hungarian education, agriculture, industry, and a boycott of Austrian goods. He warned the Hungarian people not to be betrayed into acts of violence or to abandon legality. "This," he said, "is the safe ground on which unarmed ourselves we can hold our ground against armed force. If suffering must be necessary, suffer with dignity."

The Austrian tax collector came. He was treated respectfully; he just wasn't paid. The Austrian police levied upon Hungarian property to settle the tax liens. They were not resisted. However, no Hungarian auctioneer would handle the necessary sale of the property. Austrian auctioneers came. No one would bid. It was too expensive to bring in Austrian bidders.

The Austrians decided that some sort of military occupation was necessary and tried to billet Austrian soldiers in Hungarian homes. But the Austrian soldiers so hated living with families who ignored and des- pised them, that, in spirit of no physical violence, they protested loudly against this duty.

The boycott of Austrian goods was declared illegal, but Hungarians defied the decree. The jails were overflowing. No Hungarian would sit in the Imperial parliament.

The Austrians tried reconciliation, prisoner release, and partial self government, but Hungary insisted on its full rights. For this, the Austrian emperor decreed compulsory military training, but when the Hungarians said they'd refuse, he capitulated.

On February 18, 1867, Hungary received its constitution as sought. Without arms or violence, but with patience and perseverance, the Hungarians won complete victory.

See *Nonviolence* (Miller), pp. 238-239; and *The Power of Nonviolence* (Gregg), pp. 15-16, and *The Quiet Battle* (Sibley), pp. 137-155.

CANOES BLOCK ARMS TO PAKISTAN

U.S. aid to dictatorship finally cut.

In 1971, it was U.S. government policy to support the military dictatorship in Pakistan, which was then exploiting and killing the people of East Bengal (now called Bangladesh). A group of North American non-violent activists successfully challenged and eventually helped to change this policy. Well-known performing artists like Joan Baez wrote songs to influence public opinion on the issue. Material aids support was sent by U.S. citizens directly to the people of Bangladesh. Public education on the issue brought about massive pressure on Congress to cut off military aid to Pakistan.

Not the least of U.S. activism was the formation of a "non-violent fleet" of canoes, kayaks, and other small boats. Slipping by the Coast Guard and police vessels, the fleet met Pakistani freighters in the Baltimore, Philadelphia, and New York harbors, blockading the huge trade ships to prevent them from landing.

One Pakistani ship was turned around in the Delaware River in Philadelphia. Another docked, only to encounter picketers and the refusal of the local dockworkers' union to load or unload. Many times, police were able to break through the "blockade" and get Pakistani boats in, but the news coverage of the tiny boats of the nonviolent "fleet" confronting the huge freighters was so dramatic that public opinion was swayed in favor of the activists, and U.S. military aid to Pakistan was cut off.

See "Canoes Block Arms to Pakistan," by Dick Taylor, in *Nonviolent Struggle Around the World* (WRL 1978 Peace Calendar). Also Movement for a New Society, 4722 Baltimore Avenue, Philadelphia, PA 19104.

MILESTONE TOWARD PEACE

Draft card protest.

In the spring of 1967, a special movement started among those who felt U.S. participation in the Vietnam War was wrong. A pledge campaign was launched to get 500 people, by April 15th, to agree to burn their draft cards. If the number was not reached, no one would be bound by the pledge. By the night of the 14th, only 120 had signed. At the final meeting, however, many felt that even 50 draft cards burned would constitute a significant political act. A show of hands was requested and 57 responded favorably.

The next day a huge number gathered in the Sheep Meadow of Central Park. The Cornell contingent, numbering in the thousands, was led by a large "We Won't Go" banner emblazoned in the school colors. "Burn draft cards, not people," the crowd chanted.

Even an army reservist in "green beret" uniform stepped forward and burned his card—a tremendously courageous act, most thought. More followed. According to Marty Jezer's account, 175 burned their cards that day, more than had signed the pledge.

" . . . The most important effect of the draft card burning," Marty wrote, "was that it changed the lives of those who took part. (The Movement) . . . has given people the strength to devote their lives toward the creation of a community where love of one's fellow replaces the profit motive as the highest value."

See *We Won't Go* (Lynd), pp. 220-225.

NATIVE AMERICANS ON A WARPATH

Why did they spare the Quaker home?

Quakers on the early North American frontier always left their latchstrings unsecured (the early equivalent of an unlocked door). Anyone, including all Native Americans, was welcome to enter at any time of the day or night to find shelter and warmth. One time, however, Mary and James Tyler were warned that a war party of Indians, incited by the British to burn and kill all, were on their way to destroy their settlement.

It was a difficult decision, but the Tylers decided not to change their long-standing practice. That night, they again left their latchstring out. In the middle of the night they were awakened by a war whoop. The could see and hear seven Native Americans in full war paint pull open the door and enter the house.

The Native Americans conferred briefly, then turned and left quietly, going back into the night.

In the morning, the Tylers went out and saw the burnt ruins of the other cabins nearby.

Later, as a U.S. government representative to a conference with the Native Americans, James Tyler related his story. One of the Native Americans present said he had been part of that raiding party.

"We meant to burn and kill all," he said. "We found the latchstring out. We said, 'We no burn. No kill these people. They do us no harm. They trust Great Spirit.'"

See *Safe Passage on City Streets* (Samuel), pp. 69-70.

ALTERNATIVES TO VIOLENCE

KING CHRISTIAN PROVES
intrepid nonviolence can check militance.

Contrary to the occupation agreement in 1940, the Nazis displayed the swastika flag on a public building in Denmark. The Danish king, King Christian, demanded the flag's removal. The German military officials refused. The king said he would send a soldier to remove the flag. The reply was that they would shoot him. "I am that soldier," said the king. The flag came down.

King Christian and the Danish people, without previous preparation or nonviolence training, were able to keep up this kind of defense quite effectively against the Nazis for two and a half years, until the British government persuaded them to use violence.

See *The Power of Nonviolence* (Gregg), pp. 29-30; and *Nonviolence* (Miller), p. 252.

NONVIOLENT HEROISM

King Christian defies Nazis.

At one time during the occupation of Denmark, the Nazis ordered all Jews to wear the Star of David to identify them for future deportation to the dreaded concentration camps and gas chambers. When this happened, who appeared in public with the Star of David ostentatiously displayed on his chest? None other than King Christian himself, the Danish king. Others soon took the cue: all Danes began wearing the Star of David, and the Nazis were forced to give up their plans. The king stated publicly that if a Jewish ghetto were established, he would move from his palace into such a place. He ceremoniously attended a special celebration in a Copenhagen synagogue to show his love and support for Jewish Danes. The Danish people protected and hid Jews from the Nazis. It is in fact claimed by some that not a single Danish Jew was killed by the Nazis. Could violent resistance have been so effective?

See *The Power of Nonviolence* (Gregg), p. 29; and *Nonviolence* (Miller), p. 252.

CITIZENS OF THE PLANET

Can we outgrow provincialism?

Ecology teaches us that humankind is not the center of life on the planet. Ecology has taught us that the whole earth is part of our "body" and that we must learn to respect it as we respect ourselves. As we feel for ourselves, we must feel for all forms of life—the whales, the seals, the forests, the seas. The tremendous beauty of ecological thought is that it shows us a pathway back to an understanding and appreciation of life itself—an understanding and appreciation that is imperative to that very way of life.

As with the whales and the seals, life must be saved by non-violent confrontations and by what the Quakers call "bearing witness." A person bearing witness must accept responsibility for being aware of an injustice. That person may then choose to do something or stand by, but he may not turn away in ignorance. The Greenpeace ethic is not only to personally bear witness to atrocities against life; it is to take direct action to prevent them. While action must be direct, it must also be non-violent. We must obstruct a wrong without offering personal violence to its perpetrators. Our greatest strength must be life itself, and the commitment to direct our own lives to protect others.

The Greenpeace Philosophy.

EFFECTIVE TECHNIQUE
for understanding each other.

Role playing has become a way of life in our class. First we practiced using contrived situations until the students became familiar with the procedure. Now when there is a problem within our room that requires more than a "How would you feel?" most of the children can assume the parts of character in a given situation.

For instance, during what seems like a re-occurring name calling recess, I asked Morris and Ed to stop and pretend they were one another. Amazing as it seems, since both were name calling, when each took the another's roles the situation took on a different air. Both agreed it was uncomfortable and sad. The battle was over for the rest of the recess.

It is still difficult for my students to take the role of the opposite sex without giggles, but we are working on it!

Submitted by a teacher from Akron, Ohio, city schools while taking the ALTERNATIVES TO VIOLENCE course.

NONVIOLENT COMMITMENT
takes guts when bullies strike.

The Montgomery bus boycott lasted about a year. On December 2, 1956, a Black woman celebrated 'boarding day' by riding the bus.

When she got off a young white man followed her. As the bus pulled away he went over and struck her as hard as he could in the mouth, knocking her down. He stood over her with his fists doubled.

A carload of white men pulled up, apparently looking for trouble. Blacks were in the area. All of the Black people followed their training, 'If an incident occurs, do not go to the aid of the person being attacked. If you do, this will only encourage white people to rush to the rescue of the attacker: then there will be a more serious situation.'

In spite of her burning anger, the woman who had been struck followed her training, too: 'If you are struck, do not strike back. On the other hand, do not show cowardice or fear if you can help it.' She rolled over, sat up a few seconds, got to her feet and dusted herself off, wiped the blood from her mouth, and walked off three or four steps looking away from the young man.

No one came to either's aid. The attacker did not expect this result. Embarrassed, looking around quickly, he jumped into the waiting car and they all fled.

See *Courage in Both Hands* (Hunter), p. 53.

… ALTERNATIVES TO VIOLENCE — CASE 17-B

STRAIGHT TALK
can be more effective than weapons.

The holdup man pushed a note into the young bank trainee's teller cage, demanding money. A gun was pointed covertly at her. However, ignoring the gun and the threat, she blurted out, "You can't do that. It's against the law!"

The crook was taken aback by her simplicity and directness. What could he do? Argue with her, there in the middle of the bank, with a glass pane separating him from the money he wanted? He ran from the bank.

At a completely different time and place, another young woman reacted similarly. Confronted by a thief with a knife, she said, "You can't bother me! This is my neighborhood!" The woman was as surprised and embarrassed as anyone when she told the story later. But simply **stating the obvious** has an effect. It worked.

See *Safe Passage on City Streets* (Samuel), pp. 33-35.

WIDOW COMBS VS. CAPERTON COAL

Guess who won?

On November 22, 1965, the Caperton Coal Company began strip mining the land of Mrs. Ollie Combs. But Widow Combs was ready. She sat down in front of the bulldozers and wouldn't move.

Widow Combs was 61 years old, and she lived with her five sons on Social Security and a state disability check. The only thing she owned was her farm, and she wasn't going to see it ruined. She told the company men, "We live hard. This land and this house is all we've got. Go on and leave us alone." Her neighbors came to support her stand.

However, the Caperton Coal Company was ready, too. They had a court order which said neither Mrs. Combs nor anyone else could get in their way. The sheriff came and read the order to Widow Combs. She said, "It's not worth the paper it's written on." And then she and her two sons, Jesse and Lincoln, were arrested.

Widow Combs told her sons to go on with the sheriff, but she sat till they carried her away to jail. Three times in all Widow Combs went to jail. She even ate Thanksgiving dinner there, sent to her by the people of Clear Creek. Newspapers, radio and TV all reported her story, and before long, the whole state knew about Widow Combs.

There was such an uproar, the Governor took a stand. He issued new rules and proposed new laws on strip mining. The county judge who sent Mrs. Combs to jail acted, too. He ordered the news rules enforced immediately. The Caperton Coal Company was defeated.

Widow Combs' battle against strip mining wasn't the first one or the last, but it was certainly one of the best.

See *Appalachian People's History Book* (Crowell), p. 98.

A BETTER FUTURE
starts with today's children.

The environment is a concern for many of us. As a Special Education teacher, I write individualized Educational Plans, and within those plans under Science, Health, and Social Studies annual goals, I include short-term objectives for citizenship. My objective for students aims toward good citizenship through environmental awareness, ecological diversity, and conservation.

Daily we reuse and recycle materials from office memos to lunch trays. For example, students use the backs of papers for math computations, art projects, spelling lists, etc. Lights are turned off automatically as we leave the room. When water is found running in the bathrooms, children turn it off. We encourage on another to recycle at home and conserve energy during our "circle talks."

Ranger Doug Palmer from Virginia Kendall Park is our dear friend, and we meet him each season to learn and discover more about biological diversity. As a community service, our class is in charge of Keep Akron Beautiful and Earth Day. Children feel empowered when they learn a skill and can put that skill to a functional purpose. Recycling, conserving, cleaning up are among the skills my students demonstrate daily at home and in school. Also, they love to go home to share these ideas at home.

Submitted by a teacher from Akron, Ohio, city schools while taking the *ALTERNATIVES TO VIOLENCE* course.

IDEAS TO TRY
for stimulating students' imagination.

In vocational home economics, each student is required to complete a six-hour home project (Individual Extended Experience) for each six weeks. The project counts as 1/6 of their six weeks' grade.

This year, I am planning to incorporate a lesson on environmental issues and use recycling as a choice. I will introduce the unit with samples of recycled products—toys made from recycled items and clothing that has been reused.

The students will be assigned a notebook which will demonstrate ways to save the environment:

SAVE OUR ENVIRONMENT NOTEBOOK

Using old magazines, find 2 pictures which can show conservation or recycling of natural resources in the following areas:
- electrical/natural gas
- transportation
- food
- waste/garbage
- water

Caption each picture to state how you can conserve or recycle.

Put the sheets in the above order.

Put this sheet on top to serve as a grade check off sheet. Staple notebook.

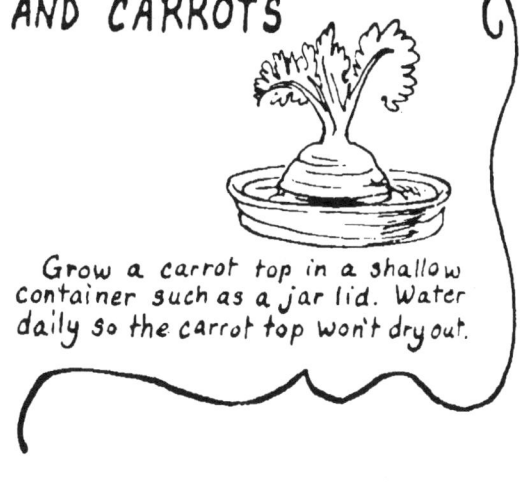

BLOCKS TO BUILD WITH... Take a milk carton. Open out, cut, stuff with crumpled newspaper and fold. An extra pinch here and here will help the block sit flat. Tape closed if desired. Try various sized cartons cut down to different heights. Supervise children when they are using scissors.

AND CARROTS — Grow a carrot top in a shallow container such as a jar lid. Water daily so the carrot top won't dry out.

Submitted by an Akron City School teacher.

We will read aloud an article which discusses how teens can help the environment. Then brainstorming will be done in small groups to get other concrete suggestions on ways to save the environment.

ORDERING INFORMATION

Schools **with purchase order numbers** for large quantity requests, please contact PEACE GROWS INC., 513 West Exchange Street, Akron, Ohio 44302; or phone with questions for PEACE GROWS INC. at 216/864-5442.

ALL others, order directly from distributor
(by credit card or check) call BOOKCRAFTERS 1-800-879-4214.
Price = $25.00 plus shipping and handling.
Make checks payable and mail to:
BOOKCRAFTERS
Attn: Order Fulfillment Department
615 East Industrial Drive
Chelsea, Michigan 48118